CAUGHT IN THE MEMORY

CAUGHT IN THE MEMORY

County Cricket in the 1960s

Stephen Chalke

with illustrations by Ken Taylor
(of Yorkshire and England)

FAIRFIELD BOOKS

Fairfield Books
17 George's Road, Fairfield Park, Bath BA1 6EY
Tel 01225-335813

First published 1999

ISBN 0 9531196 1 0

Printed and bound in Great Britain by
Bookcraft Ltd, Midsomer Norton, Bath

Dust jacket and colour sections printed by
Graphics Interface Ltd, Roseberry Road,
Lower Bristol Road, Bath BA2 3DZ

for

Bomber Wells

A people without history
Is not redeemed from time, for history is a pattern
Of timeless moments.

T.S.Eliot, 'Little Gidding'

ILLUSTRATIONS

The illustrations in this book are all of cricketers from the 1960s, but Ken Taylor has many more drawings of sporting personalities. He has already printed and distributed portraits of Fred Trueman, Ray Illingworth, Brian Close and Dickie Bird, but he can supply prints from a much wider list and in several formats. His subjects include players both from his own playing days and from the modern game.

Full details are available from Ken Taylor at The Red House, Stody, Melton Constable, Norfolk, NR24 2EB.

These colour illustrations are interpretations of black-and-white photographs. The ones of Tom Cartwright and Ron Headley are by Ken Kelly, and Ken Taylor and the publishers would like to thank him for granting permission for his photographs to be used in this way. The ones of Brian Close and Fred Trueman are with the kind permission of the Yorkshire Post. Most of the other photographs appeared originally in the now defunct Playfair Cricket Monthly magazine. The publishers have tried to find out the copyright owners of these photographs, and if any photographic source believes that any are theirs they should contact the publishers to rectify the matter.

Ken Taylor's photograph of Roly Jenkins in 'Runs in the Memory' was also based on a photograph by Ken Kelly. At the time of publication this was not known, but we are happy to acknowledge this now and to thank Ken for his retrospective granting of permission to use it.

CONTENTS

INTRODUCTION

My first book, 'Runs in the Memory', was a recreation of county cricket in the 1950s. That was a decade that began with the austerity of rationing and ended with the affluence of Harold Macmillan's 'You've never had it so good'. County cricket had enjoyed a renaissance in the aftermath of the war and, though the crowds gradually dwindled, there was not yet an air of crisis in the game. The format of the championship remained unchanged, and the England Test team went seven years without losing a series.

The pace of change quickens during the 1960s. It is a decade that begins with monkeys launched fifty miles into space and ends with men on the moon. Heart transplants are pioneered, supersonic air travel developed, the contraceptive pill made available. America's youngest President takes up the torch on behalf of a new generation, and Britain's Prime Ministers speak of 'the winds of change' and 'the white heat of technology'. There is independence for the countries of Africa. Abortion and homosexuality are legalised, capital punishment and stage censorship abolished. There are Telstar and Concorde, North Sea gas and the Post Office Tower. Motorways are laid across the country as railway lines are closed, and package holidays in Spain start to replace weeks in English resorts. Meanwhile, among the young, National Service gives way to long hair and Beatlemania, and 'Ban The Bomb' demonstrations mushroom into a culture of protest.

County cricket struggles to compete in such a fast-changing world, but it too finds its hope in radical change. A knock-out tournament in 1963, a Sunday League in 1969. The abolition of amateurs, the introduction of bonus points, the lessening of restrictions on overseas players, the list of new ideas goes on. For two years there is no follow on in county cricket, then there is a 65-over limit on first innings. A minimum of 20 overs in the last hour, a new lbw law to prevent pad-play, changes in the regulations for covering the playing area, and almost every year an alteration to the no ball law.

There are fair-sized crowds in most of the grounds, and there is still a sense that cricket is England's national game in summer. One-day cricket has not yet taken its toll on slow bowling, and the majority of batsmen still walk when they are out. England is not the supreme force in world cricket that it was in the 1950s but, when the Ashes are regained in the Spring of 1971, they have won seven and drawn two of their last nine Test series. Indeed, in the twelve winters from 1962, not one overseas tour ends in defeat. What a contrast with the twelve winters to 1999, when there will be just two series victories over New Zealand and a draw with Zimbabwe.

As in my first book, I have reconstructed twelve county championship matches. The first features a Roses match, with 34,000 spectators packed into Old Trafford on August Bank Holiday Monday 1960, and the last visits Swansea as Glamorgan strive for the title at the end of 1969. Most of the games have been chosen by the players themselves, games that have stayed in their memories for thirty and more years. Only once or twice I have influenced their choice. I wanted to ensure that all seventeen counties appeared at least once in these twelve games.

Each chapter is a tapestry woven from several strands. There is the match itself, unfolding session by session to its climax. There are the voices of the players, sitting beside the reader on the boundary edge and recalling emotions, recollecting incidents and characters, reflecting on the way of life then and now. There are the newspaper reports, so different in style from those of today, the period details and the contemporary news items that root each match in its time. And there are the glances forward: into the futures of the individual players, of their counties, and of the whole structure of English cricket.

I have recreated the matches in the present tense. It is too easy to overlay the past with the inevitability of its outcomes. If a thunder storm had not broken ... If a catch had been held ... If a hamstring had not been torn ... The charm of cricket lies in its uncertainties.

Listening to the voices of the players, I have shaped each chapter around what they have told me. The themes have changed a little from my previous book, but the enduring love of cricket is as strong. So many old cricketers have been generous with their time and their memories, and I hope this book conveys that generosity.

Again Ken Taylor contributes twelve portraits. From the fifties to the sixties, there is an explosion of colour: in motor cars and men's clothing, in the cinema and on television, and it is somehow appropriate that the black-and-white of 'Runs in the Memory' is replaced by colour in this volume.

The stories of these matches are told across the distance of thirty-something years, and sometimes they have been enhanced and elaborated with years of retelling, sometimes blurred with the passing of time. I have authenticated the detail where possible, but I am just as concerned with emotional authenticity, with capturing the pleasures that are provided by the savouring of warm memories.

The memory is not a reliable lens, but often it is our only lens. 'The game today comes second to the money that's made from it.' ... 'For all the gimmes and the cars, they don't really look very happy.' ... 'I don't think they have the fun we had.' Is it old men romanticising the past? A case of 'the older I get, the better a player I was'? Or do their memories remind us of qualities of life that we have been too careless to preserve as we enjoy the fruits of affluence, the benefits of new technology?

Whatever the answer, here are twelve wonderful games of cricket, and I hope that you will enjoy reading the accounts of them as much as I have enjoyed writing about them.

LANCASHIRE, YOU'VE LOST

Lancashire v Yorkshire

July &August 1960

chosen by Don Wilson

Don Wilson was born in Settle, Yorkshire in 1937. A slow left-arm bowler, he played for Yorkshire from 1957 to 1974 and in six Tests for England. After retiring he became M.C.C. Head Coach at Lord's for 13 years, moving in 1990 to Ampleforth College in Yorkshire where he runs the Sports Centre.

He remembers a gripping finish to a Roses match at Old Trafford.

"Len Hutton always said to me," Don remembers, "'You can play against Australia, you can play against the West Indies, but you'll never play a game of cricket like the Roses match.' And my god, he was right."

The white rose of York and the red rose of Lancaster. Five hundred years have passed since they fought for the throne of England. But for ninety years now their battles on the cricket field have had an atmosphere all of their own. "There have been matches of the utmost majesty," A.A. Thomson writes, "and there have been grim, dour, no-fours-before-lunch matches. But always there is the lust and dust of battle."

It is 1960. The average British worker has two weeks of annual leave plus these two special weekends: Whitsun and the old August Bank Holiday. The weekends set aside for these Roses matches.

Seven thousand people fly out of Manchester airport, the busiest day in its history, and long lines of day trippers form at the railway station, taking advantage of cheap day fares to Blackpool and the coast. But there are plenty more who are staying for the cricket and, though the crowds are still pouring through the turnstiles, there is *'an expectant hush'*[*] as Lancashire's Brian Statham marks out his run.

"Old Trafford was the best ground in the world to play on," Don says. "It had so much atmosphere. The crowd were knowledgeable, very Lancashire but they knew their cricket." They know that Statham has been suffering from tonsilitis since the Test match here on Tuesday, *'he is pale and full of antibiotics'*, and they are not surprised that his first over is *'an amiable loosener'*. But, when Higgs has Bryan Stott caught in the slips and it is one for one, *'the Yorkshire contingent on the popular side were flabbergasted'*, and the Lancashire crowd knows that the battle is joined.

---

[*] Quotations from contemporary newspaper reports are in italics throughout.

Yorkshire and Lancashire. Yorkshire cricket team is only for the Yorkshire born, and all but two of this Lancashire side are Lancastrians. Once Lancashire was rich with cotton mills, Yorkshire with wool, but their days of glory are gone now, and 'the luxuriance of cricket at Old Trafford' has in the words of Neville Cardus turned into 'a suspicious thriftiness'. Yorkshire cricket, like their wool, he writes, 'has a saving relish and an ability to expand at the right time.'

The white rose and the red. *'It is a good many years,'* the Times reports, *'since Yorkshire and Lancashire met while first and second in the championship. That in itself was enough to appeal to a city where cricket was once so much a part of the daily round.'* First and second for their August meeting, it has not happened since that first summer after the war, when the crowd here was so great that the captains agreed to shorten the boundaries. Here in 1960 only Lancashire's Alan Wharton remains from that match. A tough rugby league footballer, he will score over thirty centuries in his career, but he will always choose as his most memorable innings that 41 he scored in his first Roses match. Just as Ken Taylor, who now hits two fours with *'a dangerous hook and a slice over slip's head'*, will always recalls his golden duck when he first played here three years ago. Ken is not a no-fours-before-lunch batsman, but his adventurous innings does not last long as *'his middle stump was cartwheeled out of the ground by Higgs'*, and it is 20 for two. According to John Kay in the Manchester Evening News, *'the good news must have spread for within an hour the crowd had doubled.'*

Doug Padgett and Brian Close set about repairing the damage. They are Yorkshire's leading batsmen this summer, top of the averages that their captain Vic Wilson is forever providing for his chairman. "About this time, Brian Sellers had a fixation about statistics," Ray Illingworth recalls. "I would see Vic going into the committee with the latest averages. I told him it was ridiculous to go by results on paper." But Vic is Yorkshire's first professional captain, a quiet man who earns his respect by seniority, and it is not in his nature to argue with the chairman in the way that Brian Close will later do. Today Sellers sits in the pavilion, and perhaps he remembers the crowds that packed into the ground that first year after the war. His eighth year as captain, his sixth as champion county. He was at the wicket when "the game ended, not in the easy victory to which Lancashire had thought themselves entitled but in a draw, secured by Yorkshire obstinacy." Brian Close may be obstinate, too, but he is not one for averages and he is *'beyond reach of anxiety'* as he drives Higgs for two fours.

The Yorkshire committee. The county have won the title in 1959, and they are top now at the end of July. But "they never showed any delight or enthusiasm," Ken Taylor remembers. "Brian Sellers stood up at the start of one season. 'The bowling's been adequate,' he said, 'but the batting's piss poor.' And we'd won the championship the previous year. Whatever you did, they always said it had been done better before. That was the attitude." This young team carries the burden of Yorkshire's great cricketing tradition. "Tradition?" Don laughs. "Religion, more like. At the end of the season after you'd won the championship, most of the committee would still not know your name. There was one fellow called Escott, he called me Yan. He didn't know my first name from a bar of soap."

At lunch Yorkshire are 101 for four, *'an excellent morning's work for Lancashire'*, and the two captains take lunch with their committee members. Vic Wilson, the 39-year-old farmer from North Yorkshire, the county's first professional captain, and Bob Barber, the 24-year-old Cambridge graduate, the golden boy Lancashire have groomed to succeed Cyril Washbrook. Barber has succumbed to his chairman's pressure to stay in different hotels from his players, but he does not find it easy to maintain the iron discipline that the committee demands, and he longs in vain for "a friendly hand, a listening ear, some quiet advice". Still, his bowlers have taken four good wickets this morning, and a shower during lunch gives the pitch some fresh life. A win here, and Lancashire will be top of the table. But even more than that, they will have beaten Yorkshire twice in a season for the first time since 1893.

There are few left here who recall August 1893, when Yorkshire were set 57 to win and, in the words of A.A. Thomson, "flapped and floundered until, with six runs still needed, they had nine wickets down." Then Jack Ulyett sent the ball soaring to long-on, "a sixer for sure", only for Albert Ward to "lean back like a contortionist and take the ball comfortably in his huge carpet-bag hands." Brian Sellers will know the tale from his father, who was one of those who flapped and floundered that afternoon. Just as A.A. Thomson replays the action through the lens of his uncle's memory. "It is enough to say that it was one of those battles that try men's soul, and Uncle Walter was never quite the same man afterwards."

It is August Bank Holiday 1960. Newspapers carry a daily count of road deaths, and there are nineteen today. Next month traffic wardens will appear on the streets of London, and the Ministry of Transport will introduce a voluntary test for old cars: brakes, lights and steering. The first two tested in Manchester are a 1922 Bean and a 1924 Singer, and they both fail.

At Old Trafford wickets continue to fall, with Brian Statham and Ken Higgs doing the lion's share of the bowling. "Brian was fast," Don says, "but he was a very straight bowler. He once said to me, 'If you're ever bowling, aim for the middle of the bat. If they miss, you hit.'" Today he has three lbw and two bowled in the middle of the innings, and only Brian Close lasts long in an afternoon interrupted by showers. It is 146 for five when they come off for a second time, Statham at the end of his spell. But he is fresh when they resume, the wicket lively once more, and he bowls Close with an inswinging yorker. *'Close was the principal substance of the innings,'* J.M. Kilburn writes in the Yorkshire Post. *'He was never master, but he was never a servant. As long as he stayed Yorkshire had some anchorage; with his departure they were helpless to the storm.'* Yorkshire, all out for 154.

"Old Trafford," Don recalls, "was fast in those days. With bounce. There were lots of runs scored usually - unless we batted badly." And, as Vic Wilson leads the champions onto the field, they know that 154 is a poor score and that badly they have indeed batted.

With such a small total on the board, the last man they want to see following them through the gate is Geoff Pullar, England's opening bat. He scored three centuries against them last year. Then at Whitsun on a dusty Headingley track he accumulated 121 out of 210, and nobody else in the whole match reached 40. "He was a dour player," Don tells. "You never thought he was in, but all of a sudden you'd look up and he'd got 35 not out. Then, when you think you're bowling well at him, he'd be 70 or 80. And you'd think, I haven't seen him make a shot yet. Where's he got 70 from? Then he'd be raising his bat for 100."

He and Bob Barber see off the new ball bowling of Fred Trueman and Mel Ryan, and there are 26 on the board when Vic Wilson throws the ball to Brian Close. Or maybe Brian just takes it. He is a man who likes to be always at the heart of the game. Off-spin, medium pace, he will bowl whatever is required. "He bowled the most devastating full toss," Don tells. "He seemed to get a wicket every time he bowled it. We used to call him the Boston Strangler. Why he didn't just bowl full tosses, we'll never know." But today he tries another of his specialities, and Pullar swings *'a long hop high to deep fine leg'* and is caught. Yorkshire hopes rise, but they soon fall again as Bob Barber and Alan Wharton compile *'a great second wicket partnership, a mixture of zip cricket and caution'*.

It is the summer of 1960. An Old Etonian prime minister and a 'You've never had it so good' economy. A pint of beer for one and sixpence, a packet of ten cigarettes for one and eight. Salford-born Albert Finney stars as lathe worker Arthur Seaton in the film of 'Saturday Night and Sunday Morning', and Granada Television is casting for 'Coronation Street'. "There's plenty of jobs for them that will take the trouble to look for them," Elsie Tanner will tell her out-of-work son in the first episode.

Barber and Wharton, captain and senior professional, they take the score to 97 by close of play, and the twenty thousand in the ground clap them all the way back to the pavilion. How does Don remember their batting? "Bob Barber was a tall, elegant man. Maybe he was the last of the true amateurs. A great shot maker. Alan Wharton was a dour professional. Ex-rugby league. He had a nose like granite. A real trade unionist. Typical Coronation Street." *'Barber scored mainly from flowing effortless stroked drives through the covers and past point,'* Denys Rowbotham writes in the Manchester Guardian, *'Wharton from more or less the same shots more roughly hewn and powerfully punched. Where Barber persuaded, Wharton bludgeoned.'* The blending of such difference is not well handled by the Lancashire committee, but this evening their runs together offer the prospect that *'Lancashire could win not only this match but the championship.'*

"At the end of the first day we all mixed with the opposition. We didn't go off our separate ways as they do now." Saturday night. *'The best and bingiest glad time of the week'* for lathe worker Arthur Seaton. *'One of the fifty-two holidays in the slow-turning Big Wheel of the year.'* It is not such a hard-drinking evening for the Yorkshire cricketers. In Don's memory there is more singing than alcohol. He and Philip Sharpe, with their Black and White Minstrel songs. 'Back in the Old Routine' and 'When The Saints Go Marching In'. Phil on the piano or strumming the ukelele.

'Oh when the saints, oh when the saints,
Go marching in, go marching in,
Oh when the saints go marching in.'

Don is just 22 years old, and little can he guess that he and Phil will spend winters as dressers to the Minstrels, "can you imagine anything more delectable?", and that sometimes they will make up the numbers in the chorus line? "We could sing the show absolutely backwards." Or that in ten years' time, on a cricket tour of the Far East, he will be commanded to sing for the King of Thailand. "This silly Black and White Minstrel singing, it had spread to all parts of the world. I was absolutely petrified."

'I want to be there in that number
When the saints go marching in."

"It was tremendous for team spirit." And over the years there are plenty of other singers in this Yorkshire side. "There was Tony Nicholson, with his 'Sixteen Tons'. *'Sixteen tons, and what do you get? You get another day older and deeper in debt.'* And Dickie Bird, with his 'Abba Dabba'. He used to do all the hand movements; it brought the house down." And Fred? "Fred was very bass. 'Ol' Man River' was his special. *'You and me we sweat and slave, bodies all aching and wracked with pain.'* And the 23rd Psalm. He used to conduct us in the different parts. They got annoyed with us on the staircases of these lovely old hotels, but the acoustics were brilliant. We played Bud Flanagan's side at Kew once, and we all sang 'Underneath the Arches'. They were magical moments. But that was the sixties. It was a fun time, nothing nasty."

Fred Trueman and Brian Statham. They are in their prime here in 1960. "You'll have to go hundreds of years before you see a pair like Trueman and Statham again." In the public mind Fred is the hard-drinking miner's son, bristling with aggression, and Brian the quiet and clinical son of a dentist, pursuing his skill with no fuss. But appearances are deceptive. "Brian was very quiet, never said anything to anybody, but he did love drinking. He'd go to bed with a crate of ale, would Brian. But Fred couldn't drink a pint." *'Are you a sipper or a supper?'* the Brewers' Society advert will ask, and Fred will be there with his pint glass in his hand. *'"Sip it for the photograph," they said. But when I sip a pint, I don't sip, I sup.'* "He was absolutely paralytic on two pints, but he was a very clever businessman, was Fred."

Lancashire's David Green agrees. "It was all image. He would never turn down a drink, but at the end of the evening these pots would all be strategically placed behind curtains."

'The Lord is my shepherd, I'll not want,' they sing.

It is the summer of 1960. British rule is ending in Cyprus, a summons for obscenity is issued against Penguin Books for 'Lady Chatterley's Lover', and the Central Lancashire League batting averages show newcomer Basil D'Oliveira in second place behind Gary Sobers. Lancashire are in a strong position here at Old Trafford and, after a sunny Sunday, great crowds arrive on Monday morning.

"I lived in Settle," Don tells. "A little market town eleven miles from the Lancashire border. I used to come over each morning. We always had to be there one hour before the start of play but, if you had any sense, for a game like that you'd be there at eight or eight-thirty. It was a daunting sight to see them queuing. And to realise that they were coming to watch you."

Worcestershire's Roy Booth was the Yorkshire keeper here in 1955, and he still remembers the scene on Bank Holiday Monday morning. "I was batting overnight, and Vic Wilson picked me up. When we got to Old Trafford station, I had to get out of the car and run to the ground. The traffic was so packed, and there were thousands pouring out of the station. All the Lancashire members with red roses in their button holes, the Yorkshire members with white ones."

'It was just like old times,' John Kay writes in the Manchester Evening News. *'There were queues from an early hour with several hundred waiting for the turnstiles to be opened.'* "I can't describe the feeling of seeing these vast crowds," Don says. This is only his second Roses match here and, like so many old players, his first is indelibly marked on his memory. "I didn't get a bowl till five past five. Pullar and Washbrook were batting, and they had a hell of a score. And this train had stopped behind the old scorebox. There were about twenty of my people from Settle in the crowd, and they gave a great cheer. And I had to bowl at Cyril Washbrook. Cocky, thick set, with those great pads of his. He went down on one knee, and I'm looking for the ball where this train has stopped. But I've bowled him out, and I'm so elated, I'm jumping in the air like a mad fool. But we didn't have all this kissing and hugging. All I heard was this voice from Fred at mid off: 'It's a bloody good job they've closed the gates or this lad'll run all the way home to Settle.'"

There is no such elation this morning as Barber and Wharton make *'a tentative beginning'*. The embankments and stands are full to overflowing and, *'when the first venturesome juveniles darted beneath the railings to fling themselves on the grass at the boundary boards, their seniors followed them like a cascade in the widening breach in the dyke until the playing area was ranged five, ten, fifteen, twenty deep.'* "All those schoolchildren on the boundary. We signed lots of autographs. It was a great thing to have the crowd so close to you." At ten past one a cheer greets the first innings lead, and there is still just one wicket down.

There are thirty-four thousand in the ground, and receipts from the match will equal those for all Lancashire's first twelve games here. *'The people are still prepared to come to the cricket,'* the Times correspondent writes, *'but only if the fare is good and the occasion really warrants it.'* Roy Tattersall and Malcolm Hilton, two great Lancashire spinners, are at Scarborough with the second team, but this is their benefit match, and their team mate Geoff Clayton remembers sending them a telegram from the Old Trafford pavilion. 'Your prayers are answered,' it reads.

It is July 1960. It costs threepence to send a letter, three shillings for a telegram up to twelve words. It is the last year of the farthing bit.

At 157 for one, Bob Barber *'went for a big hit and didn't quite get to the ball that Wilson pitched temptingly wide'*. Fred holds the catch at mid-off, but this time such success is not quite so new and Don does not threaten to run to Settle. Lunch is taken at 164 for two, and *'the sun was shining on the gaily bedecked multitude'*. A Lancashire lead of ten runs already, the biggest Bank Holiday crowd for years at Old Trafford, and the sun shining. *'A Lancastrian's idea of bliss,'* the Times declares.

But cricket is a game of many surprises, and the Manchester weather is even more unpredictable. Vic Wilson is fielding at leg slip. "A great farmer, he was," Don says, "with hands like buckets," and he *'brilliantly caught Wharton low at short leg.'* Grieves falls lbw for five, then *'a black cloud came to roost over the ground'* and, though the players stay out long enough to be soaked, it is five fifteen before the match resumes, the scattering crowd leaving *'newspapers, sandwich wrappings and empty bottles as dismal litter on the darkened grass'*.

"We wrote letters when it rained," Don recalls. "There was this bridge club, with Illingworth and Close. It was absolutely criminal if we put Closey off playing his next card. So the rest of us had to write letters."

When they do get back out, there is sawdust everywhere, *'indicating how narrow was the margin of practicality.'* "You'd be amazed how many times we used to go out with bags and bags of sawdust," Don recalls. "It used to be like a circus ring." He runs his memories forward five years to Yorkshire's Gillette Cup victory at Lord's. "It wasn't an iota fit for playing, but it was a big crowd and we didn't even think of not going out." And to Kent's visit to Harrogate the following summer. "Colin Cowdrey rolled up his trousers to fork the ground, just so they could try to finish third in the championship. Crikey, they wouldn't even look at it now. They'd say, match off."

Here at Old Trafford the match is on again, and 187 for four is soon 203 for nine as *'the ball was lifting excitingly for Trueman and Ryan, as no doubt it would have lifted for Statham and Higgs.'* "Please, Mr Barber, declare," a voice calls out, but Bob Barber prefers to watch his keeper Geoff Clayton adding a further 23 runs, with *'a series of scarcely credible cross-batted clouts and edged slashes'*. But that is 'Chimp' Clayton for you, a great competitor but not one to be inhibited by committees or traditions. A teenage Peter Lever is pushing for a place in this Lancashire side, and he knows how good a keeper Chimp is. "A great pair of hands. His anticipation was tremendous. He should have played for England, but he kicked against all authority." At Lord's in May he played for the M.C.C. against Yorkshire, a sign that the selectors are looking at him. *'Clayton held five catches and altogether impressed,'* Wisden reports, but perhaps he does not impress where it matters. "He turned up with a black eye," Peter Lever tells, "a big shiner somebody had given him. 'What about your eye, Clayton?' some M.C.C. member said. Geoff turned round. 'What the bloody hell's it got to do with thee?'"

Today he is awarded his county cap, the leading wicket keeper in the country in only his second summer, and *'rather as a fly might torment a lion he drove Trueman to distraction'*. It is rich enjoyment for the depleted crowd but, when the last wicket falls with Lancashire 72 ahead, perhaps Yorkshire are grateful that they have only fifty minutes to bat, and *'the wicket had eased considerably from the roller and an hour's drying'*. Nevertheless, Bryan Stott and Doug Padgett both fall cheaply, and *'Taylor, who played or tried to play the last over, must have been mightily relieved at its passing without a third wicket to Statham.'*

It is 19 for two and, according to Robin Marlar in the Daily Telegraph, *'the remainder will have to bat extremely well tomorrow to prevent Lancashire from bringing off the hardest double in county cricket.'* A double not brought off since 1893. Not since Albert Ward leant back like a contortionist and took the sure sixer in his huge carpet-bag hands. Little does Don know as he crosses the border on his way home to Settle but tomorrow's finish will provide drama just as great. "I wish Uncle Walter had been alive to compare it," A.A. Thomson writes.

Don has started his working life as an apprentice joiner, but he has lost that winter employment now. Lost it on the night last January when the Thames-Clyde express train crashed at Settle and his father, an ambulance superintendent, took him along to aid the rescue. It was one day off work too many for his employers, and now he faces the coming winter with the same insecurity as so many of his team mates. Ken Taylor plays football for Huddersfield, and Doug Padgett is a wool sorter in Bradford. But Brian Close and Ray Illingworth sell greetings cards to newsagents, and Don joins them, taking on the patch that includes Manchester. "Raymond made a good business out of it; he covered the whole country. But I didn't work that hard."

Certainly not as hard as he works when he dresses the Black and White Minstrels, but then that is an affair of the heart. Like playing cricket for Yorkshire.

"We did love the game. And I can't say they look that way in this present era, even for all the gimmes and the cars. They don't really look very happy. Even the under-18s. 'I'm sorry, Don, I can't be here tomorrow. I'm changing my sponsored car.' I wouldn't have dared say that to Brian Sellers. I wouldn't have played for a month. I find that sad. The game's more important than what you can take out of it." But Don knows exactly what he has taken out of it. "It was fabulous fun. We used to be a community of men. We were there to play, we were there to enjoy it, and we were there to entertain. The players of that era, we have all got good memories." And there are few days of cricket that remain more vivid in Don's memory than Tuesday the second of August 1960.

I.T.V. is negotiating a £142,000 deal to televise football, but Tom Finney turns down an offer of £100 a match to play for P.S.V. Eindhoven. "I was given a free release by Preston," he says, "and it would be wrong for me to take advantage of it. If I had wanted to continue playing, I would have stayed with Preston."

Play starts at eleven, and by a quarter to twelve the Yorkshire score is 36 for five, and only half the first innings arrears has been cleared. It is all looking much like the game at Headingley at Whitsun when Lancashire bamboozled them twice with leg break bowling. "Yorkshire were horrified by leg-spinners, to play against or to come and play for them", and Greenhough and Barber are both England bowlers. Yorkshire, all out 96 and 117 at Headingley. Here at Old Trafford *'Sharpe batted extremely competently but both the Wilsons were in all sorts of agony against the leg-spinners.'*

Don has inherited the hot seat of Yorkshire cricket. The slow left arm bowler in the tradition of Rhodes and Verity. His predecessor, Johnny Wardle, sacked so controversially two years back, was a real entertainer with the bat. And Don's early games showed few signs of matching him. He bagged a pair against Barber and Greenhough at Headingley. "Tommy was a great character. I think he talked more people out than he actually bowled. He was always chirruping at you. In the second innings he said to me, 'Here, Wils, get a run off this', and he dollied up this great full toss. And I went and missed it and was bowled." In the next match he got another pair, and it was only at Hull in July, when somebody shouted out "Send for Wardle", that he found any form, walloping ten fours and a six in his 83. "Well done, Don," Fred said on the pavilion steps. "At last you've laid to rest the ghost of Johnny Wardle." Here at Old Trafford he props up an end for his minstrel friend Phil Sharpe, and they inch the score past 100 by lunch. *'This is the best innings I have seen Sharpe play,'* says the Times correspondent. "He got this terrible tag that he couldn't play slow bowling," Don says. "I don't think it was true."

After lunch it is Statham that makes the breakthrough, trapping Phil Sharpe *'with an appeal for lbw evidently stirring up his sore threat'*. It is his sixth lbw of the match, but then everybody knows how straight he bowls. "We never argued about lbws," Don says. "I suppose some of us might have complained if we'd seen the replay like they do today, but we were never brought up to that." Don strikes *'some skimming on-drives'*, but *'a full toss from Barber so excited Trueman that he missed a sweep and was leg before wicket, and the mere turn of a leg break was sufficient for Ryan.'* Yorkshire are 149 all out, and they have left Lancashire just 78 to score between ten past three and a quarter past five. *'In all logic there should have been no need for excitement.'*

"As the day progressed," Don remembers, "the crowd started to build. At first it was nearly empty. Because the match really should have been over by lunchtime. But the word got round Manchester that everything was becoming exciting, and there were ten or fifteen thousand there by the end."

'Lancashire's troubles were partly self-imposed,' the Times records, *'for they allowed Yorkshire to develop an astute defensive plan. Pullar batted 80 minutes for 14.'* No looking up at the scoreboard and wondering where his runs have come from today. *'Barber three-quarters of an hour for nine.'* No glittering stroke play from the amateur. *'Gradually the clock began to overtake them.'* This is Neville Cardus's *'suspicious thriftiness'*.

It is the summer of 1960, before the introduction of one-day cricket. "We didn't have all these men on the boundary like they do now. I remember Peter May saying to me in the eighties, 'We have men in set areas to stop people scoring.' And I said, 'Do you know, Peter, people used to travel miles to see you whip that ball through mid-wicket for four runs. They used to watch you hit that one, bang, through extra cover, and they'd leave the ground, saying 'Ooh, that shot of Peter May's.' It'll only be one now, and nobody remembers one."

But this is a Roses match, and Yorkshire are facing their second defeat at the hands of the old enemy. "What are you going to do?" Brian Close recalls asking Vic Wilson. "We can't do any more than try our best," Vic replies. "Vic wasn't a flamboyant captain," Don recalls, "but he knew he had x batsmen and y bowlers. It was more of a calculating way of captaining the side." But Brian Close is always one for trying something different. "Let Freddie and Mel bowl short of a length at the off stump. Set the field to save ones, and put a man on the boundary where they might get four. Then, if that works, they might panic."

It is certainly better thinking than his plan to get Gary Sobers out at Sheffield in 1963. "This chap can't play spin bowling," he announces, and he throws the ball to Don and positions himself at short leg. "He was still stood there when Sobers was 100. The best chance I had of getting Sobers out was if

Closey had been fielding in the High Street at Worksop, twenty-odd miles away."

'Having started by hardly running at all, they began to contemplate the improbable. Barber was brilliantly thrown out by Padgett, who then took a splendid running catch to send back Wharton. When Pullar was bowled by Ryan, 80 minutes had brought 31 runs, and Marner was beaten at once by a full-toss from Trueman.' 32 for four. Mel Ryan, "he was a big man, had a great heart for Yorkshire cricket", removes Collins and Statham, and it is 43 for six, only half an hour left to score the last 35 runs. *'Palms grew hot, voices shrill; the nervous tension that no other game raises to such a degree seized Old Trafford in a threat of hysteria.'*

Ken Grieves is still at the wicket. An Australian with sleeked black hair and film star looks. "A good player, he hit the ball hard." *'He took upon himself the whole burden of Lancashire's batting: directive, executant, inspirational.'* But all he has left to partner him are Dyson, Clayton, Greenhough and Higgs. At 46 for six Clayton comes through the gate, and all round the ground they begin to wonder what has happened to their number four on the scorecard, Jack Dyson. "I never had any nerves," Geoff Clayton tells. "I was brought up in the hard school. It never affected me." And Dyson? "He used to go and hide in the toilet. He was a bag of nerves. He was a good lad, but he wasn't the ideal man to have in a crisis." And this is indeed a crisis. "That Roses match, it's something you've got to play in to realise what it's like."

"I was down at third man," Don tells. "And I looked up to see this massive ground ringed with police. 'What's the problem?' I said. 'Are you expecting trouble?' 'Trouble?' this policeman said. 'If Yorkshire win this match, they'll lynch Lancashire from that pavilion balcony there.' And my god, he meant it." *'By now the players were very tense,'* Robin Marlar reports, *'and through binoculars the veins on one balding head seemed to stand out like lollipops.'* 35 in 30 minutes becomes 30 in 18. Fred and Mel Ryan have bowled unchanged for an hour and three quarters.

"Mel's tiring," Brian Close tells Vic Wilson. "Give me the ball. I'll keep it tight." But maybe Vic thinks of Brian's full-tosses, and he sticks to his opening bowlers. *'Grieves, with nine in an over off Ryan, reduced the sum to 19 runs in eight minutes.'*

Geoff Clayton is on strike. Facing Frederick Sewards Trueman, the greatest fast bowler in the world. Lancashire's Peter Lever recalls his own first entrance into a Roses match. At Sheffield in 1963. Ryan and Trueman rampant, Lancashire 53 for six, "you can imagine the Yorkshire crowd", and Geoff Clayton at the other end. "'You look after Melville,' Chimp said, 'and I'll look after this big, daft bugger at the other end.' He used to wind Fred up something. 'I'll start talking to Sewards,' he said. 'I can't understand it, Fred,' he said to him. 'The pitch is as flat as a pancake, you're bowling your guts out and every bugger else is watching. Why are they not having to bowl?' 'Blimey, you may be right,' Fred said. 'Here, Closey!', and he disappeared from the attack."

It is not so easy today and *'when Clayton opened his shoulders and heaved with all the strength of his small, squat frame, he lofted the ball over Trueman's head for J.V. Wilson, trotting round from deep mid-off to take the easy catch.'* Vic Wilson, the farmer, his bucket-like hands may be as huge as old Albert Ward's carpet-bag ones back in 1893. "This blooming thing popped up," Don tells, "and of all people he went and dropped it. It was an absolute dolly." *'It was a catch he would normally have held in the course of light and irrelevant conversation,'* John Kay writes in the Manchester Evening News. *'The sitter of the year,'* Crawford White calls it in the News Chronicle.

'Yet even after two more singles from this fated over, Lancashire still needed 16 in six minutes.' Or is it six minutes? *'At this stage it was suddenly realised in the Press box that the two clocks on the ground were not synchronised. This added mightily to the pandemonium therein.'*

62 for six and sixteen wanted. Mel Ryan's last over sees Geoff Clayton hit two fours and Ken Grieves fall on the final ball to a catch behind. 72 for seven, six to win off one over from Fred, and the pavilion clock reads five-fourteen. There is still no sign of Jack Dyson as Tommy Greenhough emerges through the gate.

'If I live to be 100,' John Kay writes in the Manchester Evening News, *'I shall never forget the nerve-tingling anxiety of batsmen, bowlers, spectators, and even the umpires as Freddie Trueman spat on his hands and began the last over. Afterwards umpire Syd Buller told me he could have heard a pin drop as Trueman ran up for each and every ball.'*

Six runs wanted, six balls to be bowled. Off the first Geoff Clayton straight drives a single. *'The next shattered Greenhough's stumps.'* Five to win off four balls and only two wickets to fall. *'This was cricket only for the robust in health.'* After a seeming eternity Jack Dyson emerges from the pavilion.

"You can play against Australia, you can play against West Indies," Len Hutton tells Don, "but you'll never play a game of cricket like the Roses match." "If Yorkshire win this match," the policeman says, "they'll lynch Lancashire from that pavilion balcony there."

It is August 1960, Lancashire top of cricket's county table and Burnley the Football League champions. There are eight Lancashire clubs in the First Division, with Liverpool so close each year to making it nine.

When Manchester City won the F.A. Cup Final at Wembley four years ago, Jack Dyson scored their third goal. In front of a hundred thousand people. But that, it seems, is as nothing, compared with coming out to bat this afternoon. "He couldn't hold a cigarette still," Peter Lever tells. "He was shaking so much." "He came out like a ghost," Don says. "There's a rumour going, and I can't vouch for it, that they'd been giving him the old calming down injection."

All afternoon, the News Chronicle tells, its telephones are ringing with inquiries about the Roses match. *There is no need for counties to be cowards when contemplating the future. They simply have to do what was done at Old Trafford and play cricket, lovely cricket.* It is August 1960. Within three months the News Chronicle will be gone, absorbed by the Daily Mail.

Five runs are wanted off four balls, and the first of them runs off Dyson's pads to Mel Ryan at fine leg. "I groaned silently," Mel remembers. "I was half-blinded by sweat and almost rigid with tension." Five wickets in the greatest of Roses finishes, this afternoon will be the highlight of his career. "But I fumbled, and the single became a two." Then Dyson jabs the ball down into the block-hole and Geoff Clayton, *'backing up furiously and roaring for a single'*, is down at the striker's end in a trice. Two to win off two balls and two wickets left. *'Clayton stuck out a pugnacious chin and chopped a single to third man.'* One ball left, one run to win, and the ghostly Jack Dyson to face it.

"Fred marked his run up," Don tells. "He swept back his hair and hitched up his sleeve. And off he went. What a sight he was! And as he got to the crease, Chimp Clayton was miles to the far end, shouting 'Run, run, run'. And Fred never let go of the ball. He held the ball over the stumps, and we as players didn't know what he was going to do. I'm short third man now, in the circle, and I remember hearing Fred say, 'Lancashire, you've lost.' And we all gasped."

"Lancashire, you've lost." Not technically a loss, it's true. But in the passion of that moment and to be run out before the ball is bowled, it must seem like a loss. "But Fred wouldn't take the bails off. He put the ball in his pocket, and he marched off back to his run-up. Whereupon the police sighed with unbelievable relief."

As Mel Ryan writes, "the age of cricketing chivalry was not yet dead."

'The frenzied crowd were suddenly quite still. Dyson crouched low, and the menacing Trueman spat on his hands. Then the fiery Yorkshireman began tearing in for his do-or-die thrust.' Hair flowing, sleeve flapping. Geoff Clayton stays in his crease, and Jack Dyson inches backwards, expecting a bumper. Don smiles. "Fred, as much as his greatness was, he never really knew where the ball was going. He used to tell you he did the off-cutter, the leg-cutter, this yorker and that yorker, but we all knew that Fred was Fred. He just ran up and bowled. And he was absolutely brilliant."

Mel Ryan puts it differently. "Fred was a great competitor. He refused to believe that any batsman could withstand him when he was absolutely determined, and he certainly was that now. I think he tried to bowl a leg-stump yorker." He has bowled unchanged for two hours, sixteen overs. A fast bowler with a long run. In an Old Trafford bubbling with emotion. And he has only conceded 24 runs. As thrifty as Lancashire's early batting but perhaps there is Yorkshire's 'saving relish' in his outsize personality.

By the end of the summer Fred will have bowled 1068 overs and taken 175 wickets. Without a hint of breaking down. But this is before they start to worry about the bowler dragging his back foot through the line. "The thing I do remember about the sixties," Don says, "was this damn no ball law. First they tried putting a disc down for the drag, and that didn't seem to work. Then they brought in this incredible law that you had to have your front foot behind the front line. It absolutely ruined the likes of Fred. Then you were allowed to break the line. And, since that moment of the front foot rule, we seem to have had more injuries."

It is 1960, the start of a new decade. John Kennedy is campaigning for the American Presidency, and Princess Margaret has married a photographer. Little does the crowd here at Old Trafford know, as Fred runs in to deliver this last ball, how many changes their game will undergo before the decade is out. And how their Lancashire will find glory as the first champions of a new instant Sunday cricket, designed to bring back the crowds. "We were against the one-day stuff," Don tells. "Brian Close said that, if we played too much one-day cricket, we'd lose the art of the game. And looking at it now, he was dead right."

Who needs one-day cricket when you can see a finish like this? *'I thought Trueman might deliver a bouncer, or bowl one slightly wide of the stumps,'* the Times correspondent reveals. *'Instead, he fired one fast and straight and full of length.'* Jack Dyson has scored a goal at Wembley, and now he gets the thinnest edge onto his pad, and the ball races away to fine leg for four. *'I don't know if there were any heart attacks or fainting cases,'* John Kay writes, *'but thousands dared not look until Clayton threw his bat yards into the air in the most dramatic, triumphant minute I have ever experienced in cricket.'*

"Defeat was a serious matter for Yorkshire in 1960," Mel Ryan writes, "but two defeats in one season by Lancashire, that was just a bit too much." *'Ryan will never bowl better or longer,'* John Kay declares. *'He was weeping unashamedly at the end.'*

'The scorebook says that Lancashire won by two wickets,' writes J.M. Kilburn in the Yorkshire Post, *'but they really won by the last straining of nerve and sinew, the last and highest conception of a cricket match. Their victory was a magnificence of cricketing fascination, with the highest honours, the deepest disappointments and the greatest anxieties shared by two teams who will never forget the experience.'*

"It was a day's cricket which will live in my mind forever," Mel Ryan writes. Don Wilson shakes his head. "How could you ever forget a game like that?"

Lancashire have done the double for the first time since 1893. And they will only ever do it once more, in 1989. But by then the people of the North will have more annual leave and more money to spend on escaping from the Manchester rain. Wool and cotton mills will have become museums and industrial estates. Bank holidays will be allocated to international cricket, and there will be Yorkshire players born in Australia, Scotland, even Manchester. The 'lust and dust of battle' will not have the same intensity. "The tradition's not the same now," Don reflects. "You know, Michael Parkinson flew his wife back to Barnsley to give birth in case it was a boy."

Lancashire are top of the table now, and the Times once more looks back to 1893. *'Yorkshire and Lancashire were lying first and second in the table,'* it notes. *'Yorkshire went on to win, with Lancashire second and Middlesex third, and one is tempted to wonder the extent of the omen.'*

It all ends just as the Times wonders, Middlesex even finishing third. Lancashire stay top for another fortnight, but by the end of the season the committee's disciplinarian regime has seen Geoff Clayton banished to the second eleven, Jack Dyson sacked, Alan Wharton seeking pastures new at Leicester, and even Bob Barber censured.

Come back here in six years. Another August Bank Holiday, and this time it will be Yorkshire who complete the double on the last possible ball. Only two of this Lancashire side will be playing, but there will still be eight here from this Yorkshire. And they will still be winning championships and singing on the stairwells.

"I wasn't a great cricketer," Don reflects, "but I got into a very successful side. I was a very lucky person to have played my cricket in that Yorkshire team of the sixties."

'You and me, we sweat and slave,
Bodies all aching and wracked with pain.'

It is forty years now since the 21-year-old Don celebrated Washbrook's wicket at Old Trafford, 'jumping in the air like a mad fool', but his hands and arms still fly in all directions, his face is still full of the same enthusiasm. "Fabulous fun," he says. "I've got so many great memories." Why, he has even sung for the King of Thailand.

'I want to be in that number
When the saints go marching in.'

LANCASHIRE v YORKSHIRE

Old Trafford. 30 July, 1 & 2 August 1960

LANCASHIRE WON BY 2 WICKETS

YORKSHIRE

W.B. Stott	c Marner b Higgs	1	c Collins b Statham	5
K. Taylor	b Higgs	19	b Higgs	8
D.E.V. Padgett	lbw b Greenhough	21	lbw b Statham	6
D.B. Close	b Statham	63	lbw b Statham	9
P.J. Sharpe	lbw b Statham	16	lbw b Statham	46
R. Illingworth	lbw b Statham	7	c Clayton b Dyson	9
*J.V. Wilson	b Statham	13	c Clayton b Greenhough	20
D. Wilson	lbw b Statham	0	not out	32
F.S. Trueman	not out	3	lbw b Barber	4
+J.G. Binks	b Higgs	4	b Higgs	1
M. Ryan	b Higgs	0	b Barber	3
Extras	b 1, lb 5, nb 1	7	lb 5, nb 1	6
		154		**149**

1-1, 2-20, 3-64, 4-93, 5-113, 6-146, 7-146, 8-147, 9-154, 10-154
1-8, 2-18, 3-19, 4-28, 5-36, 6-63, 7-89, 8-121, 9-143, 10-149

Statham	23	7	43	5	24	13	23	4	
Higgs	17.2	6	48	4	16	7	35	2	
Greenhough	15	2	46	1	16	6	43	1	
Dyson	5	2	10	0	10	6	12	1	
Barber	1	1	0	0	7.3	0	30	2	

LANCASHIRE

*R.W. Barber	c Trueman b D. Wilson	71	run out	11
G. Pullar	c Taylor b Close	11	b Ryan	14
A. Wharton	c J.V. Wilson b Trueman	83	c Padgett b Ryan	4
J. Dyson	b Trueman	15	not out	5
K. Grieves	lbw b Ryan	5	c Binks b Ryan	27
P. Marner	run out	4	b Trueman	0
R. Collins	b Trueman	0	b Ryan	2
+G. Clayton	c Close b Trueman	28	not out	15
T. Greenhough	c Sharpe b Ryan	0	b Trueman	0
J.B. Statham	c J.V. Wilson b Ryan	0	c Binks b Ryan	0
K. Higgs	not out	3		
Extras	b 4, lb 1, nb 1	6	lb 3	3
		226	(8 wkts)	**81**

1-26, 2-157 3-172 4-187, 5-191, 6-195, 7-199, 8-199, 9-203, 10-226
1-16, 2-27, 3-31, 4-32, 5-43, 6-43, 7-72, 8-73

Trueman	28	5	65	4	16	4	28	2
Ryan	33	9	69	3	15	4	50	5
Close	12	3	23	1				
D. Wilson	13	7	35	1				
Illingworth	16	6	28	0				

Umpires: John Langridge and J.S. Buller

WE'LL GO SEVEN DOWN

Nottinghamshire v Surrey

May 1961

chosen by John Clay

with Mike Willett

John Clay was born in Nottingham in 1924. An opening batsman, he played for Nottinghamshire from 1948 to 1961, captaining the county in his final year. From 1962 to 1968 he captained the second eleven, after which he worked for Boots in Nottingham until he retired.

Mike Willett was born in West Norwood in 1933. A batsman and occasional medium-pace bowler, he played for Surrey from 1955 to 1967. After cricket he went into the motor trade.

They remember a Bank Holiday match with a surprising finish at Trent Bridge.

The five-minute bell rings. The umpires take the field. Then the Surrey side, all in their chocolate-coloured caps, and behind them the opening batsmen: John and his partner Norman Hill.

Whitsun 1961. The talk around the counties is of the need for Brighter Cricket, and Wisden is clear where the responsibility lies: "There is nothing wrong that the captains cannot put right." Here in Nottingham John Clay is in his first month in charge, and he has opted to bat first on *'an ideal batting strip.'* But then, is it ever anything else at Trent Bridge?

The five-minute bell. John is 36 now, the senior professional turned captain for this one summer, and he is playing on the ground where he watched as a boy. The youngest of thirteen, he grew up in George Road, less than half a mile away, in the days before the motor car drowned out all other noise. "I could hear the five-minute bell and run and be there before the players came out."

Nottinghamshire and Surrey. In the 1880s, they dominated the emerging county championship, and the tradition began of playing at the two Bank Holidays. Between the wars one or other of them was often challenging for the title, and John recalls his childhood excitement every Whitsun: "The Surrey game was always special. People still talk about it now. The very names: Sandham, Hobbs, Barling, Gover. And they had those brown caps on, where everybody else had blue or green. That attracted me for a start."

Nottinghamshire and Surrey. It is many years now since they met on equal terms. Surrey have won eight championships since 1950 while Notts have finished seven times in the bottom three. The score in their Bank

Holiday encounters in these years is Surrey sixteen victories, Nottinghamshire one.

Bedser and Loader, Laker and Lock. Has any county ever had such a fine bowling attack as Surrey in the fifties? Lock and Surridge and Stewart, they crouch around the bat and take catches galore. And if there are runs required, there are Barrington and P.B.H. May, Stewart and now the young John Edrich. "How could you compete with that lot?" John Clay asks. "They were just better players than us."

It is not an equal contest, but at least Surrey is a team to draw a good crowd. *'Notts depend upon the visit of Surrey to provide them with a rich financial reward,'* Harry Richards writes in the Nottingham Evening Post, but a cool and cloudy day keeps the attendance down to just three thousand. These patient Nottingham supporters have not seen their county win at home for nearly two years now, not since July 1959 - when Norman Hill scored two centuries in the match against Lancashire. Here against Surrey *'Hill was soon on the offensive, driving Gibson to the cover boundary, but he did not stay long. Only 14 had been scored when, playing defensively, he popped the ball up, and fast bowler Loader dived to hold the catch.'*

"Norman fought it out all the time," John recalls. "He really struggled for his runs." It is a struggle that will see him score 2,000 this summer, with six centuries, just as he did two years ago. What a contrast with his namesake Maurice: just seven centuries to show for 484 first-class innings. Yet it is Maurice that the England selectors ask after, and it is Maurice who brings a sparkle to John's eye. "He was such a beautiful player. Even if he wasn't getting runs, he looked elegant. He played some great innings, and I remember them as much as I remember anybody's. But I don't know what it was. He just didn't have any go in him. I used to say to him, 'Maurice, I lie awake at night, worrying about you.' And he'd just smile. He was from Lincolnshire, and he had this expression: 'Don't worry, my old mate, you're all right.' And I said, 'I'm all right. It's you I'm worrying about. You should be playing for England.' 'Oh no, don't worry about it.'"

Maurice is not even in the team here today and, as Peter Loader recovers from his tumbling catch, Norman is replaced at the wicket by Merv Winfield. *'The fast bowlers Loader and Gibson were lively and hostile, often getting the ball past the bat,'* but *'fortunately Clay and Winfield were in useful form.'* The score has reached 73 by the time Merv edges Tony Lock into the slips, and lunch is taken at 77 for two. *'Good common sense batting,'* Gordon Ross calls it in the Observer.

"I worked and I concentrated," John reflects. "Most of the time I was just glad to get some runs and be in the side for the next match. That's how ordinary players like me looked at it. I can only remember one game when everything I did went right." His memory goes back to August Bank Holiday 1953 at The Oval. Simpson, stumped McIntyre, bowled Lock, 88. Clay, caught and bowled Lock, 89. An opening partnership of 159. "I'll never forget that day. Stuart Surridge was giving Locky some terrible stick, and Locky was getting redder and redder. Alec and Eric Bedser, Bernie Constable, they were all niggling at each other - in a mardy way, as we say up here in Nottingham. It was the only time I ever really relaxed when I was batting." The next day John hit another 58, *'driving and cutting brilliantly'*, but Surrey still contrived a six-run victory in the last over.

Clay and Simpson, an opening partnership of 159 in 1953. Now they are a third wicket partnership in 1961. *'After lunch Clay cover drove Loader to complete his first half century of the season.'* Glad to get some runs - though, as captain, he knows he will be in the side for the next match. *'Simpson was fairly restrained but, when Lock dropped one short, he promptly lifted it into the car park.'*

Reg Simpson. Has English cricket had a finer player of fast bowling since the war? "I've never seen a better opening bat in my life," their team mate Bomber Wells says. "I used to think I was quite quick," Somerset's Ken Biddulph says. "Then I'd come up against Reg Simpson, and he'd make me feel like an off-spinner." "He was very much a back-foot player," John explains. "He still preaches the back-foot gospel today. And if anybody bowled a bouncer at him, he'd just sway his head a fraction whereas the likes of me would be ducking. In the end they didn't bother bowling them at him."

Reg Simpson. For ten years he has captained this Nottinghamshire side, and now at the age of 41 he has given way to John and joined the committee as chairman of selectors. He is the Managing Director of Gunn and Moore, "it was more or less obligatory to have a Gunn and Moore bat," and that has allowed him to play as an amateur. "We'd go for a meal with our five shillings' allowance, and he'd sit there eating smoked salmon. We'd go down to London to play at Lord's, we'd be standing up in the third-class and he'd be sitting down in the first." Forty years on, John shakes his head. Reg is not a man of many words. He has carried the Notts batting for years, and he does not suffer fools gladly. But "he couldn't have been better to me. 'I'm chairman of selectors,' he said, 'but John's captain. He'll have the final say.'"

Reg is a great believer in Brighter Cricket, and he encourages John to take the same approach. "'Don't play for yourself,' I'd tell the blokes, 'play for the team.'" *'The tempo changed. Clay added 27 in 40 minutes after lunch, and Simpson showed something of his old charm.'* Then John is caught at short leg, and the real highlight of the day begins.

Cyril Poole, 'C.J.' "He just came in and played," John says. "He'd be the first man on the sheet for a one-day game. He'd never let the bowlers get on top of him. If he was there, something was happening. A tremendous entertainer. The crowd loved him." *'Poole was spectacular,'* R.H. Maudsley writes in the Sunday Telegraph, *'driving high and low.'* *'Through the years Poole has thrived on Surrey's bowling,'* Gordon Ross writes in the Observer.

'He scored 50 in 40 minutes with a display that fairly sparkled. Simpson was wisely content to watch him in full flight.'

"Cyril always rose to the big occasion." Like last August at The Oval. Steam was rising off the pitch after a torrential downpour, Lock and Loader were almost unplayable, but C.J. hit 64 and 66, and the crowd organised a spontaneous collection for his benefit. "He scored so many runs at The Oval that they used to give him a standing ovation when he went in to bat."

C.J. Poole. Batting against Derbyshire's Jackson and Gladwin at Ilkeston is not something Notts relished in the fifties - "I shan't bother to play at Ilkeston again," the amateur Gamini Goonesena announced after one particularly torrid match - but in 1952 C.J. hit 219 out of 337 there. Then there was the pre-season friendly when he went out with a bat that was leaning against the dressing-room fireplace. "There was a shortage of good willow," according to Bomber Wells, "and this chap came to see Reg with this thing that he said would revolutionise bat-making." A hollowed-out shell, filled with compressed sawdust. "We gave it a go in the indoor nets, but it was dead as a dodo." Ignorant of all this, C.J. strode out with it, and his team mates "rushed out onto the balcony, grinning like Cheshire cats." Again he faced Jackson and Gladwin, and again he smashed the ball all round the ground. "Did he bring out a pocketful of sawdust with him?" George Dawkes, the Derby keeper, asked in the bar afterwards. "Every time he played a shot, there seemed to be a fresh pile of it in the block-hole."

It is 186 for three, and the Surrey bowlers are struggling. But then this is not the Surrey attack of even two years ago. Peter Loader is still quick, but Alec Bedser and Jim Laker have gone, and Tony Lock has a new action. For years the bowlers have been the same but now the understudies have their chance: the *'lively'* David Gibson and today even Mike Willett, playing his 22nd championship match in his 13th summer with Surrey. "I grew up in Lambeth," Mike explains, "a mile from the Oval. As boys we were Just Williams, socks down and snotty noses, and we used to hop over the wall and watch Alf Gover and Jack Parker. I may only have played a dozen times for Surrey in the fifties, but those twelve games were like playing twelve times for England. Just to walk out at the Oval with PBH and Alec, when I'd been playing Club and Ground games at Honor Oak and Streatham, I thought, 'I want to make this my own.'" He has had offers of first-team cricket from Somerset and Gloucestershire but, like all the Surrey second team in the fifties, he has preferred to wait for his chance. "You couldn't imagine playing for any other county than the Brown Hats."

Mike is a batsman; he has never taken a championship wicket. "Loader had been bowling at four times my pace," he remembers, "and nothing had moved all day. Then I ran up. Willett the Dobber, they called me, and this ball took off. Roy Swetman was standing up, and it flew over the top of his head." Peter Loader is at mid-on, and he is quick to quote Alec Bedser's favourite expression. "Mike," he says, "you put a little in, you get a little out." "Trent Bridge was a fast bowler's graveyard," Mike reckons. "For two or three years it must have been the best batting track of all time." And Willett the Dobber has got a ball to take off over the keeper's head. "I've been pally with Loader ever since those days, and he still talks about that ball: 'I'm sure they must have put a commemorative plaque on the wicket,' he says."

Cyril Poole is in *'sparkling'* and *'spectacular'* form, but he lobs Mike's next delivery into the hands of mid-off. "Cyril was a good player," Mike says. "It must have been a good ball to get him out." Alas, that is not how Gordon Ross describes it in the Observer: *'What a disappointment it was to see Poole give himself up with a junior colt's stroke.'* It is Mike's first championship wicket, and *'he liked the idea so much that he put out Simpson and Springall in swift succession.'* Edrich has *'leapt three feet in the air to send back Simpson,'* and Barrington in the slips catches Springall *'like picking a cherry'*. 186 for three is now 191 for six.

It is May 1961. Illegal street betting gives way to newly-licensed betting shops, and minicabs start to operate in London. Anthony Wedgwood Benn becomes Viscount Stansgate and is barred from the House of Commons, Richard Beeching is appointed head of British Railways, and the government announces the creation of new universities in Coventry, Colchester and Canterbury.

Geoff Millman and Carlton Forbes add 54 for the seventh wicket. Geoff is the Notts keeper; twice in recent days he has been watched by Herbert Sutcliffe, the England selector, and he plays *'a very promising innings'* of 40. Then, as wickets fall, there is *'a top of the hill performance by the illustrious "Bomber" Wells'*. Next month at Worksop Bomber will come in at 109 for nine and hit *'a whirlwind 44'*, including a top-edged six that will send the Somerset keeper Harold Stephenson sprinting backwards in vain. "It landed in the river," John remembers, "and Steve nearly finished in it, too." According to Bomber, over half the Somerset side had sprinted backwards - third man, slips, short legs - and, when the ball splashed down, "Steve threw down a glove, stamped on it and shouted 'You lucky, lucky bugger, Bomber.'" John smiles. "Dear old Bomber. I wouldn't say his stories were apocryphal, but like all good storytellers he did tend to enlarge on things."

Bomber is wearing glasses now and, according to Gordon Ross, *'his spectacles have brought such quality to his batting that he was able to hit Loader straight past him like a thunderbolt for four and was out to a ball, which must have almost needed oxygen before it fell back to earth for Parsons to catch.'* He has scored just 17 runs, but the crowd will remember every one of them.

'How things have changed for Surrey,' Gordon Ross writes. *'Stewart as captain, Lock one for 75, and the principal bowler Willett against a Notts side which, striving to redeem its fallen fortunes, was able to score 278 by*

half-past five.' Surrey's bowling may not be what it was two years ago but, even with Peter May resting a pulled hamstring, their batting is as strong as ever. Stewart, Edrich, Barrington, Constable. On Trent Bridge's *'ideal batting strip'*, a score of 278 should pose no problems. *'In the third over Stewart was comfortably caught on the long-leg boundary, but Edrich and Barrington stayed together until the close, untroubled by the bowling.'* 65 for one. *'If the weather holds, there is no reason why they should not get a lot of runs on Monday.'*

John Edrich and Ken Barrington. How they must both love coming to Trent Bridge! Ken first played here in 1955. He grew up in Army barracks in Reading, and that Whit Monday he went out to bat with Arthur McIntyre. "They always had a military band playing during the lunch," Arthur tells, "'Come on, Arthur,' Kenny said, 'let's march them out.' So we marched out to the wicket with our bats over our shoulders like rifles. The crowd loved it. Mind you, they didn't like it quite so much when we both got centuries." Ken was awarded his county cap for that century and, within a fortnight, he was wearing an England cap. He played just two Tests that summer, but four years later he won back his place with another Trent Bridge century. That was Whitsun 1959 when John Edrich came here to play only his second match for Surrey. "My favourite cricket ground in the world," John Edrich calls it, and well he might. A hundred in each innings of that 1959 match, another in 1960, he is already 44 not out tonight. An ideal batting strip and gentle opposition bowling, what more could he want? "Everybody at Trent Bridge was always so friendly," John Edrich says. "They always made visiting players so welcome."

A year ago Bomber Wells moved here from his native Gloucestershire, and he is still acclimatising himself to the grandeur of this Test match ground. No hard benches or bare floorboards in the dressing room. A players' balcony, decorated with flowers. And lunches richer and more varied than any he has known at Bristol. "I swear we had the same salad every day there. And the sweet was always peaches and cream. Sam Cook reckoned somebody had knocked off a load of peaches and stored them in the Nevil Road kitchen."

It is not all that Sam Cook reckons. Bomber and he have made hay for years on the low, slow Bristol wicket, the groundsman forever sprinkling sand across it, and now Bomber has moved to the best batting surface in the country. "He couldn't have come from anywhere more different," John says, but Sam is blunter. "What do you want to go up there for, Bomb? You'll end up being cannon fodder."

In the summer of 1960 Bomber bowled more overs than anybody else in the country, and he proved Sam wrong with 120 wickets. It is a rare day when Notts bowl another side out, but with his cheerful grin and his one-pace run-up Bomber is happy to bowl all day. "What a character!" Mike Willett says. "He looked like Bud Abbott. The lower he went to the ground, the wider he became. And what a bowler! He didn't half spin it, and he was fairly brisk. If he hit you on the leg, he hurt you. But he just stood at the wicket and turned his arm over. John Edrich had this ritual. He always looked down three or four times when the bowler was in his run-up. Well, Bomber would be standing there, ready to let the ball go. I can see him now. 'Are you ready, our John?' he'd ask in that broad Gloucester accent, and John couldn't get his four nods in. They just couldn't get in synch." "If he'd bowled in one-day cricket," John Clay reckons, "he'd have had six overs before they knew he was on."

Here on Saturday night in the Trent Bridge Inn, the TBI, Bomber is there, and John can still imitate his burr as he asks for "a double ginger beer, please". "The social side is so important. Before the war there was a man, Sir Julien Cahn. He was a millionaire in the furniture industry, and he owned his own ground near here. He ran his own team, used to give them jobs. I've always said that, if I could have done that, the first ones on my list would have been Norman Hill, Merv Winfield and Bomber. For the dressing room, the social side."

"Notts were a very friendly side," Mike recalls. "And we had our fun, too. Roy Swetman and I had a little radiogram. We used to have it going in the back of the car. The old 78s, Sinatra and Bobby Darin, they used to melt on the back seat on a hot day. All Swinging music. We used to take the turntable into the hotel and the dressing room. It wasn't quite Sing-along-a-Mike, but it did introduce some gaiety."

'There'll be blue skies up above, everyone's in love,
Up a lazy river how happy we will be.'

Nottingham, home of lace-making and hosiery. "Everybody liked going to Nottingham," Mike remembers, "because the girls outnumbered the men four to one. There was always a bit of a battle to get in the side for the Nottingham game."

'Up a lazy river how happy we will be,
Up a lazy river with me.'

It is the summer of 1961. The Nottingham Advertiser lists day trips from the bus station: East Yorkshire Coast Tour for a pound, the seaside at Cleethorpes for thirteen and threepence, Doncaster Races for nine shillings. Elsewhere in England, though, *'100 brawling, bottle-throwing teenagers ran amok'* during Lord Montagu's jazz festival at Beaulieu, and Jersey's Battle of Flowers is turned into *'an orgy of destruction by hooligans, mostly from London.'*

Monday morning brings a temperature in the mid-fifties, *'warm for Nottingham people'*, and a holiday crowd of eight thousand gathers at Trent Bridge. Soon they are clapping Edrich's fifty, then gasping as Barrington *'hit too soon at a ball from Davison which the downcast Simpson at mid-off dropped.'* Ian Davison is leading the Notts attack today, an attack - according to John Thicknesse in the Daily Telegraph - *'widely considered to be the worst in county cricket'*, and he surprises everybody when Edrich *'shaped to drive him through the covers and got a touch.'* By his own standards, a score of 63 here at Trent Bridge is a failure, but the total is soon racing past 100 as *'Constable began in enterprising style.'*

Ian Davison has bowled for an hour - "he had a great heart" - and so has Pat Oakden, playing in only his second county match. Now it is the turn of Bomber and their newly-qualified Jamaican, Carlton Forbes. "When he laughed, he turned himself inside out," Bomber tells, "so we called him Cha Cha." "He came over as a slow left-armer," John recalls, "but we turned him into a medium-pacer."

It is May 1961. South Africa declares itself a republic, Martin Luther King is besieged by a white mob in his Alabama church, and the British government announces plans to control Commonwealth immigration.

"Some bloke said to me once, 'How do you get on with Carlton in the dressing room?' I said, 'How do you mean?' He said, 'Well, with him being black.' That anybody could say a thing like that just staggered me. He was just another bloke as far as we were concerned."

Another bloke and a good enough cricketer to score 1000 runs and take 59 wickets in this, his first season, but there is no success for him this morning. Mind you, it can never be much fun bowling at the other end from Bomber. His old Gloucester team mate, fast bowler Frank McHugh, likes to tell the story of how one day he was walking down to third man after his over, only to see the ball flash past him for four - "and it wasn't even the first ball of the over." "I tried to get him to slow down," John says, "but he never would. He just stood there, one little hop and he was away."

One little hop, and Bernie Constable is bowled. A few more little hops, and *'Willett could make nothing of Wells. On two occasions he was beaten all over the place and lucky not to be bowled.'* "It was a most confusing situation," Mike says. "You just weren't used to it." But he is still there at lunch, as is Ken Barrington on 75, and the score is 170 for three. *'The visitors were well in command.'*

Bomber from Gloucester, Cha Cha Forbes from Jamaica, Geoff Millman and Ian Davison from Bedford and Hemel Hempstead, John Springall the Cockney. How different from the days when most of the Notts side came from the pit villages. "In my early days," John says, "we were nearly all local." The area chairman of the National Coal Board is warning that mines may close if he cannot overcome the shortage of labour. Meanwhile there is talk of two new types of smokeless fuel.

Ken Barrington returns to the middle, no bat at shoulder arms today, and he drives at his first ball from Davison. *'He did not get to the pitch of it, and Poole at cover held a catch at shoulder height.'* Then Carlton Forbes has Parsons caught in the gully, and Mike Willett hits *'the gangling left-hander*

33

from Jamaica for three fours in an over.' Now it is time for the mathematicians. There are two points for first innings lead and a further two if, at the point of taking the lead, the batting side has a faster scoring rate. Mike steps up the pace, but twelve are still needed in two overs when he is yorked by Ian Davison. Roy Swetman struggles, but *'Tony Lock entered with the air of a man who did not know what all the fuss was about, an attitude he at once explained by hitting the necessary three boundaries in his first four balls.'* Four points for Surrey, an immediate declaration, and John is walking to the wicket once more with Norman Hill.

Norman Hill, not Maurice. The hard-working struggler, not the easy-going natural. Later this summer they will be at Southport, and Norman will get talking to a man who trades in nuts and bolts. "Norman didn't know anything about it," John recalls, "but he went into business with him, one thing led to another, and now he's a tax exile." Mind you, he is not the only member of this Notts side to do so well for himself. "John Springall did the same. He started buying seconds from factories. I always remember, he came into the dressing room with a pile of socks, and Maurice pulled one on. 'Hey, up, Springy, this hasn't got a foot in it.' Then he bought a co-op building in Ruddington, and his wife had a clothes shop. He's got a house in Spain now."

Carlton Forbes, too. "Dave Pullan, who was our keeper for a while, went out to Jamaica, and he happened to mention Carlton's name. Apparently 'Mr Forbes' was a very wealthy man, and after that everything was carte blanche, 'No, no, no, you're a friend of Mr Forbes', he didn't pay for anything." John laughs. "That was different from those days. When you got the cigarettes out, Carlton had always got a match ready, but he'd never got any cigarettes."

Norman Hill faces Peter Loader. Next May he will be down at Swansea, worrying about the angle of delivery of the left-arm quick bowler Jeff Jones. How they still love to tell the story thirty years on! He takes the umpire Harry Baldwin for a drink on the second evening, plies him with plenty of ale and persuades him how as a left-hander he cannot be lbw to Jones if he plays forward. Again and again the next morning the ball hits him on the front pad and Jones appeals with full voice. "Not out," Harry Baldwin replies. "Not out ... not out." The appeals continue, then suddenly the finger goes up, and Norman departs in disbelief. "I'm sorry, Norman," Harry says at lunch. "I drank so much last night, my head couldn't take another appeal." What a pity that Wisden has to spoil it all. Swansea, 1962: *'Hill, lbw b Wheatley, 27.'* Today he fares no better as *'Stewart made a gully catch many feet to his right'* to dismiss him for seven.

Again it is Merv Winfield and John, and again the runs come. *'Clay is too stiff in the elbows to be an attractive player,'* John Thicknesse writes. "I learnt to bat on the narrow path down the side of our house," he says, "with a chalk wicket on the back gate. We never dared hit to leg because it would go next door. So, though I was a very correct player, I had very few shots." John played off the front foot when he came into county cricket, scored his first century against the gentle Somerset attack, then was close to another at Worcester. "I really felt confident, but Reg Perks started bowling bouncers at me from round the wicket, and I didn't know what to do." Reg Simpson has played Test cricket in Australia, and he knows what he thinks. "You've got to learn to play back. You'll get killed if you face people like Lindwall and Miller."

That first century against Somerset, a great day for an anxious young man just making his way into the Notts side. What does John remember of that? "Bill Voce was our coach. I got out just after I'd got my hundred, and he gave me a clip round the ear. 'What sort of bloody shot do you call that?' That's all he said. The same thing today they'd all be around, hugging and kissing. It's all gone too far the other way, hasn't it? He was delighted that I'd got a hundred, and half an hour later he came over and said so. But he was right. I'd lost concentration, and we did lose the game in the end."

'Clay used his feet well to the spinners and consistently found the gaps.' Another fifty, though there are no great celebrations, just as there are none when he is caught behind off Eric Bedser. "People today see the old film, and they talk as if we weren't trying. 'You didn't seem to show any emotions,' they say. It was our living, our bread and butter. My wife needed money to buy clothes for the children, just like they do now. We were just as keen as they are. You just didn't show your feelings. It wasn't the thing to do in those days." Merv is caught in the slips in the next over, then *'Poole met the situation with a number of forthright shots'* before edging Loader into the slips just before the close. 149 for four, a lead of 146. If the captains will it, there is every prospect of an exciting day's play tomorrow.

At the Nottingham Playhouse there is a triple bill of one-act plays by Harold Pinter, John Mortimer and N.F. Simpson. *'In none of these plays is life shown from a normal angle.'*

It is the summer of 1961. Rudolf Nureyev defects to the West, George Blake the spy is sentenced to 42 years in prison, and the Berlin Wall goes up. In London an 81-year-old Bertrand Russell serves seven days in jail for his sit-down protest against the Bomb.

The day's play is over at Trent Bridge. "The first two days were Even Stevens," Bomber remembers, "high scoring, and the crowd went home happy as sand boys." There are drinks in the TBI, and the two teams go off to eat. Bomber remembers a group including himself and Tony Lock. "Bomber, you must be a glutton for punishment," Tony Lock says, "wanting to bowl spin on these shirt-fronters." And Bomber looks back at him with a deadpan expression. "It beats going out to work any day, Locky." John remembers finishing up back at his own house with another group, Micky Stewart among them. John has two daughters, eleven and seven, "They didn't even know I played; they just thought I was somebody going out to work", and his wife

Sheila is almost as ignorant, "I always joked that she thought LBW was a drug." So what do the players talk about in his front room? He sits in the same spot 38 years later, and he smiles. "Cricket. What else? You just lived it all the time."

The Surrey team make their way back to the Flying Horse, where Mike Willett recalls the doorman. "He had this magnificent copperplate handwriting, the best I've ever seen, and every morning he used to write each of us a note - on our morning paper. A whimsical forecast like, if you were not out, he'd write 'MDW, you have four, I give you eleven' or 'Surrey, you are going to lose by 23' or 'Reg Simpson will get a hundred'. It was so beautifully written, you thought it had been put on with a stamp."

It is back to work for most people on Tuesday, but there are five thousand people in the ground. In a cartoon in The Nottinghamshire Guardian, an office worker sits among the crowd. *'I only hope,'* he says, *'that my boss subscribes to the view that you can't expect brighter cricket without bigger attendances.'*

Brighter Cricket. The Nottingham Evening Post is clear about its importance. *'Every effort has been made to drill into the men who take the field behind John Clay that this is a crisis season for cricket. The emphasis must be on entertainment not results. Glorious failure is always admired more than a timid draw.'*

John walks to the ground from his home in Crosby Road, an ordinary man going to work: "We were never on TV apart from the odd half hour at The Oval." All his life he has been a walker. To and from school four times a day as a boy. The walk along the river after Sunday School. His muscles develop, his stamina grows strong, not like the children of today. "You just grow up in the era in which you're born. There's no point laying blame. But you have to give reasons for things."

John never learns to drive, and for away games he travels with his team mates - though not with Reg Simpson, if he can help it. "He was a good driver in his way, but he didn't think anybody else should be on the road. If it were your first game, you'd go with Reg. We put a bloke called Tom Atkinson with him. 'How did you get on, Tom?' we asked. "How do you mean, 'How did he get on?'?" Reg said. "'He read a book.' 'Yes,' Tom said, 'but I didn't get past the first page.'"

It is May 1961. Jaguar launches an open-top version of the E-type, and the Renault 4 is the world's first hatchback. The M1 is called the London-to-Yorkshire motorway, and there are plans now to build four fly-over junctions to give access to its Leicestershire section.

Surrey take the field for the start of the final day. Micky Stewart, Ken Barrington and Tony Lock are the close catchers: they took over 200 catches between the three of them in 1957. And out in the covers is Bernie Constable. "Dear old Bern," Mike recalls. "He had this trick. He'd pick the ball up, look at the wicket-keeper and throw to the other end. He ran a few out like that, but of course he'd do the bowlers. Alec or Loader or Locky, they'd be at the end of their run, and they'd have to hurtle back. Sometimes it would fly off for overthrows, sometimes it hit them on the knee or the head. And then the golly goshes would start."

Reg Simpson and John Springall step out to bat. Reg the Test veteran: "You're the best player we've got," John has told him at the start of the season. "I want you to play whenever you can get the time off." And John the fringe first-teamer: "He'd murder second team attacks, but he was a journeyman in the first team." *'Simpson and Springall made 62 in the first hour and a quarter.'* Simpson, according to John Thicknesse, is *'serene. At 41 he remains a wonderful placer of the ball, a wonderful judge of a run, and a wonderful hooker.'* At the other end *'Springall's part in this was largely defensive, a great deal of pad play being interspersed with sudden boundaries.'*

John Springall. "He said to us one day, 'Do you know what Charlie Drake's real name is?'" Charlie Drake the comedian, his 'Mick and Montmorency' is a highlight of children's television. "'It's Springall.' And if you'd seen John's father, he and Charlie Drake could have been brothers." "Hello, my darlings," the little Charlie says, with a twinkle in his eye. Was John a comedian, too? "Not knowingly. Reg thought he was, though. I remember after his first net, Reg came in: 'Who signed this bloke? He can't play.' Poor John had no chance." *'This was certainly the Notts professional's lucky day. He was dropped on 41, then again on 49.'* At 54 he is bowled by Gibson, and *'John Clay delayed closing the innings until Simpson had reached his century.'*

John has opened the innings many times with Reg, and he knows how in this form "he made it look so ridiculously easy. He'd take the first over against Fred Trueman, and I'd be thinking, 'Oh, it's all right today, Fred isn't so quick.' Then I'd get down there, and Fred would be just as fast as ever. Mind you, if we were 100 for none and I'd got 20, I was happy, and the crowd was happy. They were neither interested in nor watching me. But if he got out and somebody else came in, that's when the difficulty came."

Today Reg Simpson hooks Gibson for four, takes a two off Loader, and he has scored his 62nd century. "Peter Loader was a bit quick," Mike says. "He used to bowl this frightening bouncer that steepled up at your throat. But Reg Simpson hooked him out of sight. It was the finest display of batting against quick bowling that I saw." 'Reg Simpson will get a hundred,' the doorman has written. *'The crowd rose to applaud him and, while the applause was ringing out, Clay declared.'* The target is 291 in 190 minutes, a rate of 92 an hour. *'It was a memorable innings,'* John Thicknesse declares, *'and I trust it will not be misunderstood if I say I hope I never see him bat again.'*

Brighter Cricket. It all hinges on setting the right target. "I was a big one for declarations," John says. "That was always the best chance we'd got. To get off the bottom, you've got to try to win. 'Set us a target, and we'll go seven down,' that's what we used to say.' We'd never have got a decision otherwise." Bomber and Locky have talked about it over a meal, John and Micky Stewart have talked it about in John's house. Chase till you are seven wickets down, then play for a draw if you have no chance of winning. This is their way of playing Brighter Cricket. *'In the first over Davison found a trimmer for Stewart'*, the captain is bowled for three, and at lunch it is 19 for one, 272 more wanted in 170 minutes.

92 an hour. It is a steep asking rate, but John knows to take account of Bomber's 'hop and away' overs. "I got booed at Leicester for not declaring, and they won with several minutes to spare. Alan Wharton said, 'Quite honestly, John, I thought it was a bad declaration, but I didn't realise how fast you'd bowl your overs." Twenty-one an hour that day, with the ball being retrieved from all parts. "We always used to take our time by the keeper and first slip. At the end of the over they walked sedately to the other end. Nowadays they run, and they bowl fourteen or fifteen an hour. I can't understand it." Is it because the modern captain changes his field more often? "Bill Voce used to say, 'That's your field. If you can't bowl to it, you shouldn't be playing the game.'"

Bill Voce. He and Larwood were the last truly fast bowlers they have known here at Trent Bridge. Back in the fifties Bill was the coach here: "If we can't play," John remembers him saying, "at least we'll look the part." "He'd bowl in the nets for a bit of fun. Everything was up in your ribs, and he'd chuckle when he hit you. Every so often he'd really let one go, and I used to think, 'Well, fancy facing him and Loll Larwood.' And he was in his forties, having a bit of fun. I didn't think it was fun at all."

Has nobody in John's time been as quick as this? "Well, there was Cleveland Lindo. He frightened us to death in the nets. We took him to the High School to play the boys, and he frightened the life out of them. A smashing bloke, he comes to all the old players' reunions and he's still playing. But when it really mattered, he wasn't quick at all."

"Cricket's an individual game," John says. "When you're out in the middle, you're on your own. It's like a boxing match. There's nowhere else to go. I often wish it hadn't been when Fred or Tyson or Loader was coming down at me." Maybe, if he had done it in the middle, people might have remembered Cleveland in the same breath as Fred or Tyson. Instead, they remember him for the ball he bowled at the end of a second team match. "Jack Baddiley was our skipper, at the Boots ground, and the other side wanted one to win off the last ball. 'Bowl it wide,' he said. The ball flashed past second slip. We were in hysterics. We all went off to the dressing room, and Jack was still out on the middle. He flung his cap down. 'I thought you said 'bowl a wide', Cleveland said."

It is the summer of 1961. Michael Ramsay is the new Archbishop of Canterbury, the Orient Express completes its last journey, and Angela Mortimer beats Christine Truman in an all-British final at Wimbledon.

Edrich and Barrington, two great batsmen. John Edrich on his way to a hundred hundreds. "A little guy built like a midleweight boxer," Mike calls him. "He had arms like Popeye. He didn't have much of a backlift, but I think he scored nearly fifty sixes one summer. He hit Fred Trueman over the stand at Bradford in his second over, I can see it now." And Ken Barrington: in the whole history of Test cricket only Don Bradman has scored more runs at a higher average than Ken's 58.67. Taller and more upright, almost military in his bearing. "That lovely remark by the Australian wicket-keeper. When he saw Kenny come out, he could almost see the Union Jack trailing behind him. It was like seeing Winston Churchill walking towards him."

Edrich and Barrington, two great batsmen and two very different temperaments. "Like all left-handers, John used to play and miss a lot," Mike recalls. "But he didn't care. The old nut used to go down, up and down as the bowler ran in, and the next ball would whip through extra cover or off his legs. The previous ball was history. He was never upset at the wicket." And Barrington? "What a worrier! Even if Kenny got a hundred, he'd come in, light a cigarette, put his head in his hands, 'Didn't play very well today', and he'd phone you up at night, say he was worried about his innings. He never let it go."

Edrich and Barrington. By three o'clock they have taken the score past a hundred, and the crowd is clapping Edrich's second fifty of the match. Three centuries in his two previous visits here, he will be back with a double century next year. But today he misses out, bowled by Carlton Forbes, who *transformed matters with a spell of three for 12, in which he disposed of Edrich, Barrington and the dangerous Willett.'* It is 116 for four, there are 175 more wanted for victory, and *'for a time it looked as if Surrey had given up.'*

But that is not the agreement. They are only four down, so Constable and Parsons *'again raised the tempo'.* Bomber is bowling all the while, 'Are you ready now?', and, though the runs flow, he teases them both out. It is 211 for six. Roy Swetman and Tony Lock press on, *'some catches were dropped to create anguish'*, and the extra half hour arrives with 65 wanted. 'There is nothing wrong that the captains cannot put right,' Wisden suggests. This is the summer of Brighter Cricket, and Tony Lock mis-hits Bomber to be caught in the deep.

"Give us a target and we'll go seven down." That's the phrase that John remembers, and now Surrey are seven down with 57 to win in 25 minutes. "Up on the balcony," Bomber tells, "Micky Stewart gave Roy Swetman the

39

signal to get his head down and play for the draw. Unfortunately Swetters thought he was telling him to keep on going for them. So he slogged me for a six over mid-wicket, then pulled me for a four."

"Swetty hit a six?" Mike queries. "He never hit one in his life. He couldn't have done. He was like the Eighth Dwarf. And he wouldn't have misread the signal. He and Locky were two of a kind. I suppose you could call them rebels. If you said to Locky, 'Block it out', he'd go and slog. And Swetty was the same. 'Sod them up there. I'll show them what I can do.' That would be closer to the truth of it." In no time the score leaps from 234 to 256, and there are still only seven down.

Roy Swetman. He leans against the bar of his Bristol pub, and he reads the match scorecard. "No," he says, "I can't remember it at all. Who was the Surrey captain?" Micky Stewart - it is his first ever game in charge, his first step on a road that will lead in time to his becoming England's team manager, an influential figure in the modern game. "Ah well, Willett would be spot on then. Micky's a great friend of mine, but he couldn't captain a rowing boat. Some of his crackpot theories, we're still suffering from them now." So here at Trent Bridge Roy ignores the signal from the balcony. "I'd rather lose going for a win than play out a boring draw. What's the point of cricket if not to try to win?"

Bomber is the great storyteller, though. Let him finish his version. "Swetters tried to hit me for another six, but this time he got an inside edge and dragged it onto his stumps. I can remember even now that I wiped my forehead. 'Thank God for that,' I thought." In the words of John Thicknesse, *'Surrey went bald-headed for their target long after it had become a practical impossibility.'* Eric Bedser is stumped, and Ian Davison's final over arrives with 29 to win and just David Gibson to play out the six balls. *'Survival now was the only consideration.'*

One wicket. That is all Notts need now to bring off their first victory here since July 1959, their first under John's captaincy. "At that moment," Bomber tells, "you could hear the grass growing. The vast acres of Trent Bridge were as silent as night. Davo came in. The ball pitched just short of a length round about the leg stump, Gibbo went on his back foot to play it, the ball moved right across, and it was just as though Gibbo was hypnotised. He got the slightest of edges, and Geoff Millman did the necessary." Bomber's first taste of victory at The Bridge, and even John shows his feelings. "We were pretty euphoric," he remembers. "I jumped when we got the wicket, and I almost got told off for it by a committee member." *A fitting and dramatic finale to three of the best days of cricket,* the Nottinghamshire handbook records. *'The jubilant players were deserving of the general congratulation.'*

It is not just the crowd congratulating them, either. "Locky was the most competitive man in the middle," John says. "If you talked to him, I don't think he'd even hear you. But as soon as we'd won, he was the first man in the dressing room. 'Well done.' That's what the game was all about. We'd finished, the game was over. We were pros. We'd done the best we could."

Not everybody is impressed, though. *'Surrey donate 12 points for Brighter Cricket,'* the Daily Telegraph report is headed. *'The Christmas spirit was abroad today,'* John Thicknesse writes, *'with Surrey cast as Santa Claus. Personally I subscribe to the view that a match should be saved if it cannot be won.'*

"I used to watch football," John reflects, "and it never used to bother me who won or lost. It was just pro football. Now it's all so important. And everything gets picked over. Sport's been my whole life, but it's still sport, isn't it?" John is old enough to remember a world in which there were more important matters than winning at cricket and football. "My mother had six boys in the forces in the war. She didn't complain. She had to get on with her life. And after the war people were just grateful to be playing cricket. People didn't demand as much as they do now."

The sixties have hardly begun. "The basic insecurity of the workers," Labour MP Bessie Braddock says, "is the spectre of the van driving up to take away the TV set."

Victory at Trent Bridge at last - and over Surrey of all sides. There is cause for celebration here. "But, after about half an hour, Pat Oakden - he was just a youngster, it was the first time he'd ever won a game - he said, 'It's funny, I just feel like any other game now.' It's like they say:
'If you can meet with triumph and disaster,
And treat those two imposters just the same.'
And I thought, he's right. We'd done a job, and it had been good. But the next match comes tomorrow."

Tomorrow for Surrey is at the Oval, and Mike Willett drives his green Sunbeam Talbot out of the ground, Roy Swetman in the passenger seat and the radiogram playing Bobby Darin in the back. "Squash racquets, golf clubs, dinner jackets," Roy says. "We were equipped to play anything." A pair of Surrey Cavaliers, full of banter. They will still be at it almost forty years on. "I hit my fair share of sixes," Roy says. "I think you'll find I scored just as many runs as Willett." The scorebook preserves the detail of his innings: Swetman, 3,3,2,4,4,1,1,3,3,1,4,1. And there are no sixes in the Surrey innings at all.

Tomorrow for Notts is at Oxford. "That was a pretty grim road," John recalls. "The motorway finished somewhere near Lutterworth." The Nawab of Pataudi is top of the first-class averages, his 63 sets up a decent Oxford first innings, and Norman Hill arranges to sabotage his second knock. "He took him drinking," Bomber tells. "Norman was built like a barrel, he could take a few pints." But can the Nawab? "The next morning his manservant appeared, said he was out of sorts and wouldn't be coming." Another blistering knock from CJ, and it is two wins in a row for Notts.

41

Then the fixture list throws up the Combined Services, a 40-run victory, and Somerset at Yeovil, where Notts bat first and the pitch breaks up. Four first-class victories in a row. Back in the fifties Surrey managed eighteen in a row - but Notts, they have not achieved this since 1946. Is John beginning to wonder what the season has in store? "No, I had a pretty good idea we wouldn't win many more." And he is right. By the end of August they are back at the foot of the table. Won four, drawn four, lost twenty. No side in the history of the championship has lost more games in one summer. "But every game," Merv Winfield says, "the members applauded us off the field." And John Clay? How do they remember his year in charge? "I doubt if there was a captain in the country who could have done a better job," Bomber says.

Nottinghamshire will win the championship twice in the 1980s. But by then Trent Bridge will have become a different world. "Right through my playing days, there was just Captain Brown the Secretary, Ron Poulton the Assistant Secretary and a typist. That was the only administrative staff. And if they had a Test match, they brought half a dozen people in part-time." And now? "I don't know what they're all doing. I just want to watch some cricket when I go. I've made myself a member of the Taverners' Club, and we sit at mid-wicket. I don't want to get involved in the political side."

The five-minute bell rings, and the young John dashes to catch sight of Larwood and Voce, and the brown caps of Sandham and Gover. The five-minute bell rings again, and this time he is walking out with Reg Simpson, surrounded by the great Surrey side of Lock and Laker, Edrich and Barrington. A third time the bell rings, and now he is sitting at mid-wicket, watching Derek Randall and Richard Hadlee.

"Richard Hadlee came to Notts as a good bowler, and he left as a great one. He learnt from our county cricket. Yet they knock it." Traditional English county cricket as played since his childhood: "if it's so bad, how did it produce all these great players?"

NOTTINGHAMSHIRE v SURREY

Nottingham, 20, 22 & 23 May 1961

NOTTINGHAMSHIRE WON BY 28 RUNS

NOTTINGHAMSHIRE

N.Hill	c & b Loader	8	c Stewart b Loader		7
*J.D. Clay	c Lock b Gibson	71	c Swetman b Bedser		63
H.M. Winfield	c Barrington b Lock	22	c Barrington b Lock		32
R.T. Simpson	c Edrich b Willett	27	not out		100
C.J. Poole	c Parsons b Willett	59	c Barrington b Loader		27
J.D. Springall	c Barrington b Willett	0	b Gibson		54
+G. Millman	c Swetman b Gibson	40	not out		5
C. Forbes	b Loader	17			
I. Davison	not out	10			
B.D. Wells	c Parsons b Gibson	17			
P. Oakden	c Lock b Loader	2			
Extras	b 1, lb 1, w 1, nb 2	5	b 1, lb 3, nb 1		5
		278	(5 wkts, dec)		**293**

1-14, 2-73, 3-115, 4-186, 5-190, 6-191, 7-245, 8-251, 9-268, 10-278
1-15, 2-104, 3-104, 4-142, 5-275

Loader	23.4	6	66	3	18	4	58	2
Gibson	24	6	65	3	9	3	25	1
Willett	14	2	39	3	4	1	10	0
Lock	23	4	75	1	38	9	86	1
Bedser	12	4	28	0	28	8	78	1
Barrington					6	1	31	0

SURREY

*M.J. Stewart	c Oakden b Davison	0	b Davison		3
J.H. Edrich	c Millman b Oakden	63	b Forbes		51
K.F. Barrington	c Poole b Davison	75	c Poole b Forbes		47
B. Constable	b Wells	16	c Springall b Wells		37
M.D. Willett	b Davison	73	c Poole b Forbes		4
A.B.D. Parsons	c Winfield b Forbes	12	c Clay b Wells		37
+R. Swetman	b Forbes	24	b Wells		30
G.A.R. Lock	not out	12	c Poole b Wells		43
E.A. Bedser			st Millman b Davison		5
D. Gibson			c Millman b Davison		0
P.J. Loader			not out		0
Extras	b 4, lb 1, w 1	6	lb 5		5
	(7 wkts, dec)	**281**			**262**

1-2, 2-96, 3-130, 4-170, 5-198, 6-268, 7-281
1-4, 2-103, 3-104, 4-116, 5-164, 6-211, 7-234, 8-256, 9-262, 10-262

Davison	25	5	86	3	15.1	2	70	3
Oakden	27	4	83	1	12	0	57	0
Forbes	20.1	3	65	2	12	1	35	3
Wells	24	10	41	1	27	6	95	4

Umpires: R. Aspinall and D.J. Wood

WILL YE NO COME BACK AGAIN?

Hampshire v Yorkshire

August 1962

chosen by Alan Castell

Alan Castell was born in Oxford in 1943. A leg-break bowler, he made his debut for Hampshire against Oxford University in their championship-winning year of 1961. Later in his career he switched to bowling fast-medium, staying with the county till the end of 1971 when he went to work in the drinks industry from which he has recently retired.

He remembers an eventful championship debut at Bournemouth.

Dean Park, Bournemouth. "Everybody at Hampshire used to like coming down here," Alan recalls. "It was a lovely place to watch cricket, and there were always good crowds." With its six miles of sandy beach and its cliff drives, they say that Bournemouth is the only English town to be built as a holiday resort. 'The town of a million pines', and there are pines here at Dean Park amid the horse chestnuts and holme oaks. All round the ground they can be seen above the white marquees. Then behind them are the detached Victorian houses, red brick with ample gardens, that front onto the road that circles the ground. Alan stands on the square where as a nineteen-year-old he made his debut, and he looks up at the window of one house. "We lost five quick wickets once, and one of our team was in that bedroom. I think everybody on the ground saw him racing round to the pavilion, doing his shirt up. He was in terrible trouble." Alan pauses for thought. "I rang him up last night. I said, 'War secrets are released after thirty years. I think we can let this one out, can't we?'"

It is August 1962. Colin Ingleby-Mackenzie, the dashing Old Etonian who fits in his cricket between a hectic round of society parties and race meetings, is coming to the end of his fifth summer in charge here in Hampshire, and for the first time he welcomes the young Alan into his side. "Ingleby was a really genuine person. He had a way of making everybody feel important, even down to the stewards. I didn't feel isolated at all."

It is ten o'clock on a sunny August morning. Alan walks nervously into the beautiful Bournemouth pavilion, past the corner where soon they will introduce cask ale to the bar - "The first barrel exploded, and there were hops and stuff up on the ceiling for years" - and into the home dressing room. "I remember the lovely wooden boards with all the splinters. Two years later they'd still be in the bottom of your socks."

"Morning, Ingleby," comes a deep Yorkshire voice. "Who have we got on show here today?" Here in the midst of his new team mates stands Fred

Trueman. "What's going on here then?" he asks. "We're pressing for the title, going great guns, and you're fielding the bleeding second eleven." Thirty-six years have passed, and Alan can still recall his first meeting with England's most feared bowler. "And who are you, sunshine? What do you do?"

"I'm Alan Castell. I bowl a few leg-spinners, try to bat a bit."

Fred's eyes light up. He has already counted himself a hatful of wickets - "Burden, Baldry, Ingleby twice, that's six" - and now he sizes up the nineteen-year-old Alan. "Bat a bit, bat a bit. Think you can bat, do you? Can you hook? Can you hook? If not, you'll have to learn. I'm sorry, you'll have to learn."

Alan has appeared in only two first-class matches, both against Oxford University. All summer he has been playing for the Second Eleven and for the Club and Ground sides, and nothing in his life has prepared him for this match. "When you played Yorkshire, it was another world," he reflects. "A real scrap. They didn't give anything away. The atmosphere on that last afternoon, you could cut it. It certainly sticks in the mind." Alex Bannister has been the Daily Mail's Cricket Correspondent since 1947, and he agrees: *'The atmosphere became as tense as I have experienced in a county match.'*

Hampshire versus Yorkshire. County cricket clubs come rich and poor, grand counties with Test match grounds like Lancashire and Surrey and humble provincial ones like Leicestershire and Essex. From 1914 to 1960, from the end of cricket's Golden Age to the start of the professional sixties there have been only two occasions when a county without a Test ground has won the championship title - Derbyshire in 1936, Glamorgan in 1948 - and there is a sense of an order upturned when Hampshire fly the '61 pennant at their modest Southampton headquarters. And if the order is upturned, it is Yorkshire who feel it most. Champions in '59 and '60 and runners up to Hampshire in '61. At Headingley that May they played out a draw of cautious declaration and aborted run chase and, as the Hampshire players left, Fred Trueman turned to them. "Never mind," he said. "We'll have a nice friendly match at Bournemouth in August, as we'll have won the bloody championship by then."

The championship was indeed won by the time Fred arrived - but not as he anticipated. *'When Yorkshire visited Bournemouth last year,'* the Times reports, *'Hampshire had just won the championship and Dean Park was en fête.'* "I came along that morning," Alan recalls, "and the first thing I saw was Butch White's car, parked on its own, right in the middle of the road. He'd got so pissed, somebody had had to take him home." In the afterglow of those late night celebrations, few in Hampshire remember the Yorkshire match that followed. Butch White, 23 overs, nought for 106; Ray Illingworth, 49 overs, twelve for 102. But Yorkshire folk remember it well, and there are not many in the North who accept that Hampshire were the better side in '61.

'The Southern counties gave them generous declarations,' they say. 'They never gave us anything.'

"This is the most wonderful occasion of all time," Colin Ingleby-Mackenzie declared from the pavilion balcony during those celebrations. "I just hope I won't wake up tomorrow morning and find that we're twelfth in the table." Now in 1962 the whole of Hampshire has woken up, and the county is back in the familiar territory of tenth or twelfth place. It will be another six years before they even finish in the first eight. "There was a certain amount of despondency in the camp," Alan remembers, "but I think people were aware that '61 was a bit of a one-off. If anybody other than Ingleby had been captain that summer, Hampshire would probably have finished about halfway."

For this year's Yorkshire match Butch White is nursing a groin strain. With fast bowler Malcolm Heath out since early July with a damaged hamstring and Bournemouth's Dean Park a spinner's wicket, the opportunity is there for Alan's much-anticipated debut. *As Second XI supporters know,'* the Southern Echo reports, *'he looks a good prospect for the future.'*

Yorkshire's openers take strike at half past eleven, and two wickets are down at one o'clock when the fifty comes up. *'Padgett's was the first, hitting over an intended drive. Then John Hampshire, a deep chested fellow with a natural style, was caught and bowled in Burden's first over.'*

This is August 1962. The economy is booming as Hire Purchase deposits on TV sets and washing machines are reduced from 20 to 10 per cent. For the overseas traveller, a pound can be exchanged for 14 francs or 11 marks.

Dean Park, Bournemouth. Cliff Richard and the Shadows are filming their travels across Europe in a bus.
'Everybody has a summer holiday,
Doing things they always wanted to.'
But for many the English South Coast is still the limit of their holiday ambition. Yorkshire cricketers always spend the second half of August on a fortnight's tour down South, and their supporters ask nothing more than some sunshine and a county championship title.
'Fun and laughter on our summer holiday,
To make our dreams come true.'
"That particular game the majority of the crowd were Yorkshire folk."

The holiday-makers settle in their deck chairs and on the green wooden benches to watch Hampshire's Derek Shackleton bowl as tidily as ever with the new ball. Not a hair out of place, not a ball off length. "There were times you could see the red patch where he landed it all day." Thirty-eight years old, he will bowl more than 1700 overs in this summer of 1962, all between the first championship match on the fifth of May and the last day of the Hastings Festival on the fourth of September. Thirty-four three-day matches in seventeen and a half weeks, and benefit and exhibition games to fit in on

Sundays. What a contrast with 1998 - when the championship programme begins in mid-April and reaches its climax twenty-three weeks later on the 20th of September. "We're in the middle of the football season by the time it ends now," Alan says. "I think it created more interest when it finished in August."

But Dean Park is a spinner's wicket, and within the hour Mervyn Burden and Peter Sainsbury are in tandem. Off-spin and slow left arm. Alan finds his way into the scorebook when *'Sharpe tried to hit Sainsbury back over his head'* and Alan holds the catch at deep mid-off, and at lunch Yorkshire are 91 for three, Stott at the wicket with Close. "Prior to that game," Alan recalls, "these people were only names to me - Close, Illingworth, Sharpe - but Bryan Stott was an idol of mine. I remember seeing pictures of him and his equipment when I was really getting into cricket. He had these boots that laced all the way up, and I thought, 'I must have some of those.'"

Back in 1959 Alan was signed up at the age of just 16, without even a formal trial. Arthur Holt was in charge of the Colts, and the fast bowler Malcolm Heath remembers Arthur that day. "He was grinning like a Cheshire Cat. 'I've found him, I've found him,' he was saying. 'Who's that?' I asked. 'A new fast bowler?' 'No, no. I've found a real leg-spinner.'"

Leg spin. Before the war, they say, the leg-break bowler was as certain of his county place as the wicket-keeper, and even in 1949 England went into a Test match with three of them. Yet, between Tommy Greenhough's last Test in 1960 and Ian Salisbury's first in 1992, England's only specialist leg-spinner will be Robin Hobbs, with seven Tests. For cricket's traditionalists Alan is like a rare gem.

But Alan is a youngster who wants to be up with the times. "I was a bit of a teddy boy," he confesses. "In those days you wore the county tie in a tight Windsor knot. But most of the time mine was down here. And I had these slight drainpipe trousers." Desmond Eagar is the Secretary, a man whose own career spanned the Second War, and his desk is at the top of the Southampton pavilion. "We had this wonderful relationship. At least twice a week the window used to go up. 'Where's Castell? I want to see him in my office. Immediately.'" Alan remembers one conversation involving the Club President, Harry Altham, author of the definitive *History of Cricket*. "'Ah, yes, Castell,' he said. 'I've heard about you. I want to come and watch you bowl.' And reputedly I said, 'Oky, doky, mate.' Desmond Eagar was standing there. 'Oky what? Oky what? This is the President. You don't say 'Oky doky, mate.'"

It is the summer of 1962. Peter Cook and Dudley Moore star in 'Beyond The Fringe', the magazine 'Private Eye' is launched, and the Beatles sign their first recording contract with Parlophone. In November the B.B.C. will broadcast the first edition of 'That Was The Week That Was'.

After lunch Bryan Stott, for all his laced-up boots, is *'thrown out by Marshall after hesitation with Close'*, and Yorkshire are 112 for four. Then Brian Close, who has already been dropped at square leg when Dennis Baldry *'collided with the umpire and lost his prize'*, drives Mervyn Burden into the hands of Danny Livingstone at cover.

Danny is from Antigua, and his 1600 runs last summer are a vital part of Hampshire's championship success. "He had a terrific pair of hands," Alan recalls. "It was his catch that clinched the title." Here at Dean Park twelve months ago. The ball went high in the air towards long off, and so confident of him were his team mates that they were almost in the pavilion by the time he held on to it. "He was left on an almost deserted stretch of outfield," Roy Marshall writes.

Here in 1962, Brian Close drives the ball into his hands, and Yorkshire are on the verge of becoming 112 for five. But, J.M. Kilburn of the Yorkshire Post writes, *'Livingstone must have lost sight of the ball against the background of gay colours in the crowd, dark trees and hedges and the red brick of neighbouring houses. Dean Park makes a delightful setting for cricket, but the ball is not easy to follow.'* "I don't remember that," Alan says. "The backdrop was fairly clear." Whichever way, the ball pops out of Danny's hands and falls to ground, and Brian Close survives. *'Here perhaps was the day's turning point.'*

Mervyn Burden has suffered yet another dropped catch off his bowling. It is fifteen years now since he joined his footballing mates in an indoor cricket net in Swaythling. A happy-go-lucky sixteen-year-old with no great interest in the game, he ran in and bowled an enthusiastic medium pace. Back in March 1947, when the appalling winter had brought the country almost to a halt, Hampshire were looking for a new generation to build their post-war side. What was it that Desmond Eagar saw in this untutored medium pace that led him to offer Mervyn a summer on the staff? Certainly not what they saw on his first morning at the County Ground. "My first ball," Mervyn writes, "flew clean over the top of the nets and smashed one of the windows in the old dining room. Then, before I could bowl another, Johnny Arnold in the next net hit this on-drive. It caught me a terrific crack on the ankle, and I couldn't bowl for a fortnight." They send him out with the groundsman, but he upsets a bucket of whiting over the square and they decide he is better off resting at home. What a wonderful tale he makes of it in the years that follow! How sad that he will die in 1987, before the great boom in after-dinner speaking. "He would have made a lot of money," Alan reckons.

But Mervyn is not all laughter, and certainly not when catches like Danny's go down. It is August 1962, the end of his sixteenth year on the staff, and only in 1955 has he held his first-team place through a whole season. Here in Bournemouth the wicket is ideal for spin, but elsewhere he is forever sitting in the pavilion with his packet of cigarettes. Even at Portsmouth in

May 1961, when a week earlier he had taken eight for 38 at Frome. "He got very cross when things didn't go right," Alan recalls. "He was very aware that he was playing for his place all the time."

Brian Close has survived Danny Livingstone's fumble, and Ray Illingworth joins him in the afternoon sunshine as the runs start to flow, 58 in 45 minutes of *'aggressive batting which utterly wrested the initiative from the fielding side'*. Then at last it is young Alan's turn to bowl, and in only his second over, the Times reports, *'Close pulled a full toss to mid-wicket.'* Close, caught Gray, bowled Castell, 78. Alan inspects the cuttings in his mother's scrapbook. "'*A full toss.'* I think that's a bit unkind. I bowled a full length, and Closey used to paddle it round all the time. It wasn't a bad wicket to get first one." "

On one page of his mother's scrapbook the Oxford Mail is reporting Horspath against Vic White's XI, and Alan's three for 37 includes the wicket of his father. On the next page the Daily Telegraph has him bowling *'an interesting if variable spell'* against Close and Illingworth. The page after that he is at Southampton, bowling to Edrich and Barrington. "I was quite overawed by the standard. I bowled an over at Barrington, the best I could bowl, and he hit them all off the middle of the bat. On the up, too. The ball seemed to have a different sound on the bat. I was in another league."

Behind the stumps here at Dean Park is Leo Harrison. Forty years old now, and twenty-three years on from his debut here in August 1939, 'the new Bradman' as the Daily Sketch called him. "He didn't keep wicket in those days, but they say he was a hell of a cover point." Alan recalls Leo's reaction to his opening overs here. "A great guy, but he'd wink and nod his head at you all the time, especially when it was getting tense. Well, I hadn't played much with him, and he was nodding away and I thought he was saying 'Well bowled'. When he caught up with me at the end of the over, he wasn't complimentary at all." Slow left-armer Alan Wassell made the same mistake on his debut back in the days when Desmond Eagar was captain. "He bowled his first three balls wide of the off stump, the batsman left them, and Leo threw the ball back with a nod and a wink. So he bowled three whole overs in the same spot. 'I've seen enough, enough,' Desmond Eagar said. 'Get him off.'"

Ray Illingworth completes his fifty, a vital innings as Yorkshire press for championship advantage. *'In these last weeks of stress and strain,'* the Times correspondent writes, *'Illingworth is often at his best, and he played now with the utmost dash and skill.'* Then he comes down the track to Alan and is left stranded, *'a lone miscalculation in many brave sallies to meet the ball'*. "It pitched and turned," Alan remembers. "It beat him ...... and Leo dropped it." There is a gasp around the ground. At the end of his three matches in 1962 he will have taken just the one wicket of Brian Close for 163 runs. His career will have its ups and downs, but he will always wonder about this missed stumping. "I might have gone on and got ten wickets in the match. I might have represented England. It might have been the turning point of my career." A career that sees him twelve years on the Hampshire staff and never awarded his county cap. "Then again I might have stepped under a bus."

It is the summer of 1962. The last trolley bus runs in London as a new tube line from Victoria to Walthamstow is constructed. A hovercraft service operates between Rhyl and Wallasey, while in America the world's first industrial robot goes to work.

Alan's first spell with the ball is over, and his captain Colin Ingleby-Mackenzie takes him aside. "I like the look of that, Cassers, but I think that'll do for the time being. Take your sweater. Drop down there and, if you see the man with the Echo, find out the result of the three o'clock at Bath, will you?" Like all this Hampshire side, Alan recalls his captain with the greatest affection. "The best character I ever met in cricket. His attitude really appealed to me." And what happens when Alan reports back with the result from Bath? "You could tell by his expression. Sometimes he would lose his colour completely. He never had a bet unless it hurt to lose, that was his philosophy." Today Colin gulps a little and pulls himself together. "Okay, Cassers, let's get on with the game."

Vic Wilson is dropped by Leo Harrison, then lbw to Mervyn Burden. Richard Hutton, *'after a brief period of reach and prod'*, has two lives before he is lbw to Peter Sainsbury. The score is 230 for seven, and for all the missed stumping and the dropped catches - six, they have counted in the press box - Hampshire are still on level terms in the match. *'Then, into the evening, Illingworth and Trueman clinched the day for Yorkshire.'* In forty minutes they take the total to 300 as *'the bowling lost the last vestiges of command, and fielding flagged to formalities of fetch and carry.'*

The slow bowlers are the first to suffer. Peter Sainsbury, with his flighted slow left arm. "He wasn't a big spinner of the ball but he was deadly accurate," Alan tells. He pitches the ball up, and Fred Trueman *'delighted the large and sun-splashed crowd'* with a six over long-on. Like at Headingley last year when Fred mowed ball after ball from Peter to the boundary. Five balls, five fours, and Ingleby resorted to conning the umpire. "That was an expensive over," he told him after the fifth four and, amid the hubbub, the umpire called 'Over', leaving Fred fuming: "You wait till you're batting, Ingleby, one ball will be enough for thee."

Mervyn Burden blows into his cupped hands between each delivery, "he gave the ball quite a rip," and Fred Trueman, *'pounding away cheerfully like a blacksmith at an anvil'*, scatters the long-on crowd at the other end. Next week at Southampton Mervyn will be bowling to Surrey's Dick Jefferson, and the first four balls of his over will all go for six. Then the declaration will come, and he will plead in vain with the batsman. "Oh no, don't go. Stay and have the other two and put me into Wisden."

The ball is 119 overs old, the spinners have bowled 100 of them, and Colin Ingleby-Mackenzie returns to his ever-reliable Shack. "If I had won the lottery," Colin writes, "and I had been given the option of buying any first-class cricketer to play for Hampshire, I would not have hesitated." Colin is the cavalier: "We must entertain or perish," he has told the team at the start of his reign. But the key to all his success is Shack, the meanest bowler in England. "He'd happily bowl all day," Alan recalls. "He just had that lovely action. He put it on the spot, and the ball did the rest for him." And, though their origins are worlds apart, the Old Etonian son of a naval officer and the weaver's boy from Todmorden, there is something about Colin that inspires Derek. "I would have bowled to the end of the Earth for him," he says.

Who would have guessed that they would have worked so well together? Especially after Colin's first match in charge. At Bradford in May 1958. Two days lost to rain, and a game petering out into a dreary draw. Hampshire 105 for seven with an hour left to play. "I decided to give our players some bowling and fielding practice," Colin writes. "Have a bit of a run-around." Fifty minutes later the Bradford crowd was standing to applaud his sporting declaration as Yorkshire came off eight-wicket winners. "Ken Taylor hit Shack over the top of the football stand," Malcolm Heath recalls. "What a shot! If I'd have played it, I'd have retired on the spot." Then Fred Trueman hit 58 in under half an hour. "I think it won him some prize," Malcolm says. "Four hundred boxes of liquorice allsorts, or something." And Shack came off with figures of seven overs, nought for 64. "I was amazed he ever spoke to me again," Colin writes.

Here at Bournemouth Shack takes the new ball, and Trueman again tucks in, hitting him out of the ground 'with a savage cross-batted swipe'. There are not many who treat Shack like this. Alan remembers John Shippey, his mate in the second eleven, in the pre-season nets. "In the end Shack wouldn't bowl at him." But on the county circuit? "Tonker Taylor roughed him up a bit, and of course Fred. But there weren't many." And when they did hit him, how did he respond? "Suddenly Shack got a hair out of place, but he always had the last laugh." Fred's savage six has brought up the 300, but before the over is out Derek knocks back his middle stump and the mayhem is over. Ray Illingworth completes a century that is 'a revelation', Don Wilson adds a bright 23, and Hampshire are chasing a total of 346. 'The stars are in the right place for Yorkshire at the moment,' R.A. Roberts writes in the Daily Telegraph.

It is August 1962. England's cricketers have routed Pakistan four-nil, and so one-sided is the series that Fred Trueman has been rested from the final Test to allow the selectors to look at David Larter, the six foot seven fast bowler from Northampton. The talk has already moved on to the winter tour of Australia, and Fred is at the heart of English hopes.

With just five minutes left to play, he races in to bowl to Roy Marshall, who *'hit the last two balls through the covers for breathtaking fours'*. "Ooh, Roy could play," Alan sighs. "I remember him batting one evening against Larter. There were only a few minutes left, and he cut him up the pavilion steps for six. And, when you consider, Roy had spectacles and very rarely wore a cap even. But he liked the ball coming on quick." The day is over, and Hampshire are 14 for no wicket.

Hampshire have bowled 136 overs in five and three-quarter hours. Nearly twenty-four overs an hour where the modern county game has to stipulate a minimum of sixteen in its regulations. Where does all the time go? "I don't think there was the fiddling about with the field. In the recent Test Alec Stewart was changing Salisbury's field after almost every ball. I don't really think that's necessary."

The Big Show at the Bournemouth Pavilion stars David Nixon, Joan Regan and Lenny the Lion, whose television show now features pop music. "It's not that Lenny's getting any older," Terry Hall explains. "But children today have got more pocket money and know so much more about the entertainment world." There are still boys around the boundary here at Dean Park - "They used to bring the rope in for the tourist matches at Southampton" - but it will not be many years before they are gone.

Thursday morning is overcast as *'a large holiday crowd'* settles into place. "If Marshall was not out overnight," Alan remembers, "there'd be a good crowd to start with. Then if he got out and Henry Horton joined Jimmy Gray you'd see people saying, 'Let's go and have a couple of pints.'" Today there is no such early wicket but, with Yorkshire's spinners soon at work, *'Marshall took forty minutes to decide which of Illingworth's deliveries could safely be driven.'* They have scored fourteen off one over last night, and it takes them fourteen more overs to raise the total to 28.

Ray Illingworth and Don Wilson bowl in tandem, the canny off-spinner and the excitable slow left-armer. *'Before long these two made it clear that Hampshire had a fight on their hands.'* "I used to love watching Don Wilson after he let the ball go," Alan says. "Just to see the antics, the arms and the hands going. What a terrific bowler!" Marshall and Gray raise the total steadily, but with the score on 66 Don Wilson lets slip a full toss and holds *'a simple return catch'* from Jimmy Gray. Then Brian Close comes on to bowl, and with the score at 72 Roy Marshall *'skied the ball gigantically to square leg.'* Vic Wilson circles beneath it, but *'in the high wind that was swaying the trees and stretching the flags and canvas of the marquees the ball swirled into a fielder's nightmare and fell arm's length away.'* Roy Marshall is not a batsman you can afford to drop and, though Henry Horton goes at 80, *'Yorkshire's lunch-time reflections undoubtedly centred upon this mishap to their fortunes.'*

It is 1962. The Sunday Times produces a colour supplement, and Bath Museum of Costume's new Dress of the Year award goes to Mary Quant.

Here in Bournemouth the overcast skies have become *'persistent drizzle'* for the start of the afternoon session, and perhaps Roy Marshall's spectacles need wiping as *'Illingworth bowled the best ball of the day - it broke back a full nine inches - to find a gap between bat and pad.'* It is Ray's 100th wicket of the summer, and perhaps he takes a special pleasure in its being Roy Marshall. Ray is a calculating cricketer, and he will remember bowling to Roy in the Scarborough Festival last September. A 98-minute century with six sixes and ten fours. "Get Fred on," Ray pleads. "I'm top of the averages." But Trueman has other ideas. "Bloody keep him on. I've been bowling all season." They would not be Yorkshire without these exchanges, and at the end of the day Ray has slipped to third place in the national averages, 0.11 behind Flavell and Boshier.

"Without doubt," Don Wilson reckons, "Ray Illingworth was the brains of this whole Yorkshire team. He thought about the game very deeply. I was so lucky to bowl opposite him for all those years." Ray's greatest strength is his understanding of wickets, and today he knows to push the ball through faster. "I was nearly as quick as Derek Shackleton," he chuckles in the Daily Express. Too quick for Dennis Baldry, who *'found the spin beyond his assessment'*. Too quick for Ingleby, who *'edged a prompt slip catch'*, and for Leo Harrison, who *'was lbw, playing back to an off-break'*. Hampshire are in ruins at 145 for seven, still 201 behind, then *'the long-expected rain made its bleak intrusion.'*

"I am sure the Almighty never intended that cricket should be played in anything but golden sunshine," Ray Illingworth writes. But he is a Northerner, he has grown up near Bradford, and he is more at home in these conditions than his South Coast opponents. "The sun rarely shone on Bradford, but I have enjoyed some of the most fascinating cricket of my life there." No match more fascinating than the one with Hampshire in June this year. Twelve wickets for Shack, a fine 78 by Jimmy Gray as Hampshire, chasing 163, reach 156 for five, the county champions set to show the Yorkshire crowd that their title was no fluke. Brian Sellers, the Yorkshire chairman, has gone home in disgust, and he is not there when Ray bowls Hampshire out for 157. Malcolm Heath is the last man in, and *'a jubilant Trueman held a catch inches from the ground to dismiss him.'* "I remember Bradford," Malcolm sighs. "We'd be in shirt sleeves for a fortnight. Then we'd go up there, and you couldn't see the clock across the ground for the fog."

Here at Dean Park Ray Illingworth and Brian Close are sitting at the bridge table, and perhaps they are joined by Colin Ingleby-Mackenzie. In Hampshire's dressing room, Alan remembers, "we'd lob a cricket ball onto the edge of the physio's table, with a bit of spin, and try to catch it. It kept the

53

reflexes going. But mostly we used to sleep." This is Happy Hampshire, where Ingleby so famously declared, "I only ask that my team is in bed before breakfast." "It's amazing how comfortable you could get with a rolled-up pad and a sleeveless sweater." *Three hours later well-thumbed playing cards were stacked, and the players advanced gingerly into a slate-grey autumnal evening.'*

With seven wickets down and the Hampshire deficit almost 200, Yorkshire might be looking to enforce the follow-on - except that in 1962 there is no follow-on. In another experiment to brighten up the game, the county championship is in its second summer without it. The secret of success now lies in judging the declaration. Alan tells of Ingleby and Peter Sainsbury on the pavilion balcony one day. "'What are we going to do here, Sains?' Colin asked. 'Shall I bring them in?' 'I don't know about that,' Peter replied. 'Perhaps we should start to think about it.' And Ingleby was up on his feet, clapping his hands. "In we come." "No, no, not now," Peter protested, but in they came. And then of course Shack knocked a few over, and there'd be a few more points in the bag."

A side can outplay their opponents for two days and still lose - like at the Oval last year. Surrey, 356 for four and 141 for two. Hampshire, 190. Then Peter May set Hampshire 308 to win in almost five hours, and Roy Marshall *'gave a glorious display of majestic batting'*, winning with time to spare. But when Surrey visited Headingley, May left Yorkshire 298 to win in two hours. It is a contrast that is not lost on the Yorkshire supporters.

Today the boot is on the other foot, and Hampshire's hopes of victory rest on a generous declaration tomorrow from Yorkshire. *'In bleak conditions'*, certainly not the weather he knew in his Antiguan childhood, Danny Livingstone *'completed his patient fifty on the slow, soaked turf.'* "He was a superb player," Alan says, "very attractive to watch."

Danny and Alan are both rooming in the Southampton Y.M.C.A., but "normally we just talked about cricket." The rest of Danny's life is "an absolute mystery. He was a very bright guy, used to read a lot. Very meticulous, always had immaculate equipment. He had a lovely infectious laugh, but he never gave anything away about himself." 'He's always in the stars,' they say of him. "He always seemed to have access to things. 'Last game of the season, leave the champagne to me.' We used to joke that he was in on the Great Train Robbery. The county paid his retainer to an address in Stoke Newington, and one winter it came back, 'No longer at this address'. You'd have thought with money involved he'd have had it forwarded." This evening he bats with Derek Shackleton, and at close of play the score has reached 194 for seven.

It is August 1962. Jamaica and Trinidad celebrate their independence, a year after Barbados. Antigua will follow in 1967.

"Danny was the worst driver I ever experienced in my life. God knows how he ever got a licence. He turned up with this battered old Vauxhall one April. I went with him from Broadstone to Southampton and, once he got into top gear, he never changed down till he got to Millbrook on the outskirts of Southampton. 'This car's cold,' he kept saying, and we went round roundabouts in top."

But Danny never gets to take his car on away trips. There is money to be made from the expenses claims, and that is the privilege of the senior players. "Shack had this Ford Corsaire," Alan recalls. "He wouldn't let many people drive it but, if they did, it had to be at 45 miles an hour. There was only once I got my hands on the wheel. He must have been totally knackered. There I was, I'd got this lovely car, and I'd got half an eye on Shack. I could have sworn he was asleep so I started putting my foot down. All of a sudden he's leant forward and tapped the speedo. 'No more than 45, lad.' 'Sorry, Derek.'"

Butch White is Alan's first choice for a lift. "He was a very good driver, and we both agreed that the journey should be broken up so that the training could include barley, hops, yeast, that sort of thing."

It is August 1962. Licences for private cars are increasing at the rate of almost half a million a year while the government warns that it will fine pedestrians who do not use the new push-button crossings.

Friday morning sees the return of the sun, and on a drying pitch Don Wilson captures the last three wickets: Shackleton for 40, then Alan and Mervyn Burden. "Without exaggeration," Alan says, standing where he stood 36 years before, "I'd taken guard, and Brian Close was as close as you are to me now. As I was playing forward, he was trying to catch it off the blade of the bat. He was diving in front of me. I mean, I was a boy from Oxford club cricket. I wasn't used to this." Castell, caught Close, bowled Wilson, 0. Then Mervyn Burden is caught in the slips, the fourth duck of the innings, and Hampshire are all out for 233, a deficit of 113. *'Yorkshire had to score quickly before lunch and set their opponents a reasonable target.'*

Derek Shackleton runs in to bowl at 12.20 and, without a run on the board, he has John Hampshire out *'to a brilliant one-handed catch by Sainsbury.'* "Peter was the best all-round fielder I ever saw," Alan reckons, *'but Padgett and Sharpe exacted swift retribution.'* By one o'clock the score is 89 for one, the lead 202, and perhaps if Ingleby were on the balcony he would be calling them in. But Vic Wilson bats on and, according to J.M. Kilburn, *'the cricket danced to the pipes of Pan and to all appearances in the idiom of jive. The wildest mis-hits were made, the simplest catches were dropped, batsmen came and went almost too rapidly for identification, and the result of confusion thrice confused was a lunch-time declaration at 125 for nine.'* Hampshire have 239 to win, Yorkshire ten wickets to take, and the crowd is *'not far short of the first day's dimensions.'*

Alan's leg-breaks are not seen in the mayhem of Yorkshire's run-scoring. The wickets fall to Mervyn Burden and Peter Sainsbury, four each, and Alan must wait till mid-June next year before he captures another. Then here at Bournemouth in July he takes ten wickets in the match against Somerset, and his mother's scrapbook starts to fill again. "The best leg-break prospect I've ever seen," Bill Alley says. "For his age he's even better than Richie Benaud was." "Keep talking, Bill," Alan says as he hears the words again, and on the next page Denis Compton is pressing for his inclusion on the winter tour of India. By August he is in the first-class averages, but they arrive at Wellingborough, the pitch is a green top and Roy Marshall is standing in as skipper.

What was it Alan Ross wrote?
'Leg-spinners pose problems much like love,
Requiring commitment, the taking of a chance.'

"Roy, for all his attacking batting, was very defensive as a captain, not at all like Ingleby, and I had to go home. I went back on the train, I think. Back into the nets. If they'd just have let me keep on playing, I'm sure I wouldn't have had a problem. But I hardly played again that season, and I lost it completely. It was the stuff that nightmares are made of. I more or less froze and couldn't let the ball go." Three championship appearances in the next two summers. He stares at Bill Alley's words in the scrapbook. "I feel I let him down badly."

Slow bowling is not the easiest life. By the time Alan is drawing this praise from Bill Alley, Mervyn Burden will have played his last game - though Peter Sainsbury, with his batting and fielding to fall back on, will go on for many a year. He will be the only survivor of Colin Ingleby-Mackenzie's Happy Hants to play in the championship-winning side of 1973. "You'd have dived under a bus for Ingleby," Peter says.

Peter Sainsbury is a great fielder and a handy batsman, and he will have much to offer in the one-day cricket that will soon be at the heart of every county's finances. Unlike Mervyn Burden or Malcolm Heath. Malcolm has been out of action with a hamstring injury for the last two months, and Alan recalls the scene at the County ground in Southampton in September. "While the contract meeting was taking place upstairs, dear old Malcolm was lapping the ground, round and round. I can see him now in his dark track suit, knowing that the committee room was overlooking the ground. But it was not to be." By the next summer the injury will be gone, but Malcolm will harbour no bitterness. "Nowadays you can miss whole seasons, and they don't take any notice. But they did me a favour. I was twenty-nine, one day cricket was coming in, and I wasn't the greatest fielder or batsman. I remember Arthur Holt saying to me, 'County cricket might not be here in three years' time.'" Colin Ingleby-Mackenzie recommends him to Guinness, where he works for many years.

'It is a pity,' the Times correspondent writes, *'that anyone who harbours doubts as to the merits of cricket was not here at Bournemouth. The climax was enthralling, its prelude absorbing as the balance moved from hour to hour.'*

Roy Marshall faces Fred Trueman once more. He could have been facing Shack at the other end - for they have worked out that Derek was born in the Yorkshire half of Todmorden. Trueman and Shackleton: "perish the thought," Alan says. "Mind you, Marshall might have got after Shackleton, you never know." What about in the pre-season nets? Did he get after him there? Alan smiles. "I think it's fair to say that Shack wasn't much of a net bowler, and Roy wasn't much of a net batsman. They both felt the business had to be done in the middle."

At 15 for no wicket Don Wilson replaces Fred Trueman, and with his second ball he has Roy edging to slip where Philip Sharpe completes *'a lightning if lucky catch, knocking up the ball in a reflex action.'* Then Henry Horton calls for a run, and Jimmy Gray is slow to respond. "Henry was notorious for his running between the wickets," Alan laughs. "There were quite a few casualties. He used to get so excited." Plenty of casualties - and other incidents, too. Like the day at Trent Bridge when Hampshire needed one to level the scores and he edged the ball onto his pads and kicked it away. "There was a stewards' inquiry, but they let the result stand."

Henry Horton is in his fortieth year. An old footballer, centre half for Blackburn Rovers and Southampton. "He took no prisoners. Like his batting, it wasn't pretty." The crowd may love Roy Marshall's dashing stroke play, but "he was the sort of player every side should have, to occupy the crease and to get in there and graft. Nobody did it better." A tall man, he plays on the front foot, and he takes the short-pitched bowling without fuss. "I've seen him black and blue, but he had this philosophy that you don't let anybody know they've hurt you. You could see him take a real ripping blow on the inside of his thigh, and the binoculars used to be on him. And three or four overs later, when he was the non-striker, he would have a little rub." He and Danny Livingstone take the score to 100, and *'Hampshire were up with the clock and interested in winning.'*

It is the summer of 1962. At Stratford-upon-Avon Paul Scofield is King Lear, and at Coventry Benjamin Britten's 'War Requiem' receives its first performance in the newly consecrated Coventry Cathedral.

'Under the morning sun the ball had turned and lifted as petulantly as I have seen it all the season, but by now the worst of this had passed.' Danny Livingstone *'can hardly have played finer'* than in his first innings 75, and now he has another 42. With 96 last week at Portsmouth and 200 at Southampton next Thursday, he is running into the best form of his life. Alan remembers the double century well. "He was dropped first ball on a hat-trick. He said he hadn't seen David Sydenham on the boundary." It is the innings

that will kill Surrey's hopes of this 1962 championship title, and here at Bournemouth he is seeking to thwart Yorkshire's hopes, too. But he *'attempted to sweep once too often and was lbw to Wilson.'* Peter Sainsbury soon follows, and at tea Hampshire are 109 for four, two hours left to score another 130. According to J.M. Kilburn, *'the balance of probabilities had become a matter of opinion and loyalties.'* And in this large holiday crowd there are plenty whose loyalties lie with Yorkshire, plenty whose opinion is that they are the finest team in England.

At 136 Henry Horton is caught on the mid-wicket boundary, and at 155 Colin Ingleby-Mackenzie is run out by *'a superb piece of fielding'* by Ray Illingworth. Dennis Baldry, however, is *'playing with the utmost confidence'* . "For a little guy, he was a very big striker of the ball." He has come to Hampshire from Middlesex, "he idolised Denis Compton, down to the fact that he still wore the spiked gloves", but at 169 he is stumped by Jimmy Binks. The fielders are closing around the bat, and the scent of victory is in their nostrils. "I wouldn't have classed it as sledging," Alan says. "They wanted you to know that they were there and you were on your own, but in the main they were geeing themselves up. And in the middle of it all there was Jimmy Binks who wouldn't harm a fly." *'Binks's wicket-keeping,'* the Times correspondent writes, *'is an important though inconspicuous part of Yorkshire's cricket.'*

169 for seven, and *'the rest was the usual equation of time and wickets, with runs no longer mattering.'* There is no requirement for there to be twenty overs in the last hour as Derek Shackleton *'endured 18 minutes before being leg before'* for nought and, with four minutes of the extra half hour gone, Alan jumps up to take his place. "I'd gone for the door, and Ingleby said, 'Cassers, you don't go until I tell you to go.' So I waited for Shack to come up the steps, along and into the room. 'Cassers, good luck to you, my beauty, in you go.' And I was booed all the way to the wicket. I'm playing in my first game, I'm on a pair, and I'm booed to the wicket. The atmosphere was electric." In the Stop Press of the Echo, Surrey are heading for victory at Leyton, and the Yorkshire holiday-makers are desperate to claim these last two wickets and to wish their team good luck in their next match at the Oval.

Yorkshire have been in the field for little more than three and a half hours, and they have already bowled almost 90 overs. There is a new ball available and, with only young Alan and Mervyn Burden to bat with Leo Harrison, the return of Fred Trueman is inevitable. "Leo came down to me. He said, 'I don't really fancy you against Illy.' The old pro, he knew. This was 1962, Fred was still quite brisk. Look at the scorecard for the first innings. Harrison, lbw Illingworth, nought. And he didn't fancy *me* against Illingworth." Alan is on strike as Fred marks out his run. *'Running in from what must have seemed eternity to the youngster, he bowled three balls before taking the new one.'* "We're obviously doing a bit of gardening, though I couldn't do too much. But Fred with a new ball was a new experience for me. Because not only was he quick but he swung it so much. The first over I played and missed three times, I do remember that. And I knew I was going to get bounced before long."

But first Leo Harrison must survive an over of off-spin. "Illy got hold of the new ball, and he rubbed it in the dirt. You could do that in those days. He actually rubbed it in the footholds so he could get a grip on it. And Fred was standing at short leg. 'Hey, what are you doing with that?'" But Ray is a crafty cricketer and *'at 6.20 Harrison was bowled'*. It is 181 for nine. Only Mervyn Burden and young Alan stand between Yorkshire and a vital victory.

Mervyn Burden. Ten years ago, when he was learning his game in the Club and Ground side, he almost made his county debut as a batsman. But everybody on the circuit knows that "he was absolutely petrified of anything above medium pace". "Nipper," Mervyn tells Alan, "I don't care where it's going. I'm not going down that end." He takes guard to face Ray Illingworth's off-spin. "There wasn't going to be a run out, that's for sure."

It is three long days, three eventful days, since Alan first came face to face with England's premier fast bowler. "Bat a bit? Bat a bit? Think you can bat, do you? Can you hook? If not, you'll have to learn. I'm sorry, you'll have to learn." Now with the minutes ticking away on the pavilion clock he knows that the moment is coming.

It is August 1962. At the Radio Show the BBC is exhibiting colour television sets. 'Much remains to be done,' the Chairman says, 'before it becomes commonplace in our homes.' Meanwhile a government committee proposes a third television channel, to be called BBC2, and viewers receive pictures from America via the satellite Telstar.

Next week at Southampton Alan will bat at number ten against Surrey, and he will add 236 for the ninth wicket with Danny Livingstone. A Hampshire record that stands to this day. Danny may be the worst driver he has ever experienced - "Once he got into top gear he never changed" - but he is pure class as a batsman. "Batting at the other end made you appreciate what a terrific technique he'd got. Everything was in place." Danny makes 200, the highest score of a career that will lead him eventually back to Antigua as Director of Sports. And Alan will make 76, his own highest first-class score. A leg-break bowler who can bat as well, for a year or two the world is at his feet. But "I sometimes think I was born thirty years too soon or ten years too late." By 1966 he has worked his way back into the team as a fast-medium bowler, but the pages of the scrapbook will never fill so fast again. "I had a good game against the '66 West Indians, really got the ball to swing. I remember having Gary Sobers caught and bowled." Sobers is the great all-rounder of the sixties, a brilliant batsman who can bowl in three different styles. "Later in the innings Roy Marshall was going to bring me back to bowl leg spin. 'Just to show them the poor man's Gary Sobers,' he said."

The headlines and disappointments are all ahead of him here at Bournemouth as he prepares to receive Fred Trueman's bumper. "With Fred, like some of the old-fashioned bowlers, you got an idea that it was coming because they were straining a bit. Not like Malcolm Marshall, who'd just do it. And I thought, 'This is it, he's stretching.' He let it go, and I ducked down. But I left the bat up, and it hit the top of it and flew down to Padgett at fine leg."

"*'I'd never seen a real bouncer before,' gasped Castell,'* in the Daily Express, *'but he still hooked Trueman to the boundary.'* "It wasn't a hook, but it went through Padgett's hands for four. And of course then there was a confrontation between him and Trueman. And one of the Hampshire supporters picked the ball up, and he wouldn't throw it back. He was trying to kill time. It was like a scene from Hull Kingston Rovers, a great scrum of Hampshire and Yorkshire supporters fighting over the ball."

'Everybody has a summer holiday,
Doing things they always wanted to.'

Alan survives another over, and it is left to Mervyn to negotiate one last over from Don Wilson. Will he survive as he did on Tuesday against Sussex's Ian Thomson, when *'the last ball of the day flew off his bat just out of reach of second slip's outstretched arm'*? According to the Times, *'Burden knows all there is to know about last-ditch defence; he hedges and prods, and shoulders arms, and pads away.'* But Yorkshire know all there is to know about pressure, and they *'surrounded Burden to the threat of suffocation'*. There is Fred at short leg, waiting to be once more *'the jubilant Trueman holding a catch inches above the ground'*. There is Brian Close on the off-side, "diving to catch it off the blade of the bat". Philip Sharpe, the best slip in England, and Jimmy Binks, *'inconspicuous but so important'* behind the stumps. And Don Wilson at the bowler's end, gesticulating "with all his antics". "Go on, get out," they say, and the crowd hold its breath with each delivery.

'Fun and laughter on our summer holiday,
To make our dreams come true.'

In the words of J.M. Kilburn, *'The sun threw long shadows to the edge of the pitch. Cricket made magic.'*

The last ball is bowled, and the Burden bat is equal to it. The match is drawn, and suddenly the ground seems full of Hampshire supporters. *'As Castell and Burden walked tight-faced back to the pavilion and as the Yorkshire players shook their heads in anguish, the crowd swarmed onto the pitch to applaud them through a line of cheering, back-slapping spectators.'* And Colin Ingleby-Mackenzie is there to cheer as well. "Well done, Cassers, my beauty." Here is one horse that has come home a winner.

"Ingleby was a really genuine person. I always felt he would have been just the same playing dominoes in Winton Working Men's Club as attending a Garden Party at Buckingham Palace."

Alan will wake in the morning to find his name in every headline. *'Hampshire fans salute courageous Castell', 'Drama as Alan robs Yorks', 'Number Ten pips Trueman', 'The kid defies Tykes'.* In a cartoon in the Echo, a tiny husband squares up to his ferocious wife: *'Since I saw Alan Castell face up to Freddie Trueman, I'm not frightened of you any more!'*

And the Yorkshire team, what do they say in the bar afterwards? "In the time I played," Alan reflects, "we played it hard, but off the field there was a lot of friendship with the other teams. But that day with Yorkshire, we never saw the going of them."

Yorkshire's rivals do not win, either, and with a draw at the Oval and victory in their last match at Harrogate they clinch their third title in four years. And they win again in 1963; it is only Ingleby's Hampshire that has stopped them winning five in a row. Then at Middlesbrough in 1965, with Ingleby in his last year, Shack and Butch White bowl them out for 23, their lowest score this century. "The lads were saying that, when they drove out of the ground, people were eight deep, with their caps, studying the wicket. It's a different tradition. We were cock-a-hoop, but then you were always cock-a-hoop when you beat Yorkshire."

Cock-a-hoop even when you hang on for a draw. Alan relives the thrill of it all as he stands on the Bournemouth square. The town is in Dorset now, part of a great conurbation with Poole and Christchurch. The great bustle of English holiday-makers is gone, and the hotels look instead to conferences and residential training. Thirty years on from Alan's debut Hampshire decide that the charm of cricket here among the pines is no longer worth the cost of maintaining two grounds. In 1992 Middlesex's John Carr bats all day for 66, and at the end of play a spectator places a solitary rose on the wicket. With a card marked, 'Fondest Memories of Hampshire cricket at Bournemouth - Will Ye No Come Back Again?'

Alan survives on Hampshire's staff till 1971. His second career as a fast-medium bowler leaves him with a bad back, and he is glad to land a position with Gordon's Gin. "I'm sure Ingleby got me the job," he says, though Ingleby himself always denies it. "Recommend you, Cassers? Good God, no. I wouldn't recommend you. Certainly not to bloody Gordon's Gin."

HAMPSHIRE v YORKSHIRE

Bournemouth, 22, 23 & 24 August 1962

MATCH DRAWN

YORKSHIRE

J.H. Hampshire	c & b Burden	17	c Sainsbury b Shackleton	0
D.E.V. Padgett	b Baldry	3	st Harrison b Sainsbury	54
P.J. Sharpe	c Castell b Sainsbury	38	c Marshall b Sainsbury	35
D.B. Close	c Gray b Castell	78	lbw b Sainsbury	0
W.B. Stott	run out	3	c Livingstone b Burden	9
R. Illingworth	lbw b Shackleton	115	c Ingleby-Mackenzie b Burden	5
*J.V. Wilson	lbw b Burden	14	c & b Sainsbury	0
R. Hutton	lbw b Sainsbury	5	c Horton b Burden	4
F.S. Trueman	b Shackleton	44	c Baldry b Burden	7
D. Wilson	not out	23	not out	7
+J.G. Binks	b Baldry	0		
Extras	lb 6	6	b 4	4
		346	(9 wkts, dec)	**125**

1-8, 2-36, 3-80, 4-112, 5-170, 6-213, 7-230, 8-300, 9-333, 10-346
1-0, 2-89, 3-90, 4-90, 5-100, 6-110, 7-114, 8-114, 9-125

Shackleton	19	5	47	2		4	1	17	1
Baldry	16.3	3	56	2		1	0	5	0
Sainsbury	43	18	92	2		8	3	36	4
Burden	46	23	101	2		10.3	0	63	4
Castell	11	4	44	1					

HAMPSHIRE

R.E. Marshall	b Illingworth	61	c Sharpe b D. Wilson	8
J.R. Gray	c & b D. Wilson	26	run out	10
H. Horton	c Illingworth b D.Wilson	2	c Stott b Illingworth	57
D.A. Livingstone	not out	75	lbw b D. Wilson	42
P.J. Sainsbury	lbw b D. Wilson	1	c Binks b Close	2
D.O. Baldry	c Trueman b Illingworth	15	st Binks b Illingworth	35
*A.C.D. Ingleby-Mackenzie	c Sharpe b Illingworth	0	run out	9
+L. Harrison	lbw b Illingworth	0	b Illingworth	7
D. Shackleton	b D. Wilson	40	lbw b D. Wilson	0
A.T. Castell	c Close b D. Wilson	0	not out	14
M.D. Burden	c Sharpe b D. Wilson	0	not out	0
Extras	b 6, lb 6, nb 1	13	lb 3	3
		233	(9 wkts)	**187**

1-66, 2-80, 3-108, 4-109, 5-132, 6-137, 7-145, 8-229, 9-229, 10-233
1-15, 2-20, 3-100, 4-103, 5-136, 6-155, 7-169, 8-173, 9-181

Trueman	14	5	31	0		7	2	20	0
Illingworth	35	11	78	4		36	15	60	3
D. Wilson	34.2	15	70	6		34	15	66	3
Close	6	2	27	0		13	4	33	1
Hutton	7	2	14	0		3	2	1	0
Hampshire						1	0	4	0

Umpires: W.E. Phillipson and J.S. Buller

THE HUMAN ELEMENT

Middlesex v Sussex

June 1963

chosen by Alan Oakman

Alan Oakman was born in Hastings in 1930. An off-break bowler who became an opening batsman, he played for Sussex from 1947 to 1968 and represented England in two Tests in 1956. After retiring from playing, he moved to Warwickshire where he was County Coach till 1987 and where he still works part-time.

He remembers a Bank Holiday match against Middlesex at Lord's.

"Lord's was always a bit different," Alan tells. "You drove up to the gate, and they looked at you as if they might just let you in. And of course the games there were always well-covered in the press. It was the only place we ever got any photographs of ourselves. So we used to try and get in with the photographer."

Lord's at Whitsuntide. Middlesex versus Sussex. "It was packed on Saturday and Monday, equivalent to a NatWest final, and it was a nice atmosphere because they weren't biased. It wasn't like going up to Hull or Bradford where, if Len Hutton edged one through the slips, they clapped like mad, and, if you drove one through the covers, nobody said anything." His team mate Les Lenham recalls the crowds: "Lord's was already filling up by the time we arrived. And at August Bank Holiday, when we played at Hove, the seats would be full and people would sit on the grass. As a professional cricketer it was so much more fun playing in front of a good crowd."

Lord's on Whit Saturday 1963. It is Fred Titmus's benefit match, and Sussex arrive as leaders of the championship table, a championship that they have never won. "They used to say, 'In a year or two you'll have a good side,'" Alan recalls. "I think they said that for about ten years."

"The Middlesex-Sussex games were great fun," Les Lenham says. "They were a nice bunch of lads, very competitive on the field but there were a few drinks afterwards. And the sun seemed always to shine on those days." *'The sun shone down from a cloudless sky,'* Ian Peebles writes in the Observer, though in the London Evening Standard *'an east wind chilled the sunny day'*. Old Father Time the weather vane sits astride the Grandstand, and today his gaze has veered away from the cricket towards Abbey Road.

It is June 1963. In the record charts the Beatles are at number one for the first time with 'From Me To You', while outside the cinemas the queues are forming for the new James Bond film, 'From Russia With Love'.

It is fifteen years now since Alan first played in this fixture, "I joined Sussex as a bowler who could bat a bit," and in his memory he still carries a picture of one delivery he bowled that day. Middlesex in 1948 were reigning county champions, exciting a post-war, rationed England with the plentiful runs of Compton, Edrich and Robertson, and that Whit Saturday a full house enjoyed *'powerful'* and *'fluent'* centuries from Bill Edrich and Jack Robertson - but only a score of 17 from their greatest hero, Denis Compton. "I bowled him out. He pushed forward, and it turned and went through the gate. He looked at the stumps as if he couldn't believe it. I couldn't believe it for a start. I was bowling from the pavilion end, and he passed me on his way back. 'Well bowled, son,' he said. I nearly said sorry." Alan may have taken only 18 first-class wickets that summer, but that one ball ensured that his name was not forgotten. "I went off to do my National Service, and people kept saying to me, 'Oh, you're the bloke who bowled Compton, aren't you?' These things happen, and they help you on your way."

Fifteen years on Alan emerges from the pavilion as an opening batsman - *'If you can imagine a giraffe at the wicket,'* the Times writes, *'it is Oakman'* - and his off-breaks are rarely seen: 19 overs in 15 innings so far this summer. He faces John Price who *'down-wind looked pretty lively and should have caught Oakman when six off a sharpish return catch.'* At the other end Richard Langridge plays out three maidens from Don Bennett.

Oakman and Langridge are in their third season as Sussex's opening pair. Alan is at the peak of his game, 2000 runs in each of the last two summers, and Richard is starting to earn mentions as a future England player, if only in the Brighton Gazette. This evening Ted Dexter will switch from Sussex to England captain as he sits down to select the team for the first Test. *'Langridge got under way by snicking Price to the boundary.'*

Oakman and Langridge, their paths into the first-class game have been so different. Alan's parents in Hastings had no interest in sport. Eight years old in 1938, he remembers only dimly the England-Australia Test series that summer. "I didn't realise they were such important games. I used to think they were just testing each other." A teenager by the time cricket returned at the end of the war, he often walked past the Hastings ground with his mother. "I could hear noises, and I asked her what they were doing in there. 'They're playing cricket,' she said. Then the first time I walked in to watch them in the nets, I got smashed on the ankle and had to hobble home. 'It serves you right,' mother said."

Soon Alan was playing on the square in grey trousers, then helping the groundsman mow the pitch, "they hadn't got the motors then so we used to pull this thing on a rope", then playing at school and for Sussex Amateurs. "There was no coaching. I used to watch the club bowlers and try to emulate their actions." Hastings was "out on a limb", but during a rain break at their 1946 festival an enthusiastic club man button-holed Billy Griffith the Sussex secretary, and Alan was off to Hove for a trial. "Today these lads are brought up from ten, aware of what's going on. People say they've got to be hungry, they've got to want to do it. Well, they offered me a contract, and I didn't know what I wanted to do, really. Mother wanted me to go in the police: security, uniform, pension. But cricket won."

In 1946 Sussex finished last in the championship for the first time this century and, like so much of the reconstruction in post-war Britain, there was no great plan in the search for young players. "It was all a bit hit and miss."

But Richard Langridge has grown up with Sussex cricket, a father and an uncle in the county side for thirty years, and perhaps he sometimes feels the weight of their 66,000 runs. "One of the nicest young men you could meet," Les Lenham says. "He had a couple of good seasons, but he lost his confidence a bit." Alan agrees: "he wasn't a natural." *'Langridge turned Price to backward short leg, and Sussex were 27 for one.'*

At number three for Sussex is Kenny Suttle, the busy little left-hander. More impressive-looking batsmen have scored fewer runs, but then there are not many on the county circuit as determined as Kenny. "He was a single-minded so-and-so," Alan says. "He didn't think there was anybody good enough to get him out." Les Lenham agrees: "Kenny went out with the attitude that nobody could bowl at him. I wish I'd been like that. I always thought they were damn good bowlers at the other end."

In Test cricket in the sixties, England has some great batsmen: Dexter and Graveney, Cowdrey and Barrington. But in the county game there is no one who scores as many runs as Kenny Suttle, and for fifteen summers he never misses a match. Broken fingers, damaged cartilage, pulled hamstrings, he plays with them all, and in the winter he plays football. "He was one of those speedy wingers," Alan says, "and Arundel had this big fellow, a killer full back. 'You'll slow down,' we'd tell him, 'and the bugger will do you.' But 'no,' he said, 'he won't catch me.' One winter the fellow really up-ended him, and Kenny came back at the start of the season on crutches. He always limped after that, but he wouldn't admit it. But then the fielding wasn't so important in those days. You could play on with injuries. It didn't matter so much."

Most Consecutive County Championship Appearances. Wisden still records the list, with K.G. Suttle at its head, 423 appearances from 1954 to 1969. And, if Kenny had had his way, it would not have ended at 423. Mike Griffith will be captain in 1969, there will be youngsters coming through, and the story goes that Mike rings him up rather than telling him face to face. "Christ," he reports back, "he wanted to know why ten other buggers hadn't been left out before him." Kenny will have the last word later in the month when he will return to hit 127 against Middlesex at Hove.

Alan Oakman and Kenny Suttle, they are a study in contrasts. Right-hand and left-hand, tall and short, easy-going and fiercely competitive. How hard it must be for bowlers to maintain line and length as they alternate strike. Alan is always on the front foot - "Vic Cannings used to say to me, 'Oaky, when you play forward to me, don't step on my foot, will you?'" - and Kenny is happier going back, cutting and pulling. *'Suttle took three fours in an over off Hooker, two with dreadful snicks, one with a model cut. Then Oakman, driving on the laggardly surface, lifted the ball to mid-off.'* It is 53 for two, and Alan is out for 21. *'The stage was set for Dexter who appeared bare-headed, presumably either in deference to the beneficiary or in recognition of the start of summer.'*

Middlesex versus Sussex at Lord's. As the crowd gathered this morning, an announcer gave them *'a kind of potted history of the fixture - the sort of public relations at which cricket is not always brilliant,'* - and Dexter's name is prominent in all the recent contests: the winning innings last year, a century in 1960, his county cap for a fighting fifty in 1959. He is a man for the big occasion, *'and one glorious off-drive raised hopes of a great entertainment to come.'* Lunch arrives, and the score stands at 82 for two. *'A Dexter innings was an attraction calculated to sway the floating vote between Lord's and the seaside.'*

Four years ago, the loudspeaker has told the crowd, the fixture ended in its closest finish of all, Middlesex winning by one run. "Oh God," Alan groans. "I remember that." And the picture in his memory is of Les Lenham fielding. Back in the days before one-day cricket forced players to chase and dive after every ball. "I was quite quick as an out-fielder," Les reckons, "but I got upset if I got a green mark on my flannels. It cost me two and sixpence in the cleaners. Nowadays they're covered after ten minutes." Perhaps this preoccupation with cleanliness is counter-productive, though. "He would trip over a lot," Alan recalls. "One year at Swansea he fell in a pool of water. The bowler wasn't very happy, but we all fell about."

What is it Alan remembers of Les's fielding in 1959? "In those days they had a board running round the ground. A rope, then a board. Les chased the ball to the boundary, scooped it back and kept going. He tripped over the board, he was a slim man, and he disappeared out of sight. We thought he'd fallen down a hole or something. He completely vanished. Eventually his head appeared above the board. He'd hurt his ankle and was sent home."

Sussex chased 229 for victory the next day, and the young Dexter's fifty took them to 209 for four. Then with the new ball wickets fell, and captain Robin Marlar emerged as last man with ten still needed. *'Marlar parried the short bowling as if warding off angry hornets,'* the Times reported, *'but his innings was wasted when the confident Suttle perished in trying to hook a bumper.'* Victory for Middlesex by one run. "It was the last ball of the over," Les Lenham reflects. "Had I been there, they'd have been able to carry me out and stand me at the end of the pitch. Robin Marlar could have had a whack for the winning runs."

To the Times correspondent, Kenny Suttle has cost Sussex victory with his attempted hook. But Alan knows that such confidence is all part of Kenny's game. "If somebody like Fred Trueman bounced one at him, he'd walk down the pitch and pat it down near the other end. 'Bugger off,' I'd say, 'you don't want to upset him.' But he didn't care. He was a stubborn little bugger." No, in Alan's memory, the defeat is forever associated with Les's injury. "If Les had been there on the Tuesday," he says, "we might have won and got our four quid bonus. That was nearly a week's wages in those days. We gave Les a bit of stick when we got back. There was a rumour that he'd gone dancing on the Monday night."

Victory by one run for Middlesex in 1959. The closest finish in the history of these Whitsun contests. Fast bowler Alan Moss was the hero, and today he is absent, nursing a pulled leg muscle. But perhaps this is not the wicket for his pace. *'Despite the burst of tropical weather, the pitch was very much slower than was to be expected and the Sussex batsmen, fresh from a fast Hove wicket, took some time to gauge the difference.'* Ted Dexter likes a quick surface, he hit a *'bold'* 85 at Hove on Thursday, and no sooner is lunch over than his attempt to repeat his *'glorious off-drive'* is mis-timed and results in a catch at extra cover. *'Sunshine, a good sized shirt-sleeved crowd and Dexter in action, it seemed a wonderful recipe for a holiday afternoon, but it was not to be.'*

Ted Dexter is the England captain. When he sits down this evening to select the Test team, he will be looking for some changes: at the top of the batting order, behind the stumps, even perhaps with the seam bowling.

"Dexter had some funny ideas about certain players," Alan recalls. "He said Les Jackson couldn't bowl - till he played back to one at Derby and it hit him on the elbow. Then he reckoned Shackleton couldn't bowl, either." Derek Shackleton of Hampshire. At Hove on Thursday he took six for 71, including the wicket of Dexter himself. "He got caught in the covers, trying to hit him over long on. 'He's not the worst,' he said." In a fortnight's time the team for the Second Test at Lord's will be announced, and Shack will resume an England career that ended in 1951.

But who will be the England wicket-keeper? Middlesex's John Murray was first choice all last summer, but in Australia poor form and injury lost him his place to Warwickshire's Alan Smith. Among the professionals nobody is rated more highly than Northants' Keith Andrew, but his batting average of 13 does not stand comparison with John Murray's 20, still less with Jim Parks' 36. "As a keeper, Jim wasn't in the same category as Keith Andrew," Worcestershire's Roy Booth says. But Jim's batting is a valuable asset. He is another whose father and uncle played for years for Sussex, and here at Lord's he adds 42 with Kenny Suttle, 57 with Les Lenham. *'Parks is a good batsman to watch. He drives, cuts and hooks with the same leisurely flow.'* And he earns himself a photograph in the Observer: *'J.M. Parks, of Sussex, confidently sweeps a ball to leg for two runs.'*

Dexter and Parks are the stars of this Sussex batting line-up, and Alan remembers the pre-season discussion about the new Knock-out tournament. "There's a fifty pound man of the match award," Ted Dexter tells them. "What do you want to do if you win it? Do you want to keep it or share it?" "Well, we looked around the team, and we thought, 'There's only Dexter and Parks who might win it.' So we said, 'We'll share it.'" Next week against Yorkshire Jim will hit a *'stylish'* 90 - "he smashed Trueman over extra cover for six" - and in July at Northampton Ted will hit a *'masterly'* 115. The team will double their win bonuses from these man-of-the-match awards.

Tea is approaching here at Lord's, and 187 for four becomes 187 for six when Les Lenham and Graham Cooper fall to successive balls from Middlesex's captain, slow left-armer Colin Drybrough. Then after the break Jim is bowled off his pads for 71, and it is 187 for seven.

At number eight there is Ian Thomson, and Alan recalls his first game with him back at the start of 1952. "He opened the batting with me against Hampshire in a friendly. He came to us as a batter and, as we walked out, Tommy said, 'Can you take first strike?' 'All right,' I said. Then Malcolm Heath ran in and bowled me with a yorker first ball. And Tommy went on and got a hundred. I said, 'Tommy, any time you want me to help you, let me know.'" A hundred in this non-first-class match, he will never reach even 80 in almost 600 first-class innings - but he will take a hundred wickets every summer from 1953 to 1964. And, like every bowler, he will count his runs as keenly as his wickets. "He and Don Bates were always betting who would get most runs at the end of the season. So we went through a period when they wouldn't get on with it." So far this summer, the score stands at Thomson 119 Bates 10. It has only risen to 121-10 when Sussex are all out for 212.

At six o'clock on BBC television David Jacobs introduces Juke Box Jury. 'A hit or a miss?' he asks the panel, and while he is sounding his bell and hooter the wickets start to fall at Lord's. *'Gale, attempting a hook, got a top edge,'* and *'Parfitt played back at a lifter and was caught in the gully.'* At close of play Middlesex are 28 for two, Ted Dexter joins the Test selectors, and Parfitt will discover in the morning that he has been discarded.

The rest of the Sussex team drives home to the South Coast. There is an experimental fifty mile an hour limit on the roads, and this is one of their easier journeys. "We arrived at Swansea at three o'clock once," Alan recalls. "The sign posts weren't that good, and nor was some of the map reading. We'd often pass Les Lenham going in the opposite direction."

On Whit Sunday cars leave London at the rate of forty thousand an hour. Last Wednesday thirteen miles of the new M2 were opened in Kent, and this new stretch of road provides the biggest jams. In desperation police redirect traffic through the old A2 bottleneck of Rochester and Chatham.

'*England Test Team Full of Surprises,*' reads the headline in the Times. Edrich and Stewart are to open, and Keith Andrew is to keep wicket. Tom Cartwright is named for the first time, and there is a surprise recall for Yorkshire's new captain, Brian Close. '*The story of Close's cricketing life will have to be made into a film one day,*' the Times suggests. '*On ability it deserves a happy ending, though whether temperament will allow that is another matter.*' England's youngest ever Test cricketer in 1949, who here in 1963 can guess the half of what is still to come? The great success of his England captaincy and his controversial sacking, the glory years at Yorkshire and his move to Somerset, then his Test recall in 1976. His Somerset team mate Peter Robinson will be with him in the car when that final recall is announced on the radio. "He was like a schoolboy being picked for the first time. 'Do you know,' he said, 'this is the first summer I haven't put the dates in me diary.'" The Life of Brian, it is a film still waiting to be made.

Monday's play starts in '*sparkling sunshine*', and a crowd of fifteen thousand gathers to watch the Middlesex innings resume on 28 for two. "Brought up on the genius of Compton," Trevor Bailey writes, "these spectators are not content with mundane batsmanship." With a Bank Holiday crowd, and a fellow professional's benefit, Denis Compton was almost guaranteed to provide glittering entertainment: a '*forceful*' 169 for Jack Robertson's benefit, a '*sparkling*' 143 for Sid Brown, a '*superb*' 150 for Harry Sharp. Just that one failure: bowled Oakman 17, for Lawrie Gray.

"In Eric Russell," Trevor Bailey writes, "Middlesex have their most promising batsman since the Compton era." "An extremely elegant batsman," Bill Frindall calls him. "Russell combined dependable run-making with an attractive spectacle." But, according to the Times, '*the morning was ruined by Russell.*' He adds 28 in two hours, the score crawls to 91 for four, and '*if he could have heard what was being said at luncheon, he would rather have been working on the Underground.*'

"I don't remember the occasion," Eric Russell admits, but he does remember the return game. August Bank Holiday in front of a large crowd at Hove. The Middlesex innings in ruins at 82 for five, and he and Fred Titmus digging in. '*Russell gave a dour display,*' Wisden records, '*which led to four spectators demanding and receiving the return of their admission fees.*' He can still recite the newspaper accounts of that innings: "Watching Russell bat was like watching celery grow," and "I thought I was watching Lord Russell during one of his non-violent campaigns."

It is Whitsun at Lord's. Fred Titmus, '*received by the crowd as one of their own*', joins him forty minutes before lunch, but '*the inertia now really set in with Titmus a mongoose bewitched by Bell's snaking spinners, once and only once breaking out to off-drive for four and briefly hush the slow handclap.*' At one stage there are eight successive maidens, and Ronnie Bell takes lunch with fourteen runs off his fourteen overs of orthodox slow left arm.

Ronnie Bell. Last Tuesday his eight for 54 spun Sussex to the top of the table, but he is not always a match-winner when the conditions favour his bowling. "Ronnie was a hell of a nice bloke," Alan tells, "but, if we got on a pitch that was doing a bit, Dexter would say, 'Come on, Ronnie, spin them out,' and he'd lose confidence. He needed a lot of reassuring."

In two hours the score has crept from 37 to 91, and sections of the crowd have taken to the slow handclap. *'Someone must have read the Riot Act in the Middlesex dressing room,'* the Times correspondent suggests. *'The morning's batting had been a travesty, but the afternoon's brought great delight.'* Fred Titmus leads the way: *'by the time he was out, he had ensured himself of a good collection.'* Eric Russell, *'becoming positively skittish'*, joins in before being stumped. 76 runs flow in the first hour after lunch. Then, with Ted Clark and Don Bennett together, *'the best was to come.'*

This Middlesex middle order is a utilitarian one, and often they suffer comparisons with more golden days here at Lord's. But today *'Clark's innings of 71 was a class above everything else and in power, improvisation and footwork would not have disgraced a Hendren or a Compton.'* The new ball is taken, and he takes to dancing out to the quicker bowlers. *'Once Buss saw him coming and bowled him a bumper, but it was struck to the mid-wicket boundary by a species of tennis service.'* There are 88 runs added in the second hour of the afternoon, *'this was cricket worthy of the time and place,'* and the score reaches 255 for six, a Middlesex lead of 43. *'By now the spectators were glad that they had come.'*

It is Whit Monday. A 100-foot-long motorised balloon has accurately forecast the glorious sunshine, and *'it's a record Whit,'* the Evening Standard proclaims. *'What a spending spree! Seaside shops have been sold out, and hotels are full up. Crowds have had to sleep on the beach or in their cars. The Kent coast is just one vast car park.'*

The wicket here at Lord's is taking turn but only slowly, and the Sussex attack has wilted in the heat of the afternoon. Don Bates has a bad knee, Ted Dexter a bad back, and *'Bell rather lost his hold when the batsmen began to use their feet.'* Dexter even turns to Kenny Suttle for three overs, but there is no call for Alan's off-spin. There rarely is these days.

At 267 Don Bennett skies the ball to mid-off where he is *'superbly caught by Dexter, running back'* though there are no great celebrations. "Everything gets so exaggerated these days," Alan reckons. "They say, 'What a brilliant catch!' as if they've never seen one like it before. Do you remember that catch Richie Benaud took in the gully at Lord's? That was a good catch. Today they'd jump out of the window with that." Ted Clark is lbw for 71, John Murray *'played three high class shots'*, and Drybrough and Price add 35 *'with more science than luck.'* The sparkling sunshine has slowly given way to a grey sky, and Middlesex have a lead of 112. By close of play Sussex are 28 for no wicket and, with Yorkshire close to victory in the Roses match, Sussex's spell as championship leaders looks likely to be short.

Rain storms have reached the South Coast. Eastbourne sea front is deserted by mid-afternoon and, according to RAC estimates, 350,000 cars are converging on London. On the M1 lane discipline is said to be ragged. It is June 1963. At London Airport two detectives meet 18-year-old Mandy Rice-Davies who has *'returned voluntarily to assist in an investigation.'*

What do the Sussex team do on a Monday evening at Lord's? "Some years we used to stay in a pub," Alan recalls. "A bit of a one-eyed place. But some years we had to drive back home. The secretary said we couldn't afford to stay, and in those days you never argued." The secretary is Lieutenant-Colonel Grimston. "I remember going to see him once, and he said, 'I've just had a cheque from the M.C.C. for the Test match receipts. It's taken us out of the red so I'm going to pop down the bank.' Sussex lurched from one season to the next. There was no corporate hospitality, no advertising boards. You just depended on your gate receipts and your members, ordinary people not paying a lot of money. We used to have a lot of retired colonels, majors and brigadiers. They used to come on bicycles with their cycle clips on and their little bags with their lunch in. They'd call you Oakman and Parks."

The summer of 1963. There are no amateurs and professionals in English cricket now. The captains here may be C.D. Drybrough and E.R. Dexter, Oxbridge men both of them, but on the scorecard the other players carry their initials before their surnames as well. "There is one correction to the scorecard today," the Lord's loudspeaker announced a few years back. "At number seven for Middlesex, in place of F.J. Titmus, read Titmus, F.J."

"I never thought I should hear myself saying it," Les Lenham says, "but we lost a lot when the high-class amateur captain went out of the game. He was never worried about his own place in the side. His livelihood didn't depend on his results." Alan agrees: "when the professionals took over, the committees started to interfere. And the captains became concerned about their job if they lost too many matches. 'Are you going to declare?' you'd ask. 'The only chance we've got of winning is to give them a chance.' 'But oh no,' they'd say, 'you can't do that.' We had some terrible games. It's like they say. Professionals built the Titanic. An amateur built the Ark."

Yet, as one tradition ends, another is beginning. On the first Saturday in September Lord's will stage the final of the new Knock-out Competition, with a prize of two thousand pounds for the winners. "We're never going to win the championship," Ted Dexter has told them in April. "We haven't got that sort of side. But I reckon with our seam bowling attack and our fielding we can reach the final of the Knock-out."

But in the minds of most followers of the county game the championship is the only competition to be taken seriously. They listen to Ted Dexter's pre-season talk but, Alan recalls, "we'd never won anything at Sussex, not like Surrey and Yorkshire, so all we did was enjoy our cricket. Arthur Gilligan was President. He used to come down in April and wish us luck. He never mentioned about winning anything."

They may all be cricketers now, but the professionals know their place. "In the twenty years I spent at Sussex," Alan tells, "I went in the committee room once, and that was towards the end when things were changing." He recalls the tourist match at Hove. "It was the only time you saw the whole committee. You were lucky to get a seat for lunch or tea, and you were playing in the match. 'Don't worry,' you'd say, 'I'll eat in the dressing room.' After play they always invited the touring side into the committee room for drinks. They had this little balcony out the front, where they could stand, and we used to walk past on our way to the pub. When they saw us coming, they'd turn their backs and look inside."

And these are the men who each autumn decide which players to retain and which to release. "There was only Arthur Gilligan who'd played any cricket. They were all retired bank or building society managers, architects, they'd got cricket at heart but they hadn't experienced what it was like to play professionally. 'Do you think he's going to make it?' they'd ask. That's a difficult question. The only way you're going to find out is to play him."

Just as Sussex played Alan back in 1947 - one game at Northampton. "In those days Burtons the tailors always had a snooker hall on the first floor and a ballroom at the top, and our hotel was right opposite it. I was sharing a room with the scorer, trying to get to sleep, and I could hear all this dancing going on. I'd love to have been over there, but I couldn't very well, it was my first match. I just lay there, thinking about the game, waiting for them to play 'God Save The King' and 'Who's Taking You Home Tonight?'" In the match he scored three not out and took nought for 99. "Thank you very much for playing, Alan," Sussex's captain Hugh Bartlett said. "You've done well."

Sixteen years have passed, Alan has made it as a batsman, and on Tuesday morning he and Richard Langridge raise the score to 72 before he mis-hits a drive to cover and another batting collapse begins. Fred Titmus is bowling at the pavilion end, where umpire Eddie Phillipson is standing, and he has both Langridge and Kenny Suttle lbw. *'A couple of overs later Dexter played a sort of Let's Be Kind to Dumb Friends shot,'* and, when Jim Parks is caught behind, the lead is seven, and there are five wickets down - and it would have been six if the bail had fallen when Les Lenham played on.

Fred Titmus is at his best from the pavilion end, bowling his off-breaks down the slope and slipping in the deadly floater that drifts away. "He was one of the top off-spinners the game has ever known," Les Lenham reckons. "He was prepared to bowl when it wasn't turning. A real pro, a great competitor. There's been no better off-spinner on a flat pitch than Fred."

But what do the Sussex players think of the lbws Eddie Phillipson has given against them? Alan laughs. "An umpire like Arthur Fagg would give them not out because he was an ex-batsman, but Eddie was an ex-bowler, he gave them." Derbyshire's Derek Morgan agrees: "He used to boast that he was the leading umpire for lbws." "When Ian Thomson went out in the field," Alan recalls, "he always threw a piece of grass up in the air. He'd see which way it was blowing, and he'd choose his end. But if Eddie Phillipson was there, it didn't matter which way the wind was blowing. 'I'm going to Eddie's end,' he'd say." Colin Drybrough takes over at the pavilion end and, when Graham Cooper pads away the ball, he too sees Eddie Phillipson's finger. With Sussex 143 for six at lunch, the lead is just 31, and only Les Lenham of the batsmen survives.

"I always tended to bat better when the chips were down," Les recalls. "I remember marching out there, thinking, 'I've got to get my head down.' I grafted a bit early on, to resurrect the team, and then once I got in, even though I say it myself, I played some quite useful shots." *'Lenham played many handsome strokes, not only on the on-side to which he is popularly supposed to be restricted.'*

"Les was very determined," Alan says. "He had to work at his cricket; it didn't come easy to him." Like many who have to work hard at the game, he will become a great coach, and perhaps he is already analysing his skills here as he plays the spin of Titmus and Drybrough. "He was always very conscious of how he looked. If he played a shot through the covers, he'd stand and watch the ball and look at himself. 'Hang on, Les,' we'd say. 'We'll get a shot of that.' But this is Lord's, and perhaps he is hoping that the real photographers are at work. In the Evening Standard, the picture is of Fred Titmus, *'chief agent of destruction'*.

It is June 1963. 'Let the air you breathe be Springtime fresh,' the advert promises. 'Let it be pure! And pleasant - as only Airwick can make it.' 'Re Housing, see Unit,' the next advert proclaims. 'Their experience of rapid, large-scale building is unique.'

"When I went to South Africa with the M.C.C. in 1956," Alan remembers, "we were each given an electric razor - and that was really something." Here at Lord's they hope for a photograph, but in thirty years' time every player will have his game analysed on video tape. Has such technological advance helped to make cricket more professional? "You've got Test cricketers at the pinnacle of their careers, they still bowl long hops, they still bowl half-volleys. Batsmen still play back when they should play forward, they still flash at wide ones. You'll never be that professional. There'll always be the human element."

After lunch Titmus takes his innings tally to six wickets as he removes Thomson, Buss and Bell. Middlesex may have a ten and eleven who bat *'with more science than luck'*, but Sussex have no such hopes of their tail. Don

Bates is one who often takes more wickets in a season than he scores runs - "He used to have a towel in both his legs." - and, when he joins Les Lenham in the middle, the lead is 73 and there are more than three hours left to play.

"I was a reasonable player of the turning ball," Les recalls. "Somebody once asked me, 'Which was your best innings ever?' And I said, '20 not out, at Stroud in 1962.' 'Pardon,' he said. I went in at nought for three, and we were all out for 41. The pitch was like a strip of plasticene. Then there was the time I carried my bat for fifty against Don Shepherd at the worst ground in the world at Margam." *'Lenham displayed remarkable concentration on a difficult pitch,'* Wisden records. "I thought it was fun when the spinners bowled on turning wickets. You had great close catchers round the bat, and you had to work the ball through these fielders. It was interesting cricket."

What a different world from the 1990s! No matches at Stroud or Margam, and the wickets at the county grounds all covered whenever it rains. At the end of the 1998 summer the England selectors pick two off-spinners to tour Australia: Such, with 38 wickets at 38.8, and Croft, with 20 wickets at 57.2. "They wouldn't have been offered contracts with figures like that. On the other hand, if they'd played in the sixties, they'd have been bowling on turning wickets. The old pros tend to forget that. 'Hold on,' I say sometimes. 'You only got twenty or thirty wickets a year on good pitches.' Mind you, Croft and Such still wouldn't have been picked, because there were better off-spinners about: Titmus and Illingworth, Allen and Mortimore. Those guys were wonderful bowlers."

Fred Titmus, the beneficiary. Yesterday he launched a bright afternoon's batting with an exhilarating 45. Today he has six wickets. "He had what we call spin-swerve," Les explains. "When he bowled his off-spinner, it curved away before it pitched back. He started out as an away swing bowler, like Laker. You can't produce spin-swerve with an arm twelve o'clock high. It's got to be at eleven o'clock like an away swinger."

Here at Lord's Les takes his score through the sixties and seventies, and he finally finds a batsman to stay with him. *'His most valuable partner was Bates who, in the manner of modern number elevens who bat like masters, stayed 45 minutes while 38 were added for the last wicket.'* Thirty-five years on, Alan reads the report, and he sets off for the Edgbaston photocopier with a chuckle. "I'll send him a copy, it'll make his day." *'Bates outlived Lenham who eventually met a nasty one from Bennett.'* The crowd this Tuesday is a smaller one, but it applauds Les as he makes his way back into the pavilion. *'By making 85 out of 132 Lenham revived a corpse.'* Middlesex need 112 for victory, and there are two hours and twenty minutes left to bat.

The pitch is *'dusty and wildly unpredictable'*, but there should be plenty of overs to make these runs. Not like at Hastings in 1946 when a sixteen-year-old Alan operated the scoreboard and Surrey chased 47 for victory in twenty minutes. "There were all these tin plates everywhere, and I had to keep turning them over to see what number was on the back. Batsmen were coming and going. I got in a terrible state. The umpire stopped the game. It was Denis Hendren, Patsy's brother. 'Just put the scores up, son,' he said. I met him years later. 'You won't remember, but I was doing the score at Hastings.' 'Oh yes, I do,' he said. 'It was you making that bloody noise, was it?'"

The target is 112 in 140 minutes, and Sussex need ten wickets for victory. A very different equation from the game a fortnight ago at Tunbridge Wells. The first round of the new Knock-out Competition. Sussex 314 for seven, with 104 from Kenny Suttle. Kent kept their slips and gullies for the full 65 overs, but Ted Dexter had other ideas. "After about the third over the second slip went to mid-wicket, gully went into the covers, and we blocked off their shots." Peter Richardson scored 127 and won the fifty pounds award, but his batting never threatened to win the game for Kent. "Man of the Match? I'd have called him Moaner of the Match. He complained all through the innings. 'Well if this is the way you play it, you can stuff this knock-out cricket.'"

It is the summer of 1963. Kim Philby is revealed as the Third Man, and John Profumo resigns as Defence Secretary. Robbers hold up a Royal Mail train in Buckinghamshire, and bad landlords are accused of Rachmanism.

'The Middlesex innings had an eventful start. Russell was bowled by his first ball, and Gale, having been dropped in the gully, was caught at the wicket off Thomson.' At eight for two, Ted Dexter decides to switch to spin. "You never quite knew what he was going to do," Alan says. "Sometimes he got bored, but he was always game to get a result. We played Middlesex at Hove one year, they'd got behind in a run chase, so he brought Les on. Les thought he was quite a good leg-spinner, but he told him to bowl it halfway down the wicket." Les recalls the over. "I was bowling to Fred Titmus. The first two balls were short, there was nobody on the leg side, and he swept them both for four. So I pitched the next one up, it turned in the rough and bowled him. Ted gave me the biggest bollocking of all time, and of course he was right. They didn't go for it after that."

Last Friday it was Graham Cooper's turn. *'The match with Hampshire looked like bogging down into a drawn game until Dexter brought on Cooper to lure the batsmen to recklessness.'* Victory came with twenty minutes to spare, and for John Clarke in the Evening Standard the moral is clear. *'Risks are worth taking, the game is better for being won or lost.'*

So what is today's idea? "I was wandering across the pitch between overs," Alan remembers, "and suddenly I heard my name. I kept walking, and he said, 'Oaky, here, it's your turn.' He never advised me to get loose the over before. All I could do was run up and hope my feet were landing right." Alan has bowled just nineteen overs this summer, and the Daily Telegraph describes his first over here as *'rusty'*. "I got over that one, and probably the next one was a bit better. So I thought, 'That's not so bad.'"

"Oaky was a very good off-spinner," Les says. "He made it bounce. It came down from over nine feet, and he spun it. But he found it hard work. He loved his batting, and he liked standing at slip because it wasn't very energetic. But bowling made him puff and blow, and he didn't like that." Alan disagrees: "I enjoyed bowling. I wouldn't have wanted to be just a batsman and fielder. I don't think I puffed and blowed that much. Maybe the first over, getting my breath."

At the Nursery End Ronnie Bell is in action, and by the time the score has reached 34 he has captured the wickets of Parfitt and White. "Parf wasn't a bad player then. Once we got him out, we thought we were in with a chance." *'For 15 minutes the score stayed uneasily at 34 for four while a reappraisal by Hooker and Titmus took place.'* Then Ron Hooker starts *'prancing down the wicket to Oakman,'* and the score runs forward through the forties and fifties. "If we'd had a high-class spinner," Les Lenham reflects, "we'd have won the championship that year."

Who knows? Perhaps Alan might have become a high-class spinner. In his first four full seasons he took 329 wickets, and here at Lord's *'his direction was perfect, and his great height seemed to make the eccentricities of bounce more frequent.'* But in 1955 Robin Marlar took over the county captaincy, and Alan's opportunities diminished. "He said, 'I'm going to do most of the spin bowling now; I'd like you to go up the batting order.' 'Well,' I thought, 'you can't argue with the captain. At least I know where I stand.'"

It is "all a bit hit and miss" for Alan as his career unfolds. 99 wickets in 1954, but two years later he was playing for England as a batsman. "I suppose I wouldn't have got into the England side if it hadn't been for Marlar." In the second of his two Tests he took five catches to help Jim Laker to nineteen wickets, and he will tell the story of his part in that dramatic match at many a Cricket Society gathering. "My God," Jim will say to him one day, "you're not still dining out on that, are you?"

Alan's bowling is an occasional extra now, seventy wickets in the last six summers, and Sussex's attack revolves around the medium pace of Thomson, Buss and Bates. "There was no variation," Alan reflects. "We went through this period when the batsmen would pad away the spinners so we had a lot of seam bowling. It was boring to stand at slip and watch it. It's like the modern game. It's so refreshing to see Warne, MacGill and Muralitharan. You get more cricket, more action. There's an art in looping the ball and spinning it." *'At 59 Oakman slipped a quicker ball behind Hooker's legs, and the batsman was brilliant stumped by Parks.'* It is Alan's first wicket since last August, but perhaps its significance will be greater in the career of Jim Parks. *'His all round form in these three days has borne the England stamp.'* Keith Andrew will carry a slight injury in the Old Trafford Test, and the team for Lord's will include Jim once more. "It was a good stumping," Alan recalls. "I was very impressed."

Titmus and Clark take up the challenge. It is Tuesday afternoon, the great Bank Holiday crowds are back at work but *'on the free seats a former Sussex captain could contain himself no longer. Again and again he cried 'Sussex!''* Titmus edges the ball into the slips, and Alan at last catches the eye of the Lord's photographer. *'Oakman just fails to hold a catch from Titmus,'* the caption will read tomorrow morning. With 47 to win Ted Clark drives Alan for *'a full-blooded six,'* then next ball he repeats the shot, only to see Alan *'leap to take a return catch that no one else in cricket, except Larter, could have reached.'* What windows would today's television commentators jump out of at the sight of such a catch. "He hit it like a rocket," Alan recalls. "I just stuck my hand up, and it stuck." It is 71 for six, 41 still wanted, and *''Well done, Sussex,' the old sea-dog bellowed.'*

Who is this captain? "We had a committee man called Poona White. He wasn't an ex-player, but he'd been a Commander in the Navy. The old boy did a lot for Sussex. He went round knocking on doors to increase the membership. I could imagine him getting excited like that." Les Lenham disagrees. "Dear old Poona wouldn't have been a man to shout; he was a quiet, studious man." Whoever it is, at 85, he is once more bellowing. Alan may be puffing and blowing but, when Bennett drives him out to Bates at mid-off, he sees the fielder *'clutch the ball to his midriff.'* "Don Bennett smashed it quite hard, and Batesy got his body behind it. He hadn't got the best eyesight, but somehow he held on. He went quite pale afterwards."

It is 1963. The last series of 'What's My Line' is broadcast on television, the first of 'Dr Who'. American Express launches a sterling credit card, and the first British-made oral contraceptive becomes available.

"When you play cricket, it's the best years of your life," Alan says. "You won't find a job to compare with it. The camaraderie, the laughs." He runs a newsagents in Hove in winter. Soon he will move on to a sub-post office, but he knows that he will not be happy to retire to a job outside cricket. "You look at the fixtures, and you think, 'Oh they're at Bournemouth today, I remember what happened there two years ago.' It's difficult readjusting."

Perhaps it is thoughts like these that keep Fred Titmus so long in the game. Fourteen years ago, he made his debut at Bath, and he will play his last game here at Lord's in nineteen years' time. By then he will be running a sub-post office in Hertfordshire, putting his head round the dressing room door on his day off. "What marvellous timing," Mike Brearley will say. "Have you got your boots?" And on the last afternoon he will take three vital wickets. It is captaincy by hunch, just as Ted Dexter is practising today.

There are 27 runs still to win, and for 80 minutes Fred Titmus, *'all pads and bat and wrinkles'*, has *'eschewed the violence which was getting his colleagues out.'* He is the pro's pro, and he is determined to win this benefit match the careful way. "In those days," Les Lenham explains, "when the ball turned, you had to sweep the good length balls. You couldn't keep pushing,

pushing. Unless you went down the pitch, the only option was to sweep." But here at Lord's there is an added factor, a 'human element' that Fred Titmus must take into account.

Eddie Phillipson. "Dear old Eddie," Essex's Robin Hobbs remembers. "He used to give them out with a smile." He is one whose lbw decisions are influenced by the batsman's shot. "If you played straight," Alan tells, "it was not out. But if you played the sweep and it hit you on the pad, he'd give it out." There are just 16 runs to win when *'Titmus, sweeping at Oakman, was leg before.'* The celebrations start again on the free seats. *'You lovely lads, there are only two to go.'* Drybrough forces Ronnie Bell to mid-wicket for three, he drives Alan over his head for two, but he too cannot resist *'heaving at Oakman'* and is leg before. Nine to win, eight minutes to get them, and *'Loud and clear came the former captain's exhortation. 'Come on, Sussex, Sussex by the sea.''*

Five wickets in an innings for Alan. It is seven years now since he has known such success with the ball. But, when Price plays out the last ball of the over, it is Ronnie Bell who must bowl at John Murray. Is Ronnie glowing still with his eight wickets a week ago or does he need a lot of reassuring? We are down to the human element now.

John Murray, batting at number nine. He is no longer England's first-choice keeper, but he will be recalled for the Oval Test when the West Indies return in three years' time. His 112 will be only the third century scored by a number nine in Test cricket, and Wisden will declare that *'he looked every bit as good as Graveney.'* A hundred against Hall and Griffith, Sobers and Gibbs. Here at Lord's there are just eight to make against Alan Oakman and Ronnie Bell. *'He pulled the first ball of Bell's over for four.'*

The human element. The ball is returned to Ronnie Bell, and he maintains his length. "I don't envy the young players now," Alan says. "We had one style of bowling or batting, and we were broken into it." John Murray plays back the next four deliveries, then on the last ball he runs a leg bye to keep strike. Three to win, and the exhortation is becoming desperate: *"Come on, Sussex, Sussex by the sea."*

Three to win, and Alan to bowl his off-spin once more. *'Murray went down the pitch to the first and played it with his pads.'* With Eddie Phillipson the umpire the appeal is inevitable, but he has given two lbws in the last ten minutes, and this time the bat is straight. "Not out," comes the reply. *'He played the second dead-bat.'* Then that twist of good fortune for Middlesex, *'the third went for two byes.'*

John Murray. Three years ago he faced Derek Shackleton here, nine wickets down and five to win. There is no harder bowler than Shack to get away, his match figures eleven for 75 in 52 overs, but *'Murray decided upon an all or nothing policy and pulled him into the main grandstand for a towering six.'* Today it is just one to tie, two to win, and he is waiting for his chance. *'He let the fourth go outside the off-stump. The fifth he swept.'* "You had to sweep the good length balls," Les Lenham explains. *'He swept and missed.'*

Once more Alan turns to Eddie Phillipson. No third umpire, no televised replay. It is down to the human element. In the words of Michael Melford in the Daily Telegraph, *'Oakman and umpire Phillipson between them finished off the match.'* Murray, lbw for 14. "That was going down leg," he tells Alan as they leave the field. "No, it wasn't," Alan replies. "It was the one going up the hill." *'And above the cheers of the crowd came that Sussex voice. "You wonderful lads!" was the chorus now, with many a martlet joining in.'*

> *'You may tell them all that we stand or fall*
> *For Sussex by the sea.'*

Tomorrow's championship table will find them still in first place, and the headlines will belong to their occasional off-spinner. *'Hunch-man Alan keeps Sussex top by one run,'* proclaims the Daily Express.

"It's a wonderful, marvellous, bloody awful game," Alan says. "You have your good days and your bad days, but you only remember your good times."

'The memory of Middlesex's victory by one run in 1959 had become a little less painful,' the Daily Telegraph concludes.' "One run," Alan reads thirty-five years later. "I didn't realise it was that close." They will still be top of the table in late July, but by then Ted Dexter's mind will be firmly on the Test series. "He'd always got everything worked out before it happened," Alan recalls, and this summer his early season words prove prophetic. Fourth in the championship, they will return here in September to win the first Knock-out Cup. Their strategy in each round is to set defensive fields for their seam bowlers, but the Lord's wicket is a slow turner and in desperation Ted Dexter throws the ball once more to Alan. "We'd only made 168, but Ron Headley couldn't get the ball off the square." 13 overs, one for 17. "Dexter reckoned I should have won the Man of the Match award."

Two thousand pounds is the prize for the winning county. How much of it is paid to the players? "We asked the committee before the Final. 'Have we ever let you down?' they said. Well, there was no answer to that. I think we got nine quid at Christmas. There'd be all hell let loose now, but in those days you didn't argue."

The world has moved on, and today's cricketers do not drift into the first-class game as Alan did. Hastings may have felt out on a limb in the Sussex cricket of the 1940s, but fifty years later its ground will be gone altogether, redeveloped as a shopping centre. "A major step forward," one local councillor will call it, and Alan will be left only with memories. The human element. "I was standing in Marks and Spencers, trying to work out where I used to bat, but I couldn't manage it with all the clothes around."

MIDDLESEX v SUSSEX

Lord's. 1, 3 & 4 June 1963

SUSSEX WON BY 1 RUN

SUSSEX

A.S.M. Oakman	c Bennett b Hooker	21	c Price b Clark	35
R.J. Langridge	c Hooker b Price	14	lbw b Titmus	37
K.G. Suttle	c Russell b Titmus	46	lbw b Titmus	8
*E.R. Dexter	c White b Price	15	c Hooker b Titmus	2
+J.M. Parks	b Hooker	71	c Murray b Drybrough	11
L.J. Lenham	c White b Drybrough	15	c Hooker b Bennett	85
G.C. Cooper	b Drybrough	0	lbw b Drybrough	9
N.I. Thomson	c Murray b Price	2	c Drybrough b Titmus	0
A. Buss	c Murray b Bennett	18	b Titmus	8
R.V. Bell	b Bennett	4	c Price b Titmus	1
D.L. Bates	not out	0	not out	13
Extras	*lb 5, w 1*	6	*b 7, lb 7*	14
		212		**223**

1-27, 2-53, 3-82, 4-130, 5-187, 6-187, 7-187, 8-194, 9-201, 10-212
1-72, 2-82, 3-90, 4-91, 5-119, 6-142, 7-153, 8-179, 9-185, 10-223

Bennett	19.2	8	44	2	5.4	1	14	1
Price	20	8	41	3	17	4	38	0
Hooker	17	2	44	2				
Clark	7	1	12	0	3	0	19	1
Titmus	19	5	51	1	38	11	69	6
Drybrough	16	7	14	2	26	8	69	2

MIDDLESEX

R.A. Gale	c Bell b Bates	2	c Parks b Thomson	7
W.E. Russell	st Parks b Bell	77	b Bates	0
P.H. Parfitt	c Buss b Bates	1	c Buss b Bell	8
R.A. White	lbw b Bates	11	c Langridge b Bell	15
R.W. Hooker	run out	19	st Parks b Oakman	21
F.J. Titmus	c Lenham b Bell	45	lbw b Oakman	17
E.A. Clark	lbw b Thomson	71	c & b Oakman	10
D. Bennett	c Dexter b Bell	39	c Bates b Oakman	6
+J.T. Murray	c Parks b Bell	13	lbw b Oakman	14
*C.D. Drybrough	not out	19	lbw b Oakman	5
J.S.E. Price	b Thomson	19	not out	0
Extras	*b 4, nb 4*	8	*b 2, lb 4, nb 1*	7
		324		**110**

1-8, 2-14, 3-37, 4-75, 5-151, 6-179, 7-267, 8-277, 9-289, 10-324
1-1, 2-7, 3-28, 4-34, 5-59, 6-71, 7-85, 8-96, 9-103, 10-110

Thomson	40.4	13	80	2	4	1	11	1
Bates	19	5	52	3	5	1	8	1
Buss	19	3	58	0				
Bell	43	17	110	4	19	8	31	2
Suttle	3	0	16	0				
Oakman					19.5	8	53	6

Umpires: R. Aspinall and W.E. Phillipson

Brian Close

We wrote letters when it rained. There was this bridge club, with Illingworth and Close. It was absolutely criminal if we put Closey off playing his next card. So the rest of us had to write letters.

Geoff Pullar

You never thought he was in, but all of a sudden you'd look up and he'd got 35 not out. Then, when you think you are bowling well at him, he'd be 70 or 80. And you'd think, I haven't seen him make a shot yet. Where he's got 70 from? Then he'd be raising his bat for 100.

Tom Cartwright

Tom was my idol. Everybody else used to bowl. Then Tom would come on, and it was a different game. He didn't have a long run-up and he wasn't that quick, but he did so much with the ball. He hit the seam regularly, that was the secret. Hand grenades he used to bowl.

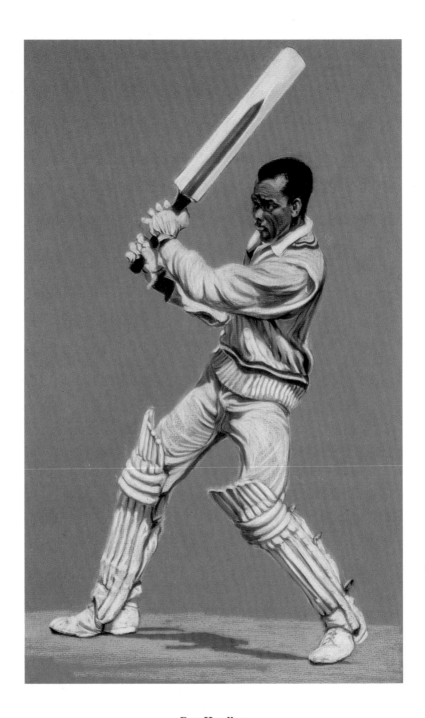

Ron Headley

Ron had six bats, and he used to line them up and take them out according to the situation. 'Big Bertha tomorrow, we want some big hitting.' 'I'll be dabbing ones today, I'll take the little Wand.'

IT'S STRANGE WHAT YOU REMEMBER

Derbyshire v Warwickshire

July 1964

with Tom Cartwright, Ray Hitchcock, Brian Jackson, Michael Mence and Derek Morgan

Tom Cartwright, Ray Hitchcock and Michael Mence all played for Warwickshire. Tom played five Tests for England, and later for Somerset and Glamorgan. Brian Jackson and Derek Morgan played for Derbyshire, Derek captaining the county in his last five seasons.

They all try to remember a game of changing fortunes at Derby.

A hundred pounds to play a Test for England.

"It's strange what you remember, isn't it?" Tom says, and his mind drifts back to Whitsun 1963 and the news of his selection in the England twelve for the first Test. Warwickshire were playing Derbyshire at Edgbaston, the traditional Bank Holiday meeting, and "Well done," Charlie Lee the Derbyshire captain said to him. "A bit of a surprise," Tom replied. "Charlie was much older than me and a teacher," Tom tells, "but he was a nice man to pass the time of day with. And he said, 'You might as well have the hundred pounds as anyone else.' And he didn't mean it any other way. Just a conversation piece. And I thought, 'He's probably right, that's about the strength of it.'"

A year has passed. Now it is Derbyshire versus Warwickshire at the Racecourse Ground, Derby, and Tom has still not had that hundred pounds. Twelfth man duties last summer for that first Test, twelfth man duties again last week at Headingley. It is mid-July, he is the country's leading wicket-taker this summer, and *'with a warm sun shining from a blue sky'* he prepares to take the field with his Warwickshire team mates.

The Racecourse Ground, Derby. *'Not entirely unconvincing as the opening set for Macbeth,'* the Guardian calls it. It is an open field to the north of the city, bleak and windswept, and there is no pavilion as such. The players change in the old jockeys' quarters and watch from the judges' box.

"We preferred playing at Chesterfield," Derbyshire's Derek Morgan reveals. "It was a lovely ground, and the crowd there was always very appreciative of what was going on. In the north of the county they're all very sports-oriented, whereas the Derby people don't really support anything. Not even the theatre or football."

"I loved playing county cricket," Tom says, "but Derby was the one place I never really looked forward to. I never got runs or wickets there, and it was such a cold place. You'd go to the dressing room, and there was a fire laid. It didn't matter what time of year it was, you lit the fire. When it was every other year at Whitsuntide, it was horrendous. We'd be wearing pyjamas under two pairs of cricket trousers, and all the shirts and vests we'd got."

Derby is always cold in Tom's memory, but this morning, according to the Times, *'the ground wore a pleasantly Edwardian air under the morning sun.'* Charlie Lee wins the toss for Derbyshire and opts to bat first. But, after Harvey is caught behind for one, he and Ian Buxton *'progressed at a pace suggestive of builders laying foundations, firmly but at a speed slower than seemed necessary.'* 48 for one after an hour and a half.

It is July 1964. Donald Campbell passes 400 miles an hour in Bluebird, the Blue Streak rocket completes Britain's first flight in space, and an American satellite sends back close-up pictures of the Moon's surface.

Warwickshire versus Derbyshire. Second in the table against second last. Both counties have plenty of seam bowling, but Warwickshire have the batting as well. Derek Morgan looks at the Warwickshire line-up: Horner, Barber, Ibadulla, Smith, Jameson - "Oh gosh, they all got on with it." Then he looks at his own side: "We were a deadly boring batting side. There was only Laurie Johnson who whacked the ball anywhere. The crowds only came to watch the bowling." *'An on-drive and straight drive by Lee and two cover drives by Buxton were the morning's only positive shots.'* Then Tom captures the wickets of Buxton and Oates in the space of three balls, and lunch is taken at 58 for three. The score was *'not impressive',* the Times records.

So what is Warwickshire's new ball attack that the Derbyshire batsmen have struggled so hard to master? Not David Brown and Jack Bannister, their regular pair, and not Albert Wright, the first reserve; they are all resting injuries. And not Rudi Webster, the tall Barbadian who took seven for six last week against Yorkshire; he is up in Edinburgh, collecting his degree in medicine. No, today it is Bill Blenkiron, the brickyard labourer's son from outside Bishop Auckland, making his championship debut, and Michael Mence, who two years ago went from the Bradfield College team to the Warwickshire first eleven and bowled Middlesex's Bob Gale with his second ball in first-class cricket. "1962 was a very special year for me," he recalls. "It seemed a remarkably easy game."

Michael Mence and Bill Blenkiron, both professionals now. "I think cricket was just something to fill Michael's time," Bill says. "He wasn't looking for the pennies like we were." Michael agrees: "I was a boy in a man's world. I had a great deal of talent, but it was never any more to me than a game." At the end of that magic summer of 1962 Mike Smith, the Warwickshire captain, took him aside. "Go to university, Michael," he said. "Don't bother about cricket, get yourself a career. If you come back to us at 24 or 25, you'll still be a better player." But Michael went for an interview at Jesus College, Cambridge, where Surrey's Dick Jefferson had failed his exams the previous year. "Dick was a Wykehamist, really quite a bright lad, so I asked the governor, 'What happens if I fail my first year exams?' 'You'll be sent down,' he said. 'Well,' I said, 'I think I can pass the exams, providing I don't play any cricket till they're over.' 'Oh god,' he said, 'we don't want you then.'" So now he is on the Warwickshire staff, in winter an articled clerk to a stockbroker, and here at Derby he is playing his first championship match of the summer.

It is 58 for three, and the players make their way to lunch. "We used to go into the base of the old Racecourse stand," Warwickshire's Ray Hitchcock tells. "The approach to it wasn't very well-lit." "It used to smell all the way along," Bill Blenkiron says. "It was like going into a dungeon."

Twenty minutes after lunch Charlie Lee *'lunged forward and edged Mence to second slip'*. At 64 for four *'Derbyshire seemed on the verge of total collapse,'* but Mike Page is at six, *'the promising Page'*, and *'with his first stroke he showed just what was possible.'* His off-drive scores just one run, but *'what was important was that it instantly transformed Johnson.'*

Laurie Johnson is a white Barbadian, whose Derbyshire debut was back in 1949. "He came over to train at Fletcher and Stewart, the big sugar machinery people," Derek Morgan tells. But he returned home for some years - "in those days the West Indian wickets were beautiful" - and it is only in recent summers that he has started to prosper in English conditions. His first century came in his 280th innings, then there were ten more in the next 120. "A superb player to watch. He played in the West Indian style. He used to go down on one knee and whack it." Here at Derby *'it was as if he suddenly realised that the bowling was ordinary and he had nothing to fear. He danced down the wicket and raced to his fifty.'* At the other end Mike Page *'was unlucky enough to drag a ball onto his stumps'*, but Derek Morgan *'joined Johnson and runs went on flowing pleasantly.'*

It is the summer of 1964. Pye has developed a high-fidelity stereophonic record player, based on transistors. The BBC is *'doing all it can'* to minimise continental TV interference, and an International Telephone Committee says that world-wide direct dialling *'should be possible'* within ten years.

Derek Morgan is at number seven. "I was only an ordinary batsman," he says. "When I started, I used to go in at nine. I played all sorts of shots and kept getting out. Charlie Elliott was the senior professional. 'Don't be daft,' he said. 'Play the shots you can. You don't get any runs in the pavilion.'" Nobody in this Derbyshire side approaches a career average of 30 and, with uncovered wickets and three-day games, Derek's runs are vital. Why, two years ago, he even topped the first-class averages late in July.

"The all-rounders in those days were a different breed," Tom Cartwright says. "They came from six, seven, eight in the order, batters in days of adversity. Every side had them: bloody-minded fighters. And I can't see it in today's cricket." Last week at the Oval Derek Morgan broke the third finger of his left hand, but today *'he batted courageously with his skill apparently unimpaired.'* *'Morgan also found his shots, and runs at last came quickly.'* 150 for five, the temperature touching seventy, and still half an hour to tea.

The Derby groundsman is Walter Goodyear. "He was the best chap I ever came across," Bill Blenkiron says. "He had a tractor, and he used to do the whole ground himself. And at the end of the day he'd take your cricket boots, and next morning you'd come back and he'd whitened them." In 1970 he will be chosen as Groundsman of the Year, though there is no such award in 1964. "In those days," Derek recalls, "the home side prepared the wickets for their own bowlers. When we played in Glamorgan or Gloucestershire, the ball turned square, but everybody accepted that. It made it far more interesting."

"The Derby wickets invariably had a bit of grass on them," Ray Hitchcock says - though the Times reports that this pitch *'remained uniformly kind to the batsmen,'* the Birmingham Post that for the bowlers it is *'a matter of waiting for batsmen to fall into error.'* In the last half hour before tea there is no such error and precious few runs either. *'The slower bowlers managed to shake loose the batsmen's grip,'* and *'the batting, which had woken with a start, nodded off again.'* According to Denys Rowbotham in the Guardian, *'it meant that Derbyshire were 164 instead of all but 200 at tea.'*

The county championship is a two-horse race this year, and yesterday at Edgbaston the lead changed hands as Worcestershire inflicted *'a hiding'* on *'woeful Warwicks'*. Somerset wickets are falling fast at Worcester, and this makeshift Warwickshire attack will need a good session to keep up with them. But the new ball is *'deflected lucratively'*, and soon the applause starts to ripple: the hundred partnership, Derek Morgan's fifty, the total past 200, then the completion of Laurie Johnson's *'stylish'* century. He falls straightaway to a catch at mid-wicket, the ever-accurate Tom Cartwright captures two lbws, but the day ends with *'two mightily clubbed sixes'* from Bob Taylor and *'three handsome boundaries'* to bring up Derek Morgan's seventh first-class century. 296 for eight. *'Not nearly enough,'* the Guardian reckons. *'A total of 400 should not have been beyond them,'* the Derby Evening Telegraph grumbles. But this is Derbyshire. It is over two years since they even reached 350 and, as Derek says, "We were always a bowling side. If we could get 250 at Chesterfield or Derby, we reckoned we could win the match."

A century for Derek Morgan. Already this summer he has 850 runs and 45 wickets. Could he have played for England? "People say he wasn't quite there," Tom reckons, "because they're looking at the first four names you'd put down on paper. But if you look at the last four, he'd come into that. He probably did deserve a chance. But it doesn't happen to some people, does it?"

Tom is only 28, but Derek is 35 now and his chance has gone - though he did have one, eleven years ago. "I came on first change for the Rest against England in a Test Trial. Denis Compton was batting. He nicked one, and Godfrey Evans dropped it." Here at Derby his keeper now is the young Bob

Taylor. "When Bob dropped a catch, everybody heard about it. 'Sorry ... Sorry ... I should have caught that ... Sorry.' But if the ball dropped out of Godfrey's glove, he just picked it up and threw it back. Nobody ever knew."

Eleven years ago - in the week before the Coronation, Winston Churchill the Prime Minister and British troops rounding up the Mau Mau in Kenya. It is July 1964 now. Newspapers print Cecil Beaton's photograph of the Queen with Prince Edward her new baby, Winston Churchill makes his last appearance in the House of Commons, and Jomo Kenyatta arrives in London as President of Kenya.

Eleven years ago - in the prime of Derbyshire's fast bowler Les Jackson. Les played once for England in 1949 and again at the age of 40 in 1961, and in the years between he was as feared as any bowler on the county circuit. At Lord's they said that his action was too round-arm, that he took his wickets on Derby's grassy pitches, that his style was not suited to Test cricket. "On tours abroad," Tom thinks, "they'd have this preconceived idea that certain people couldn't bowl in those conditions - which was utter nonsense. People who can bowl will always adapt. No matter how many windows a groundsman might close, a good bowler will always open some himself."

It is Thursday morning at the Racecourse Ground, and the players are taking the field in *'hot sunshine'*. Charlie Lee has declared, and Warwickshire must face the Derbyshire seam attack. Green wickets and seam bowling have always been the standard fare here in Derby. Through the fifties it was Jackson and Gladwin - "probably the best pair of opening bowlers in the country," Derek Morgan says. Then Jackson and Harold Rhodes, the fastest bowler in England, some reckon. But Harold is injured for this match, and today it is Jackson and Peter Eyre. Only it is not Les Jackson now. Last autumn Les received his retirement gifts - a heater and an electric blanket among them - and he passed the new ball to his namesake Brian Jackson, who at the age of 29 came here last summer from the North Staffordshire League.

From Les to Brian, the Derbyshire tradition goes on. "I always rate Les as the best seam bowler I've ever seen," Brian says. "A wonderful bowler and a very nice guy." Les is not a man of many words; he is an ex-miner who prefers to express himself through hard, physical work. "I know you can bowl, else you wouldn't be here," he tells Brian. "But if the wicket helps you, you bowl the other side out. And if you don't, there's no excuses."

"Everybody was compared to Les," Derek Morgan recalls. "Les was the benchmark. You'd get on a green wicket, and you'd say, 'Les would have bowled them out on this.'" So Brian has a hard act to follow, and it is not made easier by the coincidence of his name. "One match at Swansea I was fielding down on the boundary. I had a pint under a seat here and there, and I was talking to two or three people. 'Where's your father today?' they said."

'The name Jackson has for years been synonymous with good fast bowling at Derby,' the Birmingham Post reports, *'and it was another of the*

kind that set Warwickshire off on the wrong foot by getting Horner caught at the wicket off the fifth ball of the day.' It is nought for one, and forty-five minutes later it is 11 for two as Bob Barber, *'in the act of hooking, played Jackson with precision on to the leg bail.'* "I was brought up in the hard school," Brian says. "It may sound conceited, but I knew I could bowl. It didn't bother me if Ken Barrington came in. I didn't need any psychiatrists or people like they've got now."

It is the summer of 1964. Ken Barrington may be the most reliable, the most determined batsman in England's Test side, but nobody in the country has scored more runs in the last six summers than Warwickshire's M.J.K. Smith, and today he steps out *'as he has so often done, to face an emergency.'* There is a touch of dew still on the grass, and progress is slow. *'Pad play', 'forward probing', 'deadened bat',* the only liveliness comes with some *'short singles that wavered between the risky and the ridiculous.'*

"Mike Smith wasn't the best chappie to run with," Ray Hitchcock tells. "He used the term GO and, twenty-two yards away, you'd think, 'Did he say GO or did he say NO?' Then he used to gesticulate, a little finger movement beckoning you or a halting hand. When you've got a halting hand and you've got a GO or a NO, you don't know where you are. We were all wary of him in the end."

'The afternoon told a different story,' the Times reports. *'The batsmen no longer played as though hobbled, and their running between the wickets became less frenzied.'* Edwin Smith, the Derby off-spinner, takes over at one end - "On a good wicket," Derek says, "he just turned the ball enough to get the edge, and he had a very good straight-on ball. He was a better bowler on good wickets than bad ones." Nobody in the country plays off-spin better than Mike Smith. "He was such a terrific on-side player," Ray Hitchcock remembers. "When he scored runs on the off-side, he would infer that that was the sissy side. He really dominated off-spin."

Almost every county has a good off-spinner, and in another age several might have played for England: Edwin Smith here at Derby, Brian Langford down in Somerset. But Mike Smith hits them all to leg. Surely it is possible to set a field for his batting. "He used to place it pretty well," Ray Hitchcock says, and Somerset's Ken Biddulph recalls an innings when Mike Smith took on Brian Langford. "I was on the mid-wicket boundary, Kenny Palmer at deep square leg, thirty yards between us, and he pinged it into the gap. We got closer and closer until we were practically holding hands, and he still put it between us." This afternoon Edwin Smith bowls Ibadulla for 36, then with the score on 134 *'Smith launched a fierce, firm-footed on-drive and was thrillingly caught by Buxton.'* In no time it is 138 for six, a deficit of 158 still, and only Ray Hitchcock remains of the batsmen.

Ray is the veteran of this Warwickshire team, the last survivor of the side that won the championship in 1951, and he remembers the innings that secured his first-team place. "We were playing Gloucester at the Courtauld's ground, Coventry. My name appeared on the team sheet for the next second eleven match at Belper, and I'd still got an innings to play." *'Warwickshire's cause seemed lost,'* Wisden records, *'but Hitchcock launched a vigorous onslaught which swung the course of the game.'* "I got a fifty in seventeen strokes, and I didn't have to go to Belper." He has had good seasons and bad since then: years at the top of his county's averages and years back in the second eleven. He has even had one summer off to set up his sports shop. But he has never lost his belief that "attack was the best way for me." And he has never lost his love of the Courtauld's ground. "It was a very small ground, and it had a kind of old turf, a bit spongy, so that the ball sat up a bit." Here at Derby, with the temperature in the mid-seventies, he takes on the bowlers with *'some typically cheerful hitting'*.

Derek Morgan and Edwin Smith are the bowlers, the same bowlers that he faced nine years ago when he hit a 78-minute hundred here and was in line for the season's fastest century. "Derby was a good county for me," he says. "If I was having a bad patch, I used to look up the fixture list and think, 'Can I survive till we play Derbyshire or we're at Courtauld's?'" He is in his last season now, and perhaps he is past such insecurities. *'Fatally he tried to bludgeon a refreshed Jackson as cheerfully as he had hit a tiring Morgan',* and by tea the score is 162 for eight.

It is July 1964. The General Election is due in the next three months, and Labour's George Brown promises a charter of rights for workers, with 'safeguards against arbitrary dismissal' and 'compensation for loss of job'. On the Stock Market two million pounds are wiped off the shares of Rolls Razor, John Bloom's washing machine company.

Miller is the ninth man out, caught by Derek Morgan in the slips. "The finest catcher of a ball I've ever seen in my life," Brian Jackson calls him. "It's something I can never explain," Derek says. "If the ball went to one side or the other, I could keep looking forward and put my hand out, and the ball would drop into it. Why, I've no idea. Philip Sharpe was another, he often seemed to catch the ball after it had gone past him. And Colin Cowdrey, you never saw Colin dive for a catch, he wasn't that athletic. But when the ball was on its way, Colin was moving to catch it. You listen to the commentators, and they don't understand that. 'It's gone straight to him,' they say, but those are the most difficult ones. If it goes straight to you, you've got nothing to judge the speed, and you can't give with it."

Warwickshire's last hope of a decent score lies with Michael Mence. "I was talented," he says, "but I was never tight enough." *'After tea came the new ball,'* Denys Rowbotham writes, *'and, thanks to Mence's running himself out when batting well, that was that.'* Warwickshire are all out for 187, and Derbyshire have an hour to build on their lead of 109. Michael may be talented, but among the professionals there is no great sympathy when an innings is thrown away like this. "I got a bollocking whenever I gave my wicket away," he recalls, "but there wasn't a lot of point because I was already kicking myself anyway."

Last month they were down at Worthing, and Tom Cartwright recalls a similar reception when he was last man out, though the circumstances were very different. "It rained overnight, and the pitch was terrible," he tells. "Huge pieces were flying out. We were looking pretty miserable, and I chanced my arm." One by one his team mates fell to Ian Thomson - "He was bowling to the better end," Ray Hitchcock recalls. "Sometimes the ball didn't leave the deck at the other end. So Mike Smith told us to slog Thomson." Nine wickets, all to Ian Thomson, and Tom Cartwright still there with a fifty. "I went down the pitch to him," Tom recalls, "and I was stumped down the leg-side. When I got into the pavilion, there was only Mike in there. One or two of them had lined him up to have a go at me for giving Ian all ten."

"Mike Smith was such a likeable chap," Ray Hitchcock says. "That's why he always had the team behind him one hundred per cent." And dealing with Tom at Worthing, how did that go? Tom smiles: "I think you can say that Mike wasn't the best person at giving a bollocking, and I wasn't the best person at accepting it." "We all knew we'd got enough runs," Ray says. In the Sussex second innings Tom got on to bowl at 23 for eight, and he took two wickets with his only two deliveries. Sussex stayed on for a two-day victory over Notts, and that was the last of first-class cricket in the town of Worthing.

A council ground in Worthing, Courtauld's works ground in Coventry, the old racecourse here in Derby, these are the places where a champion county must look to accumulate its victories. This is the nursery of England's Test team. "You had good wickets and bad," Tom says. "If all the wickets are good, the bowlers have no margin of error so there's no incentive to try to do things with the ball. It was a great thing when you got that little leeway, and you could learn from seeing something happen and trying to repeat it. It's the same in every trade. Those who do it better have the ability to see things and re-enact them."

It is July 1964. No bowler in England has improved as much in the last six summers as Tom. "From an ordinary net bowler," Ray Hitchcock says, "he became a true international bowler. Through sheer hard work. And thinking. In English conditions he was terrific."

The game here at Derby is in its final hour, and the atmosphere is humid. The Derbyshire lead is 109, the new ball is in the hands of Mence and Blenkiron, and Charlie Lee decides to save his own innings for tomorrow. He sends out Oates and Harvey, and Michael Mence, *'who is heavy with cold at the moment'*, runs in to bowl. He is not a brickyard labourer's son like Bill Blenkiron, he has not worked in car factories like Tom Cartwright, and he is not one who wants his cricket to be 'sheer hard work'. "It was a huge privilege to play," he says, "but it was always just a game." His opening over is *'shocking'*, but he gets one ball close to the off stump and it *'found Oates fiddling'*. A catch in the slips, and Derbyshire are one for one. But Harvey and Buxton take the score to 24 and, according to the Derby Evening Telegraph, *'the fans settled back contentedly, reflecting with smug satisfaction that Derbyshire were poised for their second win of the season.'*

Warwickshire, champions in 1911 and 1951, a third title has slipped a little further away here today. Tiger Smith, their coach, passes wisdom down from his playing days in 1911, and Tom Dollery, the second team captain, from his in 1951. But alas George Austin their scorer died last year, after 52 years' service, most of them with the same fountain pen. "A smashing chap," Ray Hitchcock says. "He used to come into the dressing room after the day's play. If we hadn't done very well, he would say, 'Tomorrow will be a better day'. Or, if we had, it would be, 'Well done, the Warwicks.' That's as much as you got, but he loved his cricket." It is another world from the computer-generated analysis that the modern Edgbaston scorer provides the coaching staff at every interval.

'Tomorrow will be a better day.' Is that what George Austin would have said this evening? It certainly looks that way as *'Buxton was dropped at slip off Blenkiron.'* There is no debut wicket here for Bill, and he is replaced for the closing overs by Tom Cartwright. "Tom was my idol," Bill says. "Everybody else used to bowl. Then Tom would come on, and it was a different game. He didn't have a long run-up, and he wasn't that quick, but he did so much with the ball. He hit the seam regularly, that was the secret, and he had a very high action. Hand grenades, he used to bowl."

The last overs of the second day. Derbyshire have a lead of 133. By lunch tomorrow it will be 250 or 300, and Warwickshire will chase the runs on a third-day wicket. That is how three-day cricket is played, and this evening all the Derbyshire batsmen must do is to play out time.

Michael Mence runs in to bowl, *'a boy in a man's world'*, and Harvey plays *'an anxious feeling shot'* and is caught in the slips. Oates and Harvey are gone, but worse follows when Laurie Johnson *'glanced Cartwright to Barber at backward short leg'*, and it is 25 for three. Derek Morgan looks back on the dismissal. "I don't know quite how the game has changed so much. I don't know why they don't have a backward short leg now because so many people flick it round in the air, and that used to be caught. I can't explain that."

Derbyshire, *'their batting order turned upside down'*, now send Mike Page out of the jockeys' quarters and immediately he plays *'a stabbing back shot'* to Michael Mence and gives a catch to Alan Smith. *'Derbyshire were on the way to squandering a wonderful opportunity.'* "Things like that used to happen sometimes," Tom says. "I can remember one night at the Oval, bowling Surrey out for 60, and another time at Edgbaston when Shack got about six of us in half an hour. You go out there, thinking 'Well, we'll sort it out tomorrow,' and you suddenly find everybody's been and gone."

Not everybody, though. Ian Buxton has watched the procession as non-striker, Charlie Lee is only now emerging to bat, and there is always Derek Morgan to rescue them if necessary. It may be 26 for four, but the lead is 135 and *'the pitch is still playing true'*. There is all to play for tomorrow.

But the day is still not over as Tom removes Ian Buxton and night-watchman Bob Taylor. 24 for one has become 33 for six. No 'tomorrow will be a better day', it's all 'well done, the Warwicks' now. *'Oh Derbyshire!'* the Evening Telegraph groans across its headline. *'This crash was inexcusable.'* Charlie Lee has held himself back, but even this backfires in the final over when he is *'bowled middle stump by the irrepressible Mence.'* 33 for seven. *'A flood of almost incredible disasters,'* the Times calls it. *'Was this good bowling or deplorable batting?'* Denys Rowbotham asks. *'For once, with Mence and Cartwright achieving school story-book analyses, cricket had moved too fast for logical deduction.'*

'The irrepressible Mence' may be heavy with cold but *'it might perhaps be said that four for 14 is not to be sniffed at.'* He will play another summer with Warwickshire, then two with Gloucestershire, but he will never again turn a game with a spell of bowling as he has done here this evening. How does he celebrate his success? "We always had beer together, generally in a public area," he remembers. "Indeed it was written into my contract. I've still got it somewhere. 'To bowl in the nets when required', and 'to mix with the public after the game'."

Drinking after the game. In two years' time he will join Gloucestershire, and the drinking there will go beyond contractual duty. "We weren't a very good side at Gloucestershire, but we were very affable. There were three or four who used to drink 12 or 14 pints a night." And in thirty years' time, how will he look back on it all? "There were three hugely talented young cricketers at Edgbaston. There was Dennis Amiss, who played for England." Eleven Test centuries, and now Warwickshire's Chief Executive. "There was John Jameson, who played for England." 18,000 first-class runs, and now Assistant Secretary of M.C.C. "And there was Michael Mence, who runs a pub."

It is July 1964, and Michael is just twenty years old. This evening in London there is the premiere of the Beatles' first film, 'A Hard Day's Night'.
'It's been a hard day's night,
I've been working like a dog.'

"I loved the sixties," Tom Cartwright says, "and I like this programme 'Heartbeat' with all the music. It was a smashing time. A very comfortable time. I suppose I was still young enough, and I was breaking into Test cricket. Things were reaching a pinnacle."

Tom has grown up in Coventry with the motor car industry, and he has found cricketing success through hard work. 91 wickets so far this summer, though he cannot lift his bowling arm out sideways beyond the horizontal. Next week at Old Trafford he will finally get to wear that England cap, and what a first two days he will have. Alec Bedser, the great medium-pacer, is a selector now, and Tom recalls the nets on Wednesday. "I can remember Alec getting changed and coming out to bowl. He always had that aura about him, and he was such a great, great bowler. Even at that time he could still run up and bowl convincingly in the nets. That was the start of wondering. 'What am I doing? ... Why isn't he still playing?'" By close of play on Friday, Australia are 570 for four, Simpson on his way to a triple century, and Tom with figures of two for 118 in 77 overs. "Hard work," he says, "and a lot of nervous energy, too." *'A dozen times or more he beat the bat,'* the Times records, *'and hardly a single stroke of positive assurance was played against him.'* Can any bowler in Test history have worked so hard in their first two days? *'At the start of the week Cartwright was a respected county bowler. Now he seems sure to go to South Africa. It has taken him a long time to make the grade.'*

Paul McCartney gives his father a racehorse. Drake's Drum, he calls it.
'It's been a hard day's night,
I should be sleeping like a log.'

It is July 1964. Petrol rises by a halfpenny a gallon; *'a blow to the motoring community,'* the AA calls it. Spending on roads has risen from 5 million pounds ten years ago to 145 million now, and Transport Minister Ernest Marples refuses calls to impose a 100 mph speed limit on motorways.

Tom bowls 77 overs in two days on his Test debut, but in the space of 23 days in August 1967 he will get through 383 overs and take 61 wickets. "An amazing three weeks," he says, and he still recalls the scene at the end of the match at Dover. "It was very hot, we'd fielded all day, and we lost the match right at the end." And the fixture list will have them at 11.30 next morning in Middlesbrough. "Somebody set the showers off, and we just ran through them. We were literally throwing on our shirts and ties, I can see us now getting into taxis to the station, and they held the train up. We were half-dressed. Then we had to go across London and up to Darlington. We stayed the night there, opposite a night club that was still going strong at four in the morning. Then we had to get up early to catch the train to Middlesbrough."

This is the county championship, the nursery in which all the great English cricketers have developed their skills. "David Cook had opened the bowling in Dover, and he'd gone off on his own in his two-seater sports car." The last of the amateurs, Tom calls him, and at Middlesbrough they receive the message that he is not feeling well and has gone home. "Of course we lost the toss, and I had to take the new ball." 73 more overs in the next two days, and he still cannot lift his arm out sideways above the horizontal.

Here at Derby there are not so many overs for Tom to bowl on Friday morning. The temperature approaches eighty, but there is no rearguard action from Derek Morgan. Within the hour Tom and Michael Mence have five wickets each, and, although *'the tail did its best'*, Derbyshire are all out for 71, a lead of just 180. Norman Horner falls again to Brian Jackson, but *'only one outcome looked possible'* as Barber and Ibadulla take the score to 61 by lunch. *'Only a blackening sky threatened them.'*

Bob Barber has come to Warwickshire from an unhappy Old Trafford, and this summer he is shaking off his dour reputation. *'I have generally thought of him as an unadventurous batsman,'* the Times writes. *'Not now, though.'* "Bob was a different character at Edgbaston," Ray Hitchcock tells. As Lancashire's amateur captain he has been forced to stay at different hotels and play the disciplinarian, but life under Mike Smith is a different world. "I don't think we let him get away with too much initially, and he was soon one of the boys." Soon an England player again, too. *'Barber hooked Eyre from outside his off stump, a shot as commanding in aspect as it was crushing of any Derbyshire hopes. Henceforward, everything overpitched Barber drove fluently and stylishly, and everything short he continued to hook.'*

"He played his cricket in a far more relaxed way," Ray Hitchcock says, and he will never be more relaxed than on the thirtieth of July 1966, World Cup Final day. Warwickshire versus Worcestershire at Edgbaston. "As we came out after lunch," Worcester's Bob Carter tells, "Bob was still batting, and he said to us, 'I think I've got more chance of watching this football this afternoon than you lot.' And sure enough, at five to three, up went his head, and over the lot went." Barber, bowled D'Oliveira, 84. "Cheers, chaps."

It is July 1964. Barry Goldwater wins the Republican Party nomination for the American Presidency, Ian Smith hopes for independence for Southern Rhodesia, and Nelson Mandela begins a sentence of life imprisonment.

The Racecourse Ground, Derby. The players disappear into the 'dungeon' under the stand for lunch, and *'the blackening sky'* and hot, humid air combine to deliver the threatened rainstorm. It is three o'clock before the contest resumes, the requirement is 120 at a run a minute, and the first ball back *'rose spitefully, and for minutes everyone wondered.'*

Brian Jackson may not be Les, but he is a fine bowler and next summer Harold Rhodes and he will finish first and second in the national bowling averages, Brian at 12.42 and Harold at an extraordinary 11.04. Only one bowler this century has taken 100 wickets at a lower average: Les. "I got 120 wickets," Brian tells, "and, when I went to the club dinner, the chairman couldn't remember my first name."

Here at Derby the pitch displays no further spite, but the loss of time has *'upset the natural rhythm that Barber and Ibadulla had built up.'* Barber calls a single, Ibadulla refuses it, and Barber is run out for 33. *'Perhaps the over-the-shoulder glance he gave his partner precipitated the sequel.'* The very next ball Ibadulla is lbw, and *'a brand new association had to be built up.'* This time Mike Smith and John Jameson. With his 'GO' and 'NO', his beckoning finger and his halting hand, Mike Smith *'took charge of the running and transformed Jameson's lumberings into almost brief sprints.'* The hundred comes up, and Warwickshire are back on course - or would be if it were not for *'a flash of lightning, followed by a second and a third now nearer and more violet in hue.'*

The English weather. It will return to defeat Mike Smith at the end of the summer. Warwickshire will reach the second Gillette Cup Final, and there will be a heavy mist as their supporters drive down the motorway to Lord's. "Win the toss, win the game weather", Ray Hitchcock calls it, "but we didn't know that in those days." When Mike Smith and Ted Dexter toss up, they both plan to bat first. So it is "win the toss, lose the match" for Mike as Sussex's Ian Thomson takes four for 23 in the damp. "When Tom Cartwright came on in the afternoon, the atmosphere had changed completely."

Here at Derby *'the fourth flash was fainter, the thunder receded and, barring accidents, Warwickshire were home.'* But John Jameson mis-hooks Peter Eyre, it is 122 for four, and Tom joins Mike Smith with 59 needed for victory. *'As Smith drove and cut late and square, Cartwright kept the scoreboard moving with an admirable series of supporting deflections.'*

There are only 25 runs needed in the last half hour, 13 in the last 15 minutes, *'a mere five from the last ten'.* But, as Denys Rowbotham writes, *'perhaps the match would have contradicted its weird character had there not been a last shred of excitement.'* Mike Smith completes his fifty, then falls to a catch at mid-on, and it is left to Ray Hitchcock to score the winning runs against his favourite opposition.

Ray Hitchcock. Fifteen years ago he was working in a sports shop in Christchurch, New Zealand, and he worked his passage here on a Liberty cargo boat, chipping the rust off the decks and the lifeboat. "It took about seven weeks to get here, and I was paid off at East India Docks with about eleven pounds." In his first Club and Ground game he was out for a duck, given lbw by Tiger Smith. His team mate John Campkin did not score, either: "I've come all the way up from London for this nought," he said, and "I had to console him that I'd come 12,000 miles for mine."

Ray Hitchcock. It was not easy for him to understand the nuances of English society. "Freddie Brown was the captain of England, and he was going to report me for calling him by his Christian name." But his fellow countryman Tom Pritchard interceded: "Young Hitchcock's only a raw New Zealander." It was just as difficult when Eric Hollies invited him across for a pub meal near his home. "Eric was very Black Country. 'There's only one good thing that's come out of Yorkshire,' he used to say, 'and that's the road to Old Hill.' Well, it was terrific to be invited, but all I'd got was the clothes I was in. So I went to Thrussels, a man's shop in Birmingham, and I got a bit of credit to hire a suit. I went out to Eric's place, only to realise that faggot and peas didn't warrant a suit. A cloth cap would have been better. I felt more embarrassed than ever, but it was a wonderful evening."

Ray Hitchcock. The penniless, young New Zealander becomes the driving force of the Warwickshire Supporters' Association with its football pool lottery that pays for new seating and the indoor school and helps to bring Test cricket back to Edgbaston. The county won the championship in his first summer in the team, and now here at Derby in 1964 he can score the runs that will take them back into the lead. He races from the judges' box, and Tom, *'an imperturbable part of the proceedings'*, deflects the single that brings the scores level. "Tom was a fair bat," Ray says. "Unfortunately he let it go a bit. He could have been a great all-rounder."

There are four balls left and one run to score, but Ray is not looking for the little dab. He receives *'a long hop'* from Derek Morgan, and he greets it with *'a full-blooded hook'* that sends the ball flying away for a glorious match-winning boundary, or does it? Alas, it is *'brilliantly caught'* by Ian Buxton. It is 180 for six, and another batsman must sprint to the wicket.

Alan Smith. He has played for England as a wicket-keeper. "He was a good all-rounder, a dangerous man in county cricket," Ray reckons, "but I'm not surprised that he only played a few Tests. He was dreadfully untidy. His pads used to flap about, he had an unusual gait and he was knock-kneed, but he could win a game with the bat by slashing a few. And he wasn't the world's worst bowler." As Essex will discover next summer when he takes off his pads to record one of cricket's most improbable hat-tricks. "He was full of confidence." It is a confidence that will see him end up as Chief Executive of the Test and County Cricket Board. But is it a confidence that will put his county back on top of the table tonight? *'With the grandstand clock already on five, A.C. Smith simply edged his first ball to third man, and Warwickshire again were the leaders.'*

Tom Cartwright and Mike Smith will be off to Old Trafford for the fourth Test, and Bob Barber and Tom will be at the Oval for the fifth. In their absence the Derbyshire seamers will be too much for them in the return match, and the following week at Southampton their last championship hopes will *'slip away like a liner up the Solent'*.

But Tom will be in the England party that leaves for South Africa in October, along with the veteran Ian Thomson and a young Mike Brearley. "It was the first time the M.C.C. had flown out for a tour," Tom says, "and everybody was still very conscious of the Munich air crash. So we went out in two separate groups." Tom and Mike Brearley are in the second group, waiting on the pavement opposite Lord's on General Election Day. Quintin Hogg the local MP drives past with his loud-hailer, and just a minute! Those hecklers are wearing England blazers, aren't they? "It was a good time," Tom recalls, "and for me the turn-around in the politics made it even better."

Turn-arounds. The game at Derby has been full of them. A game almost lost at six on Thursday is almost won by seven, and Tom has been in the thick of the collapse. The temperature has soared into the high seventies, and the championship lead has been regained in a last-over dash. Tom's memory is rich with the incidents of his long career. What does he recall of this topsy-turvy match? "I honestly don't recall that game," he says, "and I should because they were the one county I never did anything against. I only remember it being cold there."

Derek Morgan? "Certain things stick in your memory for no particular reason. I remember playing Warwickshire at Derby one year when Alan Ward was bowling. It was the fastest spell of bowling I ever fielded to. Bob Taylor and I were miles back, and Billy Ibadulla nicked one. I caught it at second slip, it went right into my palm, and I closed my hand around it. Next day the back of my hand was black and blue. I shall never forget that." But this match, with his only championship century at Derby? "I'm sorry. I don't think I can be of much help to you at all."

Ray Hitchcock? "Can I have a look at the scorecard?" he asks. "No, this is not a familiar game to me. But I do remember batting with Mike Smith at Burton-on-Trent one year. It was a low-scoring game on a green wicket, a real seamers' paradise, and the last over before lunch Donald Carr the Derby captain decided to bowl an over of chinamen. Mike came down to me, and in all seriousness he said, 'We mustn't waste a delivery. Hit the first one for three, and give me the bowling.' We got seventeen off the over."

Brian Jackson? "I got eight for 18 against Warwickshire one year at Coventry. I should have got nine, but Peter Eyre dropped some bugger at slip. The ball dropped in front of him, the guy was out of his ground, and Peter threw the wicket down." Wisden reveals the detail: '*Coventry 1966, R.V. Webster, run out, 2.*' It is Dr Rudi Webster, en route from Barbados to a medical career in New Zealand. "A bit of a romancer," Tom calls him. "He reckoned he could limbo under two feet till we got down to Southampton for the last game of the season. We were in the Great Western. We had wives and girl friends there, and we tied all our ties together to make the rope, got Rudi to fulfil his boast. But of course he couldn't. He ended up in a heap every time he tried."

And Michael Mence? His career is the shortest, and this is its highest point: his best ever bowling figures, a match-winning performance to put his county back on top of the table. He stands in his pub in the Isle of Wight, and he searches into the corners of his memory. "Oh lord, no, it doesn't ring any bells at all. My only recall of the Racecourse Ground was, as a seventeen-year-old, playing in one of my trial matches there. Peter Eyre was the first chap to bowl me a bouncer. I do remember that. And of course the bitter cold."

It's strange what you forget.

DERBYSHIRE v WARWICKSHIRE

Derby, 15, 16 & 17 July 1964

WARWICKSHIRE WON BY 4 WICKETS

DERBYSHIRE

*C. Lee	c Cartwright b Mence	25	b Mence		3
J.F. Harvey	c A.C. Smith b Mence	3	c Cartwright b Mence		7
I.R. Buxton	lbw b Cartwright	24	c A.C. Smith b Cartwright		19
W.F. Oates	c Ibadulla b Cartwright	0	c Miller b Mence		1
H.L. Johnson	c M.J.K. Smith b Ibadulla	101	c Barber b Cartwright		1
M.H. Page	b Mence	5	c A.C. Smith b Mence		0
D.C. Morgan	not out	103	b Mence		7
E. Smith	lbw b Cartwright	5	lbw b Cartwright		9
T.J.P. Eyre	lbw b Cartwright	0	c M.J.K. Smith b Cartwright		15
+R.W. Taylor	not out	22	b Cartwright		0
A.B. Jackson			not out		6
Extras	*lb 7, nb 1*	8	*lb 1,w 1, nb 1*		3
	(8 wkts, dec)	**296**			**71**

1-7, 2-48, 3-48, 4-64, 5-96, 6-232, 7-253, 8-253
1-3, 2-24, 3-25, 4-26, 5-33, 6-33, 7-33, 8-45, 9-49, 10-71

Mence	26	5	71	3		22	11	26	5
Blenkiron	21	3	42	0		5	0	15	0
Cartwright	34	13	67	4		16.5	9	23	5
Ibadulla	30	7	81	1		1	0	4	0
Barber	5	0	16	0					
Miller	6	2	11	0					

WARWICKSHIRE

N.F. Horner	c Taylor b Jackson	0	c Taylor b Jackson		8
R.W. Barber	b Jackson	9	run out		33
K. Ibadulla	b Smith	36	lbw b Jackson		27
*M.J.K. Smith	c Buxton b Smith	73	c Buxton b Jackson		51
J.A. Jameson	c Taylor b Morgan	15	c Jackson b Eyre		28
T.W. Cartwright	b Smith	2	not out		22
R.E. Hitchcock	c Johnson b Jackson	17	c Buxton b Morgan		0
+A.C .Smith	lbw b Smith	5	not out		2
M.D. Mence	run out	14			
R. Miller	c Morgan b Jackson	12			
W. Blenkiron	not out	1			
Extras	*lb 1,nb 2*	3	*b 2, lb 7, w 2*		11
		187	(6 wkts)		**182**

1-0, 2-11, 3-109, 4-134, 5-138, 6-138, 7-160, 8-162, 9-178, 10-187
1-12, 2-74, 3-74, 4-122, 5-179, 6-180

Jackson	20.3	8	30	4		18	2	51	3
Eyre	13	3	28	0		13	1	41	1
Buxton	14	7	18	0		10	1	20	0
Smith	25	9	52	4		5	3	6	0
Morgan	18	3	56	1		14.4	2	53	1

Umpires: T.W. Spencer and A.E. Fagg

OF SKILL AND LAUGHTER

Essex v Worcestershire

May 1965

chosen by Robin Hobbs

Robin Hobbs was born in Chippenham, Wiltshire, in 1942, his family settling after the war in East London. A leg break bowler, he played for Essex from 1961 to 1975 and in seven Test matches for England. He came out of retirement in 1979 to captain Glamorgan, for whom he played till 1981. He still lives in Essex where he runs the county's under-12 side.

He remembers a fine game of cricket at Brentwood.

"We never won anything at Essex till 1979," Robin reflects. "So nothing was expected of us. After the first month of the season, we'd be fourteenth in the table and, well, we had another three months to drink and to go out with the girls, didn't we?"

Nothing expected of them and not even a county ground to call their own. It is May 1965, a Wednesday morning in Brentwood, and the spectators are settling on the temporary seating around the ground. "The seats were just long planks - held up by bricks, probably." The portable scorebox has been driven in, and the ground staff are putting the numbers in place. Just as Robin did here five years ago when Oxford University stormed to a thrilling victory, with centuries by Burki and Green. "Magnificent batting. I was up and down the scaffolding, moving all the signs."

Essex versus Worcestershire. The first match of this year's Brentwood week. Essex are a struggling side, beset by financial difficulties, and by the end of the season their playing staff will have been reduced to twelve. But Worcestershire are the reigning county champions, and this summer their squad has been strengthened by the qualification of Basil D'Oliveira.

Essex versus Worcestershire. Yesterday the two teams were playing each other at Worcester. Now for the second round of championship fixtures they are playing at Brentwood. Worcestershire have travelled down on their club coach, but the Essex team has made its way back in private cars. "A good four and a half hours," Robin remembers.

It is May 1965. British Rail has published its plan to halve the rail network, the British Medical Association recommends a new offence of drink driving, and Roger Miller tops the record charts with 'King of the Road'.

"Clacton to Swansea was the worst journey," Robin says. "I used to drive the kit van with Paddy Phelan. You knew you wouldn't get there till two in the morning. It was a fact of life. You just accepted it; it didn't really bother you. If you had a late night, you could get away with it. There wasn't so much pressure. Now with all the money and the press, every game is serious."

The late nights are not just caused by the travelling between games, either, as Robin discovered four summers ago, a teenage boy embarking on the adventure of a cricketing life. "Paddy Phelan used to look after me. My first county game away from home was at Stroud, and we stayed at the Station Hotel. What did we do in the evening? Well, Paddy's idea was, you took the Essex van down to the bus station and waited till all the buses had left. Then you knew you had a chance of picking up one of the girls and taking her home. That was his idea of fun. It worked quite well, actually."

Here at Brentwood the sun is shining, the midweek crowd is settling on the planks, and the Essex openers are making *'a bright start'*, 26 runs in the first half hour. There is little in the pitch, it seems, for Len Coldwell and Jack Flavell, Worcestershire's feared new ball attack. "Coldwell bowled inswingers," Robin recalls, "but Jack was ferocious. On uncovered wickets with no helmets on. The Essex tail used to hide in the lavatory."

Coldwell and Flavell. All their lives they will be the best of mates, but Roy Booth has kept wicket to them for several summers and he knows how different they are. "Len was an intelligent bowler, he would talk about his grip, and he kept the ball really well. But Flav just used to stick it in his hand and come up and bowl. He might rub it once on his flannels, but that was all. 'Flav, look after the ball,' Len used to be calling from fine leg. But Jack didn't bother; he had a natural action, and he bowled close to the wicket."

Roy Booth is out of this match, suffering from sciatica, and his deputy John Elliott is playing only his second championship match in seven years. "Flav was the quickest bowler I ever kept to," John says, and he takes a *'fine low catch'* to dismiss Barker. "One-handed. I remember that." The breezy start continues when Bear greets D'Oliveira *'with a straight drive over the sight screen'* but, when he is caught in the leg trap, it is 48 for two and, writes Tony Goodridge in the Daily Telegraph, *'the batsmen became suspicious.'*

Essex are a travelling side with no headquarters, and their batsmen never quite know what to expect from their pitches. Trevor Bailey is captain, and he has a reputation for ordering green tops. Like the one three years ago at Ilford when Jim Laker made his Essex debut. "Go and have a look at the wicket, Jim," Trevor suggested. "See what you think." Robin was not playing, but he knows the story well. "'Where the bloody hell's Jim?' Trevor said after a long wait. Then he found him on the square. 'Well, Jim, what do you think we should do?' And Jim said, 'I don't know, I haven't found the pitch yet.'"

"Ilford was quite pleasant," Robin reflects. "A good quick wicket, though the outfield was terribly bouncy. Fielding at Ilford was quite a challenge, still is." Though a different sort of challenge from Leyton. "I disliked Leyton intensely. The local boys used to throw fireworks into your turn-ups. Fielding at third man or fine leg at Leyton was a nightmare."

Fireworks in your turn-ups? Surely this is not what Robertson Glasgow had in mind when he wrote of Essex cricket, 'Its keynote is its intimacy, its sense of companionship. It is Community Cricket, a share-out of hopes and disappointments, of triumph and reverse. All of which makes for the best kind of entertainment. For entertainment is the healthy child of skill and laughter.'

Community Cricket, and the pitches are prepared by the local groundsmen. "If we went to Brentwood, we didn't know what to expect." Next year Keith Boyce will take thirteen wickets on his county debut, and in four years' time Kent will dismiss Essex for 34 - "it was a horrendous wicket; great chunks were flying out of it." - and that will be the end of Brentwood. Warwickshire Supporters' Club will lend Essex the money to develop a headquarters at Chelmsford, the A12 will be thick with passing traffic, and a new telephone exchange behind the pavilion will spoil its rural charm.

"Brentwood was the old country town. It's not now. It just sprawls." Here in 1965 its cricket ground is surrounded by trees, and on the far side there are splashes of colour from the red hawthorn blossom among the elms and planes. "It was a lovely place to play. It was so peaceful." And the pitch in 1965? "It turned from the start, but it certainly wasn't a nasty wicket." *The pitch took a certain amount of spin, and it may be that Worcestershire's decision to include both Gifford and Slade added to the batsmen's disgust.'* Keith Fletcher is bowled for 12 and, when Barry Knight is run out *'going for an utterly improbable run'*, Essex take lunch at 66 for four. The sun is shining, and county cricket is back in the routine.

It is the twelfth of May, less than a month since Robin arrived back from the M.C.C. tour of South Africa. He has stayed on for six weeks with John Price, "we drove down from Port Elizabeth to Cape Town in this Volkswagen, it was magnificent", and he has brought home the kit on the Edinburgh Castle liner, "the most fabulous fortnight". So he only arrives halfway through Essex's three weeks of pre-season training. "We went to the Old Blues rugby ground at Fairlop. There were a couple of cricket nets there. We never went for runs. We just practised batting and bowling." Chelmsford's Indoor Cricket School is years away in 1965. "Behind the nets there was this chicken run. If people bowled short, you'd get a top edge straight over into the chickens."

Worcestershire are the county champions, but their facilities are little better. Bob Carter is twelfth man today, making way for the extra spinner, and he remembers the régime. "There was no indoor school at Worcester. Come January we used to go up to Edgbaston every Monday night. But there was no penalty if you didn't go. Your contract stated that you would arrive at the ground in April 90% fit." And on that first morning at the ground? "You put your overcoat on, stood outside in the rain, had your photograph taken and went home. But by the early seventies you took your track suit on the first day, and it didn't matter what the weather did, you were tearing about."

Tearing about in April, not on the morning of the game. "You can't do an hour and a half before a match," Bob Carter thinks. "What you're doing is taking a bowler's first spell out of him." And Jack Flavell's first spell can last till lunch. "A lot of the bowlers were fitter in the legs," Roy Booth thinks. "Then there was the footwear. Flav had boots that would have done for mining, big leather boots with thick soles. One boot would easily weigh more than both boots now. It's incredible to think of all the injuries bowlers get these days. Flav and Len used to bowl a thousand overs a year. I put it down to being stronger as young men, not watching television all the time and not getting into cars. Walking to school, playing out at night."

Robin has grown up in Dagenham and been to grammar school in Stepney. "I had an hour by bus and a three-mile walk each way. Every day." And his own son? "His nibs is fetched and carried. It's all expected. You think you're doing the right thing, giving them extra time to do their homework. But you realise you're a fool, because they never do do the homework." And could his son walk home from Brentwood like forty years ago he walked through the streets of Stepney? "You can't walk over the fields. There are so many nasty characters around. You don't want to be around Brentwood on a Saturday night. It's a no-go area."

It is May 1965. The House of Commons is voting for the abolition of hanging, the House of Lords for the legalisation of homosexuality, and a Speakers' Conference is considering lowering the voting age to eighteen. Bob Dylan is touring Britain, his 'Times They Are A'Changin'' in the top ten:

'The present now will later be past,
The order is rapidly fadin'.'

The old order endures here at Brentwood as Trevor Bailey resumes his innings after lunch. His Test career is long over now, but he still enjoys his reputation as Barnacle Bailey. *'For-ever Trevor took half an hour over his first run,'* Pat Marshall writes in the Daily Express, *'two hours to reach double figures and two and a half hours before hitting his first boundary.'* At the other end Geoff Smith *'opened his broad shoulders for 49 enjoyable runs'*, and Brian Taylor, or 'Tonker' as they call him, *'played one or two authoritative shots'* in a quick 24. But Trevor Bailey has come in at 54 for three, and he has 17 to his name when the sixth wicket falls at 154.

The next batsman is John Wilcox, the young schoolmaster. Last summer his headmaster in Bakewell gave him the term off to play for Essex, and his ten matches saw him finish top of the county's batting averages. "I think the headmaster thought there would be some kudos for the school," he remembers. "But when I asked him again the next year, he told me to make up my mind. Did I want to keep the job or to play cricket?" He has decided on the cricket for now, and here at Brentwood he joins Trevor Bailey at the crease. Just as yesterday he joined Tonker Taylor at Worcester. 239 to win there, and he scored a steady 22 not out while Tonker smashed a belligerent century. But they finished 21 runs short with four wickets standing, and Trevor Bailey was not best pleased when he drove the young schoolmaster home. John remembers the conversation. "I think you ought to have put your foot on the pedal a bit. Tried to get your runs quicker." "I thought so, too, but Tonker carefully instructed me that I was to stay in and he would get the runs." "Ah," said Trevor, "Tonker's a good cricketer until he starts to think."

There are so many ways to read a game. In Trevor's mind, John has cost them the victory at Worcester. But Wisden? *'Victory would probably have been theirs had Bailey showed even a modicum of the enterprise of Taylor. Instead, he prodded along to 16 in one hour thirty-five minutes.'* John reads the lines and laughs. "Oh, he had a cheek then, saying anything about me."

"Trevor was a good cricketer," Robin says, "but he did like to be up in the averages. I wouldn't say he was a selfish cricketer, but he didn't like to lose. He'd rather draw a match than try and win it."

Worcester to Brentwood. A four-and-a-half hour journey. "We stopped the coach at a little pub on the way to Broadway," Worcester's John Elliott remembers. "Trevor and I stopped for a meal in a transport caff," John Wilcox recalls, and he is still amazed by the contrast between Trevor the batsman and Trevor the travelling companion. "I've never known anyone who was always in quite such a hurry. I'd had about three mouthfuls, and Trevor was standing up, lighting a cigarette, saying 'Come on, we've got to go.'"

Bailey and Wilcox, here at Brentwood. Wilcox and Bailey at Clacton eighteen years ago. John's father Denys, Essex captain before the war and Trevor's prep school headmaster, guiding his protégé through a century partnership. Now Trevor is the captain, and in the early evening the Brentwood crowd is clapping another century stand. "He'd put on a hundred with both father and son," John reflects. "That was nice." *'Instead of Essex out for under 200, the Bailey-Wilcox (or Svengali-Trilby) combination blossomed into a sparkling 139 seventh wicket stand. Not that Bailey did any of the sparkling. It was young Wilcox, encouraged by his mentor, who supplied the glitter with ten beautifully driven boundaries.'* Svengali and Trilby? Will the old manipulator create genius in John's cover drives to rival Trilby's beautiful voice? John's father died twelve years ago, and this would be a poetic way for Trevor to repay his personal debt. "It would have helped greatly if my father had been alive," John reflects. "I realise it now, I didn't then, but I resented anybody else telling me how to play."

John Wilcox. At the start of the month his wife gave birth to their first son William, and he still treasures the photograph of the three of them beside the Brentwood sight screen as he waits to bat. His father Denys inherited the Alleyn Court headmastership from his grandfather, and in thirty years' time this baby boy will inherit it from him. It is the family vocation, but for now he is enjoying the adventure of county cricket. "I was going to be the headmaster of our prep school," he reflects. "This was just a bit of fun in between."

The pitch is taking slow turn but, by the time Slade bowls Bailey, it is 293 for seven, and Robin Hobbs strides out, eager to maintain the flurry of runs. "I always thought I was a smashing batsman. And I got out to Dougie Slade's arm ball. I was fed up to the back teeth." The first duck of the day, "I got three first-ballers in a week at Westcliff once," he laughs, reciting the names of the non-descript bowlers who did for him, and Edmeades soon follows suit. There is only Paddy Phelan left to help John Wilcox to a maiden century. But alas *'Wilcox drove Slade to long-off and Kenyon took a catch which ended a good innings of 87 runs.'* "I did play well that day," John reflects. "I went home with Tonker. 'We were on song today, John,' he said to me." Essex are 302 all out, and there is time for two overs before the close.

Worcestershire are county champions, and they have the best top six in the country. Kenyon and Horton to open. Headley, Graveney, D'Oliveira and Richardson to follow. "I'll be perfectly honest," Robin admits. "I wasn't looking forward to bowling against this lot."

Don Kenyon is the Worcester captain, and he has led them to their first ever championship. Now he is an England selector, too, though it is a mystery to many how he only ever played eight Tests himself. "He came from the wrong county, didn't he?" suggests his team mate Ron Headley, a Jamaican by birth. "And he wasn't a social animal. He never really talked, he just batted." And his captaincy? "He was the biggest influence on my career. He said, 'Ron, you've got the shots, play them.' I had eighty-odd at close of play one day, and I played back this half-volley last ball. 'Come Monday morning,' he said, 'the first delivery could pitch leg and knock out your off stump. You've just thrown away four runs.' That was his positive attitude. He didn't think like an Englishman, 'I mustn't get out.' He had the mentality of a West Indian; he liked to attack." Here at Brentwood Don Kenyon has one over of Barry Knight to face, and he clips a two before falling lbw.

"Then Trevor Bailey came up with this masterstroke of captaincy," Robin tells. Robin is a leg-spinner, almost the last of a dying breed, and Trevor has stood by him, nurtured him to the verge of an England place. "He threw me this shiny red ball, and I opened the bowling." To Martin Horton, who has scored a double century against Essex in his time. "Trevor liked to do the unexpected sometimes," John Wilcox remembers. "Often opening batsmen are very poor players of wrist spin." So what delivery does Robin select from his repertoire? "I can see it now," he says. "It was halfway down the wicket, and he went to pull it. It came down for a second bounce and bowled him." It is two for two, and with two night-watchmen at the wicket, *'eight close fielders were clustered round like vultures waiting to pounce on the corpse.'* There is no more drama, but Robin has got his duck out of his system. "It obviously brightened my evening up, getting Horton out."

It is a Wednesday evening in May 1965. At eight o'clock television viewers can choose between 'Z Cars' on BBC and 'The Fugitive' on ITV.

'The trend towards series and serials is growing at an alarming pace,' Milton Shulman laments in the Evening Standard. *'Even the most thick-headed executive must realise that all human activity cannot be portrayed as a dripping tap going on relentlessly and fruitlessly from week to week.'*

Next morning Don Kenyon trains his cine-camera on the portable scorebox. His movie of the season will show their three for two in reply to Essex's 302. *'Is it Don's intention to run the film through to his players,'* the Worcester Evening News wonders, *'to prevent swollen-headedness?'* If he had waited till five minutes after the start, he could have filmed it at five for three as Slade *'skied an intended drive'* in Robin's next over.

Thursday morning, the temperature rising into the seventies. There may be more traffic on the passing A12 than when John's father played here but, John says, "when you've got a reasonable-sized crowd, there's always that hum of activity on the ground, and that would have masked the traffic. And there were quite a lot of people watching, certainly by today's standards."

It is May 1965. Essex's County Development Plan proposes 3250 new homes, eight new schools and a range of shops and offices. "Without some remnants of the countryside which has inspired and warmed the hearts of generations of British people," the Duke of Edinburgh warns, "life in these islands is going to be reduced to the level of animals on a factory farm."

The pitch is taking turn, and Essex have Robin's leg-breaks and Paddy Phelan's off-spin. So there is plenty of bowling for the two of them. "You knew before the season started," Robin explains, "that you were going to bowl seven hundred overs. And if you were out of form, you bowled yourself into form. You didn't get left out. It wasn't like now when they're only playing one game a week." By next summer the playing staff here at Essex will be down to twelve, and there will be even less pressure on their places. "We played at Portsmouth, and David Turner hit this bloody thing back at me. He was only a little guy, and I never got the right length to him. And it smashed my finger. But I still went up to Worcester for the next game." Worcestershire 405 for six, Graveney 166, D'Oliveira 126. "I fielded third man both ends, with my finger strapped up, and I never bowled a ball. We had nobody else."

Centuries for Graveney and D'Oliveira at Worcester in August 1966. There were centuries for them last Saturday at Worcester, too. Tom Graveney, the elegant timer of the ball, and Basil D'Oliveira, with the short back-lift and the strong forearms. "Graveney was very gifted, a touch player," Robin reflects, "but Basil hit it like a tracer bullet. Nowadays they have heavier bats, and they all smash the ball. I used to field cover, and there weren't many where I thought, 'Oh I don't fancy it if this bloke hits it.' But Basil was one."

This morning it is Ron Headley's turn to demonstrate the all-round strength of this Worcester batting side. *'Worcestershire were struggling from the beginning,'* Tony Goodridge writes, *'and only a splendidly aggressive innings by Headley made batting look comparatively simple.'* Is he a touch player with a light bat or a big smiter with a heavy one? Worcestershire's twelfth man Bob Carter tells the story. "He wasn't a powerful man, he was very willowy. But Ron was full of theory. He had six bats. I changed next to the bloke for twelve years, and he used to line these bats up and take them out according to the situation. 'Big Bertha tomorrow, we want some big hitting.' 'I'll be dabbing ones today, I'll take the Little Wand.' How the hell you can work with different weights unless they're balanced identically, I don't know." *Headley was in dominating mood. While his colleagues struggled for occasional singles, he proceeded majestically by fours.*

"Ron was a beautiful timer of the ball," Roy Booth says. "But he was a bit too complicated, was Ron. He had one awful patch, a string of ducks, one year. He used to come back into the dressing room. His bat was hung loose. He'd sit in the corner. He'd look as if he was going to burst into tears. Then somebody would say, 'It'll come right, don't worry about it.' He wasn't dropped. I think, if he'd have got dropped, it could have ruined his career."

Ron Headley will play 30 three-day matches this summer, Robin 33. Plenty of opportunity to find form. And both of them enjoy captains who believe in them. "Trevor was very good to me," Robin says. "He backed me to the hilt." The county game of the sixties is not always easy for the leg-spinner. "With somebody else handling me, I might have dropped out of the game after two or three years." Just as Paddy Phelan, bowling his off-breaks at the other end today, will go in the end-of-season cost-cutting. "Trevor was such a good cricketer himself. When Paddy came into the side, he just couldn't accept that he couldn't put six balls an over on the spot." It is 61 for four when Fletcher, *'with sweet-flowing pick up and throw'*, runs out Gifford. Then, *'as if a cloud had spread over the cloudless sky, Graveney mis-swept at Phelan, and the wicket-keeper took a good leg-side catch.'*

Tom Graveney. Last summer he was the leading run-scorer in the country, and he scored a fine century at Worcester last Saturday. *'The disappointment of many at Graveney's early departure was probably more than compensated by the value of the dismissal,'* Tony Goodridge writes. *'Nevertheless an innings by Graveney on a beautiful day such as this might well have matched the beauty of its setting on this extremely pretty ground.'*

"They were good cricket writers in those days," Robin thinks. "Now everybody's got an old player. These guys wrote better. When you read it, you thought you'd been there. I don't think you do now."

Graveney is gone to *'a good leg-side catch'* by Tonker Taylor, and lunch is taken at 71 for five. Trevor Bailey may be Essex's Svengali, captain and secretary, but Tonker is the no-nonsense sergeant-major, always well turned out, his Cockney voice barking away. In two years' time he will be the unlikely inheritor of the captaincy, forever wrestling with the antics not just of Robin but of a whole new generation of pranksters like Ray East and J.K. Lever. *'Entertainment is the healthy child of skill and laughter,'* Robertson

Glasgow wrote of Essex cricket, and Robin is still happy to entertain the world with his fund of Tonker Taylor stories. And none of them, it seems, involve good leg-side catches.

"We were playing at Northampton. And Ray East, who wasn't one of his favourites, had had a night out. Tonk made him bowl on a very hot day for three hours on the trot, and he hadn't turned a ball. He ran up and bowled this thing. It pitched leg stump, turned and went for four byes. Raymond stood in the middle of the wicket with his arms raised. 'I've turned one at last,' he shouted out. At the end of the over Tonk got him by the neck. 'You did that on purpose to make me look a fool.'"

Tonker is one who likes his wicket-keeping simple. Like the time at the Scarborough Festival when he first has to keep to Derek Underwood. "He said to me, 'Bring your mate over here.' Dear old Derek, his wicket-keeper was Alan Knott, and he'd never come across anybody like Brian. 'Right, Derek,' he said. 'See these gloves.' Derek said 'Yes', as Derek would, 'Yes, Brian'. 'Well, they ain't followin' the ball. You've got to find 'em. They're stayin' exactly where they are.'"

"I can remember Tonker stumping Asif Iqbal at Leyton in a Gillette match. Easty bowled this ball, and it bounced and lodged under his armpit. And he fell full length on the stumps. And it was given out. 'I pay for all the equipment, Robin, I may as well use it.' Cor dear, oh lord." Laugh if you will, but only five keepers in the history of the game have more dismissals to their name than Tonker.

"Tonk was a brilliant guy," Robin says. "He had a heart of gold."

71 for five at lunch, it is soon 135 all out. Ron Headley has scored over half the runs, *'his footwork and alertness were in sharp contrast to the more sluggish movements of his colleagues'*, and Robin has taken five for 46. Essex lead by 167, but *'the shrewd Bailey did not enforce the follow on.'* "This pitch will get worse the longer the game goes on," he tells Pat Marshall. "I'd rather Worcester be chasing runs on the last day than us." Soon his openers are giving the Worcester bowling *'a considerable hammering'*, then the young Keith Fletcher straight drives and pulls D'Oliveira for four sixes, three in one over. Keith is only twenty years old, and Trevor Bailey already knows that he has a future England player on his hands. "He was only a small guy," Robin says, "but he hit the ball a long way. Trevor took him under his wing and said to him, 'If you're going to play Test cricket, you've got to keep the ball on the ground more.'" But maybe in May 1965 this is a conversation yet to be had. Or maybe the Brentwood ground brings out his attacking flair. "You had trees at the back, you see. Batsmen like to see the ball hit into trees, don't they?"

It is 149 for two, a lead of 316, when Len Coldwell returns to bowl Fletcher for 40. Then next ball Tonker swings and is caught at mid-off, "What am I, Robin? ... I know, I know", and suddenly the wicketless Coldwell is on a hat-trick.

Freddie Jakeman and Buddy Oldfield are the umpires today. They are old Northants players, earning this meagre living. "There weren't so many people waiting to come on the list. There wasn't the money in it," Robin says. "If Freddie Jakeman got a bad report, it didn't matter. There wasn't anybody to take his place. It was more of a family. You talked to them in the bar. These days everything's gone through with a fine toothcomb."

Robin knows that in this family there are bowlers' umpires. Slow bowlers' umpires, especially. "People like Sam Cook, Lawrie Gray. Sam was great, he always used to help me. In my last season I got Gordon Greenidge out stumped. He'd got a hundred, and he came down the wicket to this slow leg break. I lobbed it up so much, he got back before the ball arrived. 'That's out,' Sam said. And we all went off for tea. 'Here, Sam,' Greenidge said, 'you must need your eyes testing.' 'That was out,' Sam said. 'He needs a bit of help.' 'All right, if you say that,' Greenidge said. And he accepted it. They did in those days."

Coldwell bowls to Geoff Smith, and he hits him on the pad. Is it Buddy Oldfield, "he used to blink a lot", or is it Freddie Jakeman, 'he should have had a longer playing career,' his Wisden obituary records, 'but he lacked concentration'? Whichever it is, the finger goes up and Len has grabbed the headlines with the first hat-trick of the season. John Wilcox is bowled by Jack Flavell for seven, and Essex declare, setting Worcester 338 to win and leaving their openers another tricky few minutes to negotiate before the close. This time there are no mishaps, and at the end of the day it is 13 for no wicket.

"You'd stay at the ground," Robin recalls, "and talk cricket with the opposition. Nowadays they don't. The minute the game finishes, they're off in their sponsored cars. They don't want to talk cricket. I don't blame them, but I think they miss something. Every county had somebody who was interesting to talk to, and you could learn so much. I think nowadays they'd rather have the money."

The only money Robin earns when he is not playing cricket is selling pink paraffin in the winter, round the streets of Walthamstow. "It was always a race with the Esso Blue man. Paraffin was ten bob for five gallons. The people in those days were so trusting. They'd leave a ten shilling note by their cans. But if you didn't get there by a certain time, he'd beaten you there, taken the ten bob and given them Esso Blue. Nowadays you wouldn't leave anything out, would you?"

Skill and laughter. The players drink and talk. They might be comparing bowling grips or discussing fellow cricketers on the circuit. "We played for Derek Robins at Eastbourne one year, and we were playing Yorkshire the next match. So we told all these county players how we were going to get Boycott out. He was going to be bounced out off the third ball of the first over. And what happened? We get down to Chelmsford, he's bounced out, he's got this great nick, straight through to Tonk, and he's dropped it. It's rolled to

Fletcher at first slip. 'Did he hit it?' Tonk said. Did he hit it! He went on and got a hundred." *'The perpetual run machine ticked inexorably on to 121,'* the Sunday Telegraph records. "You can imagine all these county players picking up the paper in the morning."

In his previous two visits to Essex Boycott netted 260 not out and 233. "Both at the Garrison Ground, Colchester," Robin says, and he recalls Boycott's dismissal in the second of these games. "It was Sam Cook umpiring. I liked to bowl at his end, and I had him lbw. It was no way out. 'That's out,' Sam said, and Boycott was running this leg bye. 'No, no, no, Sam,' he said. 'That can't be lbw.' 'That's out,.' Sam said, and he turned to me. 'I think we've seen enough of *him*.'"

It is the summer of 1965. The first mini-skirts appear in Mary Quant's boutique, the Beatles are awarded the M.B.E., and Cosmopolitan magazine is relaunched with the slogan, 'Have fun, be single and have sex.'

Friday morning arrives, and the sun shines once more, the temperature reaching 81 degrees by early afternoon. Worcestershire's championship pennant is flown for the first time from the Brentwood pavilion, and Essex can become the first team to beat them since last July. Trevor Bailey leads out his men. He is forty-one now, and later in the summer the committee will ask him to become full-time secretary. But he will decline, still convinced he has more to offer the club as a player. By the end of Brentwood week he will have 21 wickets at an average of 9.57, even if this does include the match against Cambridge University. "There he was, captain, five for three against his old university," Robin remembers, "and he took them all out for a meal at the Hawks Club. Dined and wined them. And why not?" Here at Brentwood Robin has taken five for 46, including Horton, Headley and D'Oliveira, but Trevor's five for three will place him higher in the national averages.

"To see Trevor get ready to go out to play in those days," John Wilcox recalls, "was really very amusing. He was strapped together all over." Only one run has been added to the overnight 13 when *'Bailey, with dive and victory roll, held on to a fine slip catch as Kenyon snicked at Knight.'* Then Martin Horton and Ron Headley complete the first 50 of the 338 they are chasing. "By the third day," Robin recalls, "the ball was turning prodigiously", and he is soon in tandem with Paddy Phelan again. Only this time it is Paddy who makes the breakthrough. *'He had Headley lbw in his first over and immediately had Graveney caught at short leg.'* "We were worried about Graveney. He was one of the great players of off-spin, and he got a hundred up at Worcester. But look what he scored. Caught Taylor bowled Phelan, one. Caught Smith bowled Phelan, nought. It's a funny old game." By lunch Paddy Phelan has added the scalps of Horton and Richardson, and the score is just 123 for five, only Basil D'Oliveira left of the recognised batsmen.

Basil D'Oliveira. Five years ago he languished in the ramshackle conditions of the cricket for Cape Town coloureds. Last summer he was qualifying in the Worcestershire second eleven, and his eight first-class innings outside the championship saw him to second place in the national averages. Now he has played his first championship match at Worcester, with scores of 106 and 47, and the bookmakers have cut the odds on him being first to a thousand runs from 75 to 20-1. He only made 19 here in the first innings, but he lunches now with 40 to his name. In time the whole circuit will know how he likes to play carefully for an hour, to get the measure of the pitch and the bowling, but here at Brentwood they are still finding out. "It was an advantage to be an unknown quantity," John Wilcox reckons. "Because county cricketers are so good at finding out people's strengths and weaknesses. Especially Trevor."

Trevor Bailey, the typically English captain. "He was a very intelligent cricketer," John says. "The drawback was that he'd got everything worked out before it happened. And if you know what's going to happen before it happens, then it's difficult to inspire the people you're leading to anything more spectacular." Don Kenyon has a different style of captaincy, but even he cannot expect to inspire his remaining batsmen to victory.

It is May 1965. At Runnymede Jacqueline Kennedy and her children are guests of honour as the memorial to her husband is unveiled.

Basil D'Oliveira. "He hit the ball hard with a very short backlift," John Wilcox remembers. "The advantage of that is that on a slow wicket you can wait and see the ball turn, very late. If you've got very strong forearms, you can hit the ball where you want. He could commit himself to the shot very late." He reaches his fifty, and there are 200 runs wanted in three hours. "He played me very easily," Robin recalls. "Brentwood's on a slope, and there's an old people's home on the far side of the ground, called Merrymeads. I remember he square cut me into Merrymeads." He adds 28 with Slade, who scores six, and 80 with Gifford, who scores 14, but they too fall to Paddy Phelan. *'During the early afternoon,'* Tony Goodridge records, *'he had a succession of what might politely be called sleeping partners.'* *'A millionaire among paupers,'* John Clarke calls him in the Evening Standard. By the time John Elliott joins him, it is 226 for seven, 112 to win, and D'Oliveira has completed his second century this week against Essex.

Two centuries in a week for D'Oliveira, two double centuries for Boycott at Colchester. These innings stay in Robin's memory. "Boycott would play you, he'd do nothing out of the ordinary. You'd probably get a couple of maidens. D'Oliveira was a different ball game. If you bowled a good length ball, quite likely it would end up out of the ground. A lot of players in this era played the ball on its merit. If it was off the wicket, Kenyon would cut it. If it was well up, Graveney would drive it. But if it was a good length ball, most of them would play it back to you. But not D'Oliveira."

Robin is a fine leg-break bowler, and he will play seven Tests for England. In twenty years' time people will look back to him as the last of an extinct breed - "I didn't think they'd come back" - but perhaps in another age he would not win such high honours. "I was an average leg-spinner, but I was always a good social man so they tended to pick me for tours." In 1965 he has no googly, and he does not enjoy bowling to Basil D'Oliveira.

Thirty years on it will be much the same when he turns out for the Old England eleven. "If you can get away with the first over against a reasonable club player, it's okay. But if the first two balls are short and get clattered for four and you're only playing once a month, desperation sets in. You get the shakes, you know. It was the same in county cricket - only you played so much, you could bowl yourself back into form."

Basil D'Oliveira is in his thirties before he starts his county career. Is it possible in the modern game that he could make such a late entrance? "Today," John Elliott says, "he'd be playing for South Africa." But if he were in England, playing in the Lancashire League, is it possible he would take so long to be spotted? "In today's cricket he'd have been scoured out earlier. There was a lot more talent around in those days." Thirty years on John is chairman at Worcestershire, always on the look-out for new talent. Where does he think it has gone? "There's too much money in other sports for the multi-talented sportsman to take up cricket. In today's world Ian Botham would have played football."

Here at Essex so many of their cricketers play football as well. Tonker Taylor for Brentford, Gordon Barker for Southend. Even Trevor Bailey has an Amateur Cup winners' medal for Walthamstow. Then there are the West Ham lads: Eddie Presland, Geoff Hurst - which Essex bowler got a hat-trick for England and never took a wicket for his county? - and Worcestershire's Jim Standen. Next Wednesday Standen will keep goal in the European Cup-Winners' Cup Final at Wembley, and by Saturday he will be at Worcester, twelfth man for their Gillette Cup match.

"Cricket was the 'in' game," John Elliott says. "You got six months of comradeship. And there was no big money anywhere else in the world." Here at Brentwood he is given out caught in the leg trap, and D'Oliveira has just Coldwell and Flavell left to prop up an end for him. Their absent team-mate Roy Booth knows how little prospect of support they offer. "Tail-enders are very useful if they can get a few," he says. "But neither Len nor Jack were batters that you could even think, 'He might stop in for half an hour.' Jack hit a fifty at Dudley once, but it was just a case of whack, whack, whack, and the ball went all over. Maybe Len was a little better." The Playfair Cricket Annual 1965 sells for two shillings and sixpence, and any spectator who pulls it from his pocket here at Brentwood will find in the career batting averages, Coldwell 6.34, Flavell 6.59. And there are 90 runs still to score.

The pitch is taking turn, and Paddy Phelan has taken seven of the eight wickets to fall. There is no break for tea, and the finish is set for 5 or 5.30, leaving time for the Worcestershire coach to get on the road to Headingley.

With his short backlift and his powerful forearms, D'Oliveira plays '*a succession of flowing off-drives*', and the ground staff on the scaffolding add another 37 to the total by the time the umpires signal the extra half hour. D'Oliveira 163, Coldwell 4. Since lunch the total has risen by 162 runs, and D'Oliveira's partners have contributed just 26 of them. "There wasn't very much effort to keep him away from the strike for most of the time," John Wilcox recalls. "I don't think anybody thought they were going to get the runs. I don't really remember feeling anxious. In retrospect I think I should have done." 53 to win now, and 30 minutes left to play.

"The thing about Basil," his team mate Bob Carter says, "is that the tougher the game got, the better he performed." And later in his career Robin will play with another with the same fight in him. "If I had to put my last hundred pounds or a noose on my neck for somebody to get me a hundred, it would be Javed Miandad. He was magnificent. The last game I ever played, when I was with Glamorgan, we were playing at Colchester, and we wanted 350 to win - on a road. He got 200 not out. We put on 43 together, and I never got a run." Javed has grown up in the back streets of Karachi, "they're playing at fifteen, sixteen there, they've got nothing; we're too cosseted here," and D'Oliveira has come to England from the Coloured quarter of Cape Town, where the police carted boys off to jail for playing cricket in the road.

Robin's 37 overs have left him wicketless, and Trevor Bailey takes the new ball and switches to his seamers. '*With the first ball in the extra half hour, D'Oliveira made his one big mistake - playing back to Barry Knight and missing. The shriek of an appeal for leg before must have rolled down Brentwood's crowded High Street.*' "When D'Oliveira got out," Robin tells, "Don Kenyon marched onto the field and awarded him his county cap." Next summer Don Kenyon the selector will be calling him into the Test team. The crowd here at Brentwood have seen the birth of a new star, and in the next over they see their old star Trevor Bailey, '*who manipulated this match like a marionette master*', bowl Coldwell to give their near-bankrupt team victory over the champions. '*A match to remember,*' Pat Marshall declares. The sun beats down as the spectators make their way out of the ground.

"As a game of cricket, it had the lot," Robin says. "Dare I say it, it had reasonable leg-break bowling, fine swing bowling by Coldwell, a magnificent innings by D'Oliveira. The sun shone; everything was right about the game. A very good county cricket match. It's always stood in my memory."

'*I'm not sold on this one-day cricket,*' the former England captain Norman Yardley writes in the Worcester Evening News. '*What's really needed to relieve cricket of its worries is not drastic change of structure but a spot of good warm weather and a decision from captains and players to put their third-day skills and excitements into their first-day's play.*'

John Wilcox has hit an exciting 87 on the first day, and he retains the press cuttings in the scrapbook his mother kept of his playing days. A smaller book than perhaps he dreams of here at Brentwood. Failure in the next game here, then failure at Taunton, and he will find himself in the second eleven. There he will stay all summer until he calls it a day and returns to teaching. Never again to be Trilby to Trevor's Svengali.

The last twist of John's cricketing career will occur in two years' time, in the first summer of Tonker Taylor's captaincy. Trevor Bailey will still be strapping himself together to play but, when he finally limps away in mid-August, it will be to John that they turn to replace him. "They were nearly broke. That's probably why I played. I'd spent the whole term teaching, and I had to go up to Scarborough to open the batting against Freddie Trueman. It was damp, and there was this fret off the sea. He bowled this ball. It started on the line of leg stick and just removed the off bail. We were nought for two. Then Trueman got food poisoning, and he couldn't bowl in the second innings." John will make 27 out of an opening stand of 87, the match's highest partnership, and his runs will help Essex to a thrilling nine-run victory over the county champions. Just as his 87 here at Brentwood have played their part in victory over another champion county. But it won't lead to invitations to play in future years. "It didn't really work. It was the sort of thing that was done before the war." By 1965 county cricket is a game for professionals. Even if Essex can't afford them.

By 1970 there will be no Brentwood week; it will be gone, just like Peterborough and Stroud and Pontypridd. "We looked forward to playing at those grounds," Robin remembers. "Rather than at Old Trafford and the Oval. But the modern player would hate it. It's all got to be dead right."

Phelan, seven for 80. Hobbs, nought for 95. "I was standing in the showers afterwards with Paddy," Robin recalls, "and I remember saying what an unfair game it all was. I mean, how can you get nought for 95 after getting five for 46? It seems crazy, but that's cricket, isn't it?"

"You look back," John Wilcox says, "and you understand the things you didn't understand at the time. It's like an impressionist painting. If you stand right up close to it, it makes no sense at all."

Robin inspects the black-and-white pictures of his bowling at Brentwood that Friday afternoon. The photographic fix is failing, and brown marks are spreading across his whites. Twenty years a first-class cricketer, these are the only action pictures in his possession. The spectators on the long plank seats, the trees behind them, and Basil D'Oliveira waiting with his short back-lift.

'The present now will later be past.'

"If I played in county cricket now, I'm sure I'd get wickets. I'd get hit harder so I'd push it through a bit more. But I wouldn't particularly want to play now. I don't think they have the fun we had. It was a great way of earning a living."

111

ESSEX v WORCESTERSHIRE

Brentwood. 12, 13 & 14 May 1965

ESSEX WON BY 48 RUNS

ESSEX

G.E. Barker	c Elliott b Flavell	15	b Gifford		28
M.J. Bear	c Headley b D'Oliveira	22	c Slade b Gifford		36
K.W.R. Fletcher	b Gifford	12	b Coldwell		40
B.R. Knight	run out	15	not out		53
*T.E. Bailey	b Slade	74			
G.J. Smith	c D'Oliveira b Slade	49	lbw b Coldwell		0
+B. Taylor	b Horton	24	c Graveney b Coldwell		0
J. Wilcox	c Kenyon b Slade	87	b Flavell		7
R.N.S. Hobbs	b Slade	0			
B. Edmeades	lbw b Slade	0			
P.J. Phelan	not out	2			
Extras	b 2	2	b 1, lb 5		6
		302	(6 wkts, dec)		**170**

1-26, 2-48, 3-54, 4-65, 5-118, 6-154, 7-293, 8-295, 9-295, 10-302
1-66, 2-74, 3-149, 4-149, 5-149, 6-170

Flavell	14	2	45	1	8.1	1	28	1
Coldwell	15	3	27	0	12	3	34	3
D'Oliveira	24	7	52	1	13	3	51	0
Gifford	29	15	71	1	10	5	23	2
Slade	31.2	10	68	5	5	2	20	0
Horton	11	3	37	1	6	3	8	0

WORCESTERSHIRE

*D. Kenyon	lbw b Knight	2	c Bailey b Knight		9
M.J. Horton	b Hobbs	0	c Fletcher b Phelan		47
D.N.F. Slade	c Knight b Hobbs	3	c Edmeades b Phelan		6
N. Gifford	run out	11	c Taylor b Phelan		14
R.G.A. Headley	c Fletcher b Hobbs	74	lbw b Phelan		14
T.W. Graveney	c Taylor b Phelan	1	c Smith b Phelan		0
B.L. D'Oliveira	c Wilcox b Hobbs	19	lbw b Knight		163
D.W. Richardson	c Fletcher b Phelan	1	c & b Phelan		5
+J.W. Elliott	lbw b Phelan	4	c Fletcher b Phelan		4
L.J. Coldwell	not out	11	b Bailey		4
J.A. Flavell	b Hobbs	3	not out		4
Extras	b 5, nb 1	6	b 13, lb 5, nb 1		19
		135			**289**

1-2, 2-2, 3-5, 4-61, 5-66, 6-102, 7-108, 8-114, 9-122, 10-135
1-14, 2-51, 3-51, 4-88, 5-118, 6-146, 7-226, 8-248, 9-285, 10-289

Knight	7	3	5	1	10	2	20	2
Hobbs	25	11	46	5	37	14	95	0
Edmeades	6	2	15	0	8	1	27	0
Bailey	5	2	12	0	9.2	3	23	1
Phelan	24	8	51	3	35	11	80	7
Smith					8	1	25	0

Umpires: N. Oldfield and F. Jakeman

Robin Hobbs

We played at Portsmouth, and David Turner hit the bloody thing back at me. It smashed my finger. But I still went up to Worcester for the next game. I fielded third man both ends, with my finger strapped up, and I never bowled a ball. We had nobody else.

Colin Milburn

I said to him one day, 'Why don't you drink halves instead of pints?' He got 150 that day, and it was only about three o'clock in the afternoon. 'What are you having to drink then, Colin?' I asked. He said, 'Two halves, please, guv.'

Fred Rumsey

Big Fred had probably had a few pints of cider the night before, and he used to sweat profusely. 'Look at the big tart,' Bill would say in the gully. 'He's knackered already. He's only been going three overs.' And Fred would start, 'Is he talking about me? What's he saying?'

Jack Flavell

When I look back, all I seem to remember is that we've declared, and Flavell and Coldwell are bowling that last half hour. It was a key period of the game. We must have batted at that time, but I can only remember Flavell and Coldwell bowling. And the crowd roaring them on.

AN ENGINEER AT THE HELM

Glamorgan v Northamptonshire

August 1965

chosen by Keith Andrew

Keith Andrew was born in Oldham, Lancashire, in 1929. He kept wicket for Northamptonshire from 1953 to 1966 and played two Test matches for England. A Mechanical Engineering graduate from the Manchester College of Technology, he returned to the game in 1975 as Director of Coaching, then Chief Executive, of the National Cricket Association.

He remembers a vital match at Cardiff between the two teams at the head of the county championship table.

"Heads," Keith calls, and the coin spins upwards from the fingers of Glamorgan's Ossie Wheatley. It is a sunny morning here in Cardiff, pleasant weather for batting, but the pitch is not an easy one to fathom. "When we got to the ground," Keith recalls, "one end of the wicket looked very brown, the other end very green. It looked to be a wicket that wasn't going to produce a lot of runs."

Glamorgan versus Northamptonshire. August 1965. Who at the start of May would have imagined that, with just four weeks of county matches left to play, this would be such a crucial contest in the summer's fixture list? Top of the table versus second. "We all thought that, if we won this match," Keith remembers, "we'd win the championship." And that is something Northants have never done. Bottom ten times, next to bottom another nine. But never county champions. Never top of the table in August.

The town of Northampton, famous for its shoe manufacturing. A fast-growing town with new industries, enjoying the prosperity of Britain in the sixties. "The town had a lot going for it," Keith tells. "It still has." And in 1965 nothing symbolises its success more than its sporting teams. A football club that has risen in four seasons from fourth division to first, a rugby side with the best playing record in the country, and now a cricket team at the head of the county championship. Who would have predicted such glory back in August 1961? The football club embarking on another season in the bottom division, the cricket team twenty points adrift at the foot of the table with just two matches to play.

August 1961. Glamorgan versus Northamptonshire. Four long years ago. "Heads," Keith called that day, too.

August 1961. Cricketers were still classed as amateurs or professionals. "I could never come to terms with that," Keith says. "I was friends with many of the amateurs, and most of them were paid indirectly. Through expenses or as pseudo assistant cricket secretaries. It was divisive to treat them differently, because of the school or university they'd attended. It really was ridiculous."

In thirty summers from 1947 Glamorgan have four captains - five, if you include the Eton schoolmaster so bizarrely recruited in 1958 - and all five are Cambridge graduates. There was also a Cambridge man in charge at Northants in 1961, Raman Subba Row, but he retired in mid-August, with the county firmly at the foot of the table. Keith Andrew took over for the last four matches, and everybody expected the 1962 captain to be Roger Prideaux, another Light Blue, joining the county as Assistant Secretary so that he could retain his amateur status. "They said, 'Roger Prideaux's coming down.' I said, 'Where from? Heaven?'"

August 1961. Four games for Keith to make his mark as captain. Two draws in Northampton. Then the trip to Wales, to the St Helen's ground in Swansea. His chances were running out, and he was desperate to win the toss and bat. High in the pavilion he grabbed his team mate Peter Watts. "Come on down to the wicket, Peter, you can pretend to be Ossie Wheatley. Go on, turn up your collar, and toss the coin until you get four consecutive tails. Then when it comes to the real thing, I'll call heads." "I suppose it helped to relieve the tension in the team." Peter threw his four consecutive tails, and Keith called a confident 'Heads' as Ossie flipped the coin. And down it came, another tail. Keith smiles at the memory. "But Ossie put us in. And we won the match. And we won the next match at Dover, too." It gave them just enough points to leap-frog over Nottinghamshire into sixteenth place. "I'll never forget the feeling. It was something like I imagined winning the championship would be. Little did I know what lay ahead. If we hadn't won those two matches, I doubt if I'd have kept the captaincy. And I'd never be sitting here, telling this story."

August 1965 now. "Heads," he calls, and this time the Queen's head shines upwards in the sunlight. In this championship run-in he will win 12 out of the last 13 tosses. *'When Keith Andrew won the toss on a wicket that was dry at one end and wet at the other,'* the Northampton Chronicle reports, *'he had a difficult decision to make.'* As in 1961 he wants to bat, but at 16 for two he begins to wonder about his decision.

It is August 1965. George Brown is Labour's Secretary of State for Economic Affairs, Frank Cousins Minister of Technology. Old Etonian Alec Douglas-Home stands down as Conservative leader, and in the party's first ballot of MPs he is replaced by grammar school boy Edward Heath.

Colin Milburn and Roger Prideaux are the next batsmen, but their partnership is soon brought to an unlikely halt. It is the Queen Mother's birthday, her 65th, and from the grounds of the nearby Cardiff Castle a 21-gun royal salute begins. *'As the echo of the birthday salvo resounded across the Arms Park,'* the Western Mail reports, *'batsman Roger Prideaux said the noise impaired his concentration. So, while Glamorgan players Shepherd and Hedges waved white handkerchiefs in mock surrender, the umpires agreed to "guns stopped play".'* The Times correspondent elaborates the story: *'Elderly spectators grumbled about modern youth's lack of spirit under gunfire.'*

There is no lack of spirit about Colin Milburn, and he is soon adding his own gunfire. *'Milburn, from the start, seemed determined to hit his side out of trouble and he quickly collected a huge six and two fours off Miller.'* Is this one of those days that Keith has bet him that he can't play out a maiden over? "I used to win every time. I'd be watching in the dressing room, and he'd look back up with a grin as the ball sailed over the boundary." In 1965 Colin is yet to play Test cricket, but in Northampton they know what a fine player he is. It is three years since his maiden championship hundred at Buxton "on a pig of a wicket". Going out to bat at 23 for four in the second innings, a deficit of 124 and Les Jackson near unplayable. A hefty 20-year-old with big brown eyes and an ever-cheerful smile. "Look out there," Keith said to his team mates in the gathering gloom. "You're seeing one of the greatest players you'll ever see." He hit eighteen fours in a magnificent century that day at Buxton, when the whole side only managed 182. "The lad didn't play Test cricket for another four years. It's still hard to believe."

Keith looks back. "I never, ever gave Colin any real advice. I knew I had a special player on my hands, and I knew I wasn't going to tell him how to quell that great spirit. It would have been a sin." But he does know what will get Colin into the England team. "I told him to lose weight and to start getting more hundreds." And did he take the advice? "Getting hundreds wasn't a problem." But the weight? "I said to him one day, 'Why don't you drink halves instead of pints?' He got 150 that day, and it was only about three o'clock in the afternoon. 'What are you having to drink then, Colin?' I asked. He said, 'Two halves, please, guv.'"

Thirty years have passed, but the thrill of playing with Colin Milburn in his prime still glows in Keith's memory. No innings more than his double century at Clacton in 1966. He will play the first four Tests that summer, with a century at Lord's and an average of over fifty against Gary Sobers' mighty West Indian side, but, while England play at the Oval, he will be back with Northants at Clacton. Keith shakes his head in disbelief. "He hooked Wes Hall for six in front of square, and two matches later he'd been dropped." Keith still recalls that morning at Clacton. "I liked a bite to eat and a cup of coffee at the start of play, and that day they only had these pork pies available. So I sat down with my pork pie. At twenty-five past twelve, they hadn't been playing an hour, and there was nobody on the off-side in any acknowledged position. There was no mid-off, no cover point, no gully. There were four men on the boundary, Barry Knight was bowling, and they were giving Colin a single. Before the end of the first hour. I was so absorbed that I hadn't even started my pork pie. He'd got 200 when he came in at teatime, and it was like he'd got a sweat suit on, I've never seen so much water when he was standing in the dressing room. It was as though somebody had poured a bucket of water over him."

Colin's attack on Miller brings the first bowling change of the day. On comes Don Shepherd, the nagging off-spinner who is so hard to force away on Glamorgan's slow, turning wickets. Nobody in the history of the game has taken more wickets and not played Test cricket. "If they'd played Test matches at Cardiff," Keith says, "he'd have been my first choice." But perhaps here in Wales there are more important things than playing for England. *'Actually,'* the Western Mail declares, *'the plain fact of the matter is that Glamorgan can afford to let England have Jeff Jones, Alan Jones, Tony Lewis or Jim Pressdee, but please don't take Shepherd while we are hot in the running for the county championship title.'* Colin Milburn is no respecter of reputation, though, and to his first ball from Shepherd *'he drove much too lustily and was caught at mid-wicket.'* 29 for three.

As Colin Milburn returns to the pavilion, he is replaced by David Steele. What unlikely sporting heroes this Northamptonshire team throws up! In twelve months' time Colin will be hooking Wes Hall in front of square at Lord's, but it will be ten years before the bespectacled and prematurely grey David Steele makes his England debut at Lord's, standing up to the full fury of Lillee and Thomson in their prime. Just an ordinary towel for thigh protection and dirty old gloves with holes at the top. On his way from the dressing room he goes down one flight of steps too far and finds himself in the toilets. Then, as he passes through the Long Room, he hears an M.C.C. member's voice: "Bloody hell, he's very grey, isn't he?" Rodney Marsh is keeping wicket for Australia and he is just as surprised by what he sees: "Who the hell is this? Groucho Marx?" But cricketers come in all shapes, David averages over sixty in his three Tests, and at Christmas he is named B.B.C. Sports Personality of the Year.

Milburn and Steele from unfashionable Northamptonshire, how they will both come to capture the public imagination! But would either of them even rate a mention in a meeting of today's Test selectors? Colin with his great weight, David aged thirty-three.

Here at Cardiff David is just twenty-three, his England career a distant dream, and he and Roger Prideaux settle to a dour session of rebuilding the Northants innings. *'Prideaux was often troubled by a damp spot that first Wheatley and then Shepherd exploited for lift, and in his first hour scored only five runs, but the partnership lasted until luncheon, when the score was 81 for three.'*

It is August 1965. Prime Minister Harold Wilson is off for his holiday in the Scilly Isles while Robert Maxwell is seeking to win a place on Labour's National Executive, with the slogan "Modernise the party machine".

'The scoring rate improved immediately when play resumed. Both batsmen began to trust their strokes, even though the wicket was taking off-

spin.' As Glamorgan's wickets generally do, especially for Don Shepherd. With the ball turning into him, the right-handed batsman is always conscious of the leg trap fielders, none standing closer than the tall, angular figure of Peter Walker. Each month Brylcreem give a pair of gold-plated cuff-links and a bottle of champagne to the fielder with the most catches, and Peter always looks for his main rivals in the county scores. "I won it lots of times," he recalls. "I'd end up chasing a skier down to deep square leg, pushing him away and saying 'It's mine.'" And 'mine' it is when Roger Prideaux cannot keep down *'a lively, lifting off-break from Shepherd'*. At the other end, David Steele plays no shot to *'a violent off-break'* from Euros Lewis, and the Northants innings starts to subside. The Watts brothers, Jim and Peter, add valuable runs, but the ever-accurate Don Shepherd takes six wickets and the final total is just 186. The county game of the nineties will stipulate a minimum of 104 overs for such a day's cricket. Yet here in Cardiff in 1965, with the pavilion clock not yet at ten past five and the close set for seven o'clock, Ossie Wheatley has taken the final wicket in the innings' hundredth over. But then the spinners have bowled 68 of them.

Keith Andrew leads his men onto the field. His premier fast bowler David Larter is at the Test at Trent Bridge so the attack is led by little Brian Crump. Larter and Crump, six foot seven and five foot four, the out-and-out quickie and the gentle medium-pacer, is there a more disorienting new ball combination on the county circuit? In the early fifties Keith came down to Northampton from Lancashire with the legendary Frank Tyson, and he knows the power of speed. Like that day here in 1957 when Frank took seven for 25. Frank is a calm and thoughtful man, but Keith laughs at the memory of that game. "He was the only bowler of any real quality who was quicker and better when he was angry. I used to try and rile him sometimes. Apparently the night before he'd gone out somewhere. I know it sounds ridiculous, but somebody cut his tie off. He was really upset. Glamorgan had got to bat the following day, and we were on our way home just after lunch."

Tyson is part of the folk memory now, part of that golden age in the fifties when England won back the Ashes and held them in thrilling style down under. Now they are trying to make a new Tyson out of David Larter, but his great frame is forever breaking down under the strain. Yet unnoticed at the other end Brian Crump bowls on and on. "David Larter would not have played for England if it hadn't been for Brian Crump. I'll tell you that. If they got two an over off Crump, things were serious. With Larter anything could happen. He'd give away ten runs in the first over." And giving away runs is never part of Keith's game plan. Especially not on this wicket with a total of 186 on the board. *'Crump and P.J. Watts opened the attack, and in 40 minutes conceded only 15 runs.'*

Keith turns to the slow left arm of Malcolm Scott, and Glamorgan's Alan Jones, after three successive boundaries, is *'deceived by the slower flight. Andrew took the ball wide and, reversing on one foot, brought off a*

117

fine stumping.' Yet more evidence for those who argue that Keith is the outstanding keeper of his generation. "He was never like old Godfrey Evans," David Steele writes, "who would throw himself all over the place. Keith would just stand there and take everything. People simply didn't realise what a job he was doing." But even in the sixties, in these days of specialist skills, there is a preference for a keeper who can bat, and Jim Parks is at Trent Bridge, preparing to leap in all directions as David Larter runs in to bowl.

Northants have never won the county championship, but Glamorgan did once some seventeen years back. In the days of Wilf Wooller's captaincy. Wilf is secretary now, at the very heart of the county's cricket, and he is doubtless one that the Times correspondent has in mind when he writes, *'Cricket fever in Wales is beginning to approach the temperature of 17 years ago. None of the 1948 champions remains in the side, but there is no lack of them around the ground, wistfully ready to take the field again if the call came.'* Bernard Hedges was playing for the second eleven by the summer of 1949 and here in 1965, *'with his hard square cuts and lofted on-side shots, he was the most successful attacker of the day.'* He is gone by close of play, though, lbw to David Steele the bowler, and at 90 for three *'honours were about even.'* Peter Walker and Tony Lewis are together at the wicket, *'hedged about by fieldsmen'*.

What is there to do on a Wednesday night in Cardiff? Keith Andrew is off for dinner with Ossie Wheatley, "we had a lot of fun - that was part of my reason for playing", Colin Milburn enjoys himself wherever he is, but Brian Crump and David Steele? "I remember one night Roger Prideaux and I were just leaving the hotel to go out, and Crumpy and Steely were in the lift with a bottle of milk. 'We're going to bed,' they said." The Milk Machine Kids, they call them. Wilf Wooller's Glamorgan may have won the 1948 championship as a disciplined unit, but in the Britain of 1965 Keith wants his Northants side to win the title by expressing their individuality. "He was a greatly under-rated captain," Colin Milburn writes. "He managed to be disciplinarian, friend and psychologist to all the players. Some captains try to deal with the whole team as one, but he had a way with every member of the side."

Julie Andrews stars in 'The Sound of Music' at the Capital Cinema while at the Odeon the Beatles' new film 'Help' is showing. The title song has just become their eighth number one hit. *'Help me if you can, I'm feeling down,'* they sing. *'Help me get my feet back on the ground.'*

There will be many years for Northants and Glamorgan to get their feet back on the ground, but for now they have dreams of glory to chase. The game is well poised, the county championship at stake, and the Arms Park's largest crowd for ten years clicks through the turnstiles. It may not be the most attractive ground in the country, dominated by the adjoining rugby pitch, but in the heart of the city it has a great atmosphere. "You were part of their way of life," Keith reflects.

The morning starts with confident batting by Lewis and Walker, and by 12.15 the score stands at 129 for four. But this is not a wicket on which a batsman can ever feel he is fully in, and one end has that awkward, drying patch for Jim Watts to hit. Tony Lewis is surprised by some extra bounce, and within half an hour Peter Walker is surveying the wreckage of Glamorgan's hopes. 158 for eight, and *'in a neck-or-nothing effort to get the vital runs he danced down the pitch to Jim Watts, who accepted a magnificent return catch only inches off the ground.'*

"More often than not, if you went to Glamorgan, the wicket did something," Keith reflects. "I thought that was good. The wicket should do something in every game, which is testing the skills of different players. Some of these bland wickets, where people like me can go in and get fifty, are no good to anybody. That's one of the problems you have now. I'd love to see, when assessing players for Test selection, their averages on away grounds. I think a lot of people make their reputations on their own wickets."

Don Shepherd and Ossie Wheatley have no reputation for batting, not on anybody's wickets, though there are days when Don's swinging bat connects spectacularly. Like his sixteen-minute fifty against Derbyshire here in 1961. Today, however, there is a championship at stake. Amid rising tension they inch the score to 178 for nine at lunch, nine runs away from the psychological advantage of first innings lead.

The Northants players take lunch, together with Jack Mercer, their scorer, and Jack Jennings, the masseur. This is the full extent of their back-up team for away matches - unless you include the coach driver. "He used to disappear during the game. We suspected we knew where he went, but we never asked."

There are no sports psychologists or spiritual advisers, but within the fun of the Northants dressing room perhaps the psyche and the soul are looked after. Jack Jennings, 'Zatopek' they call him, is "a footballer from way back, a tough, hard man" with none of the equipment of the modern physiotherapist. Just a couple of aspirins and an instruction to "run it off" is his usual response. "He used to have a surgeon's coat. We made him President of our Push Ha'penny League." If it is medicines you want, you are better off going to Brian Crump's room. "When he was in digs in Northampton, it was like the inside of a chemist's shop, but it never stopped him playing. He bowled Tom Graveney with one of the best deliveries I've ever seen, and all he could say was, 'Oh, I'll have to go to the doctor before the next match.'"

Jack Mercer, the scorer, reads out the bowling figures, and Brian Crump, for all his aches and strains, has already bowled 39 out of 88 overs. How many twinges and strains does he run off in his 1115 overs this summer? Only the evergreen Derek Shackleton bowls more overs in the county championship. Jim Watts has bowled 28 overs, and he and Brian will enjoy their lunch, knowing that there is just this one wicket to take and then they can put their feet up.

Jack Mercer. He is already 72, and he will be scoring at Northampton for another sixteen years. With his West End address, his tales of life in the White Russian lines in the First World War and his Magic Circle conjuring, he is a vital part of Keith's happy team. He takes Keith into his confidence with some of his tricks. Like the great playing card that step by step he reduces to a tiny little one. Keith recalls the rainy day at Wellingborough when he entertained the Pakistanis. "You should have seen them. I think they would have carried him off to Karachi. They were spell-bound."

A wonderful entertainer - but a cricketer, too. He has spent eighteen seasons between the wars down here in Glamorgan, and Keith still treasures the scorecard of the day he took all ten wickets at Worcester. "He was a great reminiscer." And here at the Arms Park Jack loves to point out the window, high in a block of flats, where he once hit the ball. The window was wide open, but the occupant, snapped from his reverie by the approaching ball, slammed it shut for protection. He has not long moved over from being the county's coach, though there is little technical input in Keith's memories of his coaching. Back in the days when Colonel Coldwell was the secretary, a man whose interests also extended well beyond the world of county cricket. "I'd been there about three weeks when I said, 'Who's that down there?' A smart chap with a suit and a trilby on. I knew he was a bit deaf because, when you spoke, he never answered. 'That's Jack Mercer, the coach. He doesn't do much coaching, but he gives the Colonel a lot of tips.'"

Now the team owns a greyhound. Lady Be Good, they call her. "We bought it from one of Crumpy's connections." And they play a card game called Shoot. "A devil of a game." There are two tables on the team coach, and they play on the way down here to Cardiff. "Jack always used to be losing but, as we were coming into town, we'd find that he'd got it all back. He never took any money off us. Never."

Jack Jennings, masseur for nearly forty years. Jack Mercer, coach and scorer for almost as long. Northampton may be "a progressive town", but in the sixties employers are not forever restructuring their workforces, looking for fresh blood. "I loved these two men. They really were special."

Soon the bell rings, and it is back to the tension of that last wicket partnership. *'The tenseness of the six thousand crowd could almost be felt when Shepherd faced Crump. The batsman played the first ball to cover, the next missed the wicket by the proverbial coat of paint, causing Crump to throw his arms in the air in despair, and off the next Shepherd survived a confident appeal for lbw. Then, off Scott's fourth ball of the next over, Shepherd was greeted by a tremendous roar as he cracked the four which put Glamorgan in front.'* Ossie Wheatley is soon bowled, and the lead is just three runs.

It is August 1965. Television advertising of cigarettes is banned, and there are proposals to introduce a 70 mile an hour speed limit on all roads.

Micky Norman and Brian Reynolds are the Northants openers, the only two Northamptonshire-born players in the side. Brian, his great appetite has earned him the nickname of 'Waddy', is the no-nonsense senior professional at Keith's side. Even his National Service was in the Northamptonshire regiment, and he is still on the staff at the county ground in 1998. "He was the sergeant-major for me. He made my job so much easier." Brian's reliable discipline and Keith's twinkling sense of fun. At first Keith's captaincy leans towards Brian's ingrained caution, but by 1965 he is his own man. "I'd say, 'Okay, Waddy, how many do you think we should leave them?' '85 an hour,' he'd say. And I knew straightaway we'd got to make it 75."

Reynolds and Norman. What a great player you would have if you could combine Brian's determination with Micky's stylish talent. "Micky was a great team man, a brilliant fielder, but he didn't believe in himself as much as he should have." He takes guard to Ossie Wheatley, his *'hoodoo man'* according to the Western Mail. Ossie has had him five times running for just 22 runs - including that terrible game at Swansea last year when Micky fell to the first ball of each innings and on the same day, too. Up and down, up and down the ninety-odd pavilion steps. "I reckon I knew every one of those steps by the end of that day." Here at Cardiff, with three runs to his name, his middle stump goes back, and he walks away, his last innings for the county played. At least the bowler is Miller this time.

Worse is to follow for Northants. *'From Miller's next delivery Pressdee at second slip leapt to his right to hold a superb catch, and Milburn was out.'* Reynolds, Steele and Prideaux all follow in quick succession, and the score stands at 19 for five. Poor Jim Watts has barely had time to rest his feet from 28 overs of bowling and, when brother Peter is caught behind, it is 32 for six. "Some of our chaps were looking to pack their bags," Keith remembers.

But Jim Watts is a determined man, "a fine cricketer, very under-rated", and in partnerships with Lightfoot and Crump he sets about reconstructing the innings. Don Shepherd bowls unchanged for 31 overs, but *'Crump was impatient and lifted Shepherd over mid-wicket for six before taking three fours off E. Lewis.'* Suddenly the score has reached 131 for seven. In a low-scoring match such blows can make all the difference.

Peter Walker hovers at short leg. His two catches in the first innings have taken his Glamorgan total to 389. Only Wilf Wooller, watching the contest anxiously from the pavilion, has more with 391. *'The tireless Shepherd held one end for most of the innings, and Walker brought off three superb close catches.'* The record-beating third ends Northants' resistance at 141, and Glamorgan, after playing out a maiden over, have all Friday to make 139 to win.

121

What is the secret of such close catching? "You have to have very soft hands," Peter explains. "If your hands are firm, bang, it's gone. So you learn to give with the ball - and try for everything. That's a maxim I always carried. No matter where the ball was." And how did Peter learn all this? "Where I was lucky - and I'm not sure the modern player gets this - was the tutorials I got from my peers. I was lucky to stand at short leg between Wilf, who was brave beyond belief, and Allan Watkins. I learnt a lot from them, not just in conversation but by watching them." But how did he come to be standing in such a vital position? "The way I got to stand at short leg was typical of the kind of luck of every sportsman in every era." And he tells the story of a game here at Cardiff early in his career. The batsmen piling on the runs, Wilf in one of his tetchier moods and he a youngster, going every over from third man to third man, "a run of a hundred and fifty yards at least." A change of bowler, and a chance of a new position. "Well, skip, where would you like me to field now?" "Wilf looked at me with hate in his eyes. 'For Christ's sake,' he replied, 'you can spit in the air and go where it lands.'" For eighteen years he stands where his spit landed, the greatest close catcher in an age of specialist short legs. "Not everybody was expected to field like today. There were a lot of bad fielders around. But the close catching brigade was infinitely better than now. Simply because you played on uncovered wickets, and you played with attacking bowling to attacking fields. In low-scoring matches." Just like here at the Arms Park in 1965.

Glamorgan, nought for no wicket and 139 to win. The sun has shone brightly on an enthralling day's cricket, but *'Northants will have a hard fight to prevent Glamorgan from drawing level at the top of the county championship.'* The wicket is easier now, and Keith and Ossie assess the prospects in a radio interview. "Well, we're certainly far from favourites," Keith says, "unless there's a rain storm and the wicket becomes a lot more difficult." "Well, I'm sorry to tell you, Keith," the interviewer replies, "the forecast is very good."

Keith returns to the Grand Hotel, overlooking the Arms Park. In the Northants side he has a reputation for his forgetfulness, but he still recalls in detail the events of the following morning. "I was shaving. It was very dark, and I switched the light on. I thought it was going to be a beautiful sunny day, but dark clouds had come over. It rained for about half an hour in the middle of all this sunshine. It was absolutely unbelievable. The pitch certainly wasn't covered. I thought, this is a prayer come true." Don Shepherd recalls the rain, too. "I remember staying with friends, and it didn't rain in the outer parts of the city. We came into the ground, and the Arms Park was sodden."

Keith completes his morning shave, and immediately he thinks of Wilf Wooller and hurries down to the ground. "Believe me, you've never seen anything like it. There must have been every roller that was available to Glamorgan County Cricket Club within miles of the ground, rolling the outfield till it looked like glass. They were making it as fast as possible. It was typical Wilf Wooller. I liked him immensely, he was a great sportsman, but he was up to every trick. But I liked playing against men like that; you knew you had a game on. I said, 'Come on, Wilf.' He said, 'We're going to get the runs, anyway.'"

Glamorgan versus Northamptonshire. Back in 1938, when Wilf made his debut, in the dying days of Jack Mercer's career, this fixture would have been the battle for the wooden spoon. Now in 1965, with the Welsh Nationalist Party only months from winning its first Westminster seat and Northampton Town a thriving industrial centre just off the M1, this Friday will do much to settle the destination of the championship pennant. Middlesex are their nearest rivals, and they are losing at Canterbury.

"For the first hour and a half, the ball did as I was hoping. It was jumping all over the place, and Crumpy was magnificent." All five foot four of him. "We always knew him as the fast-medium dwarf," Peter Walker recalls. "We had a lot of slow wickets at Cardiff then. No matter where he pitched it, he kept hitting the bottom of the bat." "If he'd been six inches taller, he'd have been as good as Bedser," Keith believes. "I stood him up to him on the basis that, if I could keep them in the crease, Crumpy could hit a spot where the ball was lifting. I've never been so bruised." *'The nightwatchman Evans did a good job for fifty minutes this morning with Jones, but then the pitch, influenced by sun and wind, began to work for the bowlers.'* The effect of the roller is wearing off, it seems. *'Occasionally the ball jumped, sometimes it kept low, and the batsmen were constantly on tenterhooks.'*

The first two days have brought just 516 runs in 264 overs, and there is many a modern one-day game that will produce more runs in 100 overs. Matches like this one are as much a part of the past now as the mechanical engineering that Keith studied at the Manchester Institute of Technology. "Maybe the mathematics is the same, but now you don't need the same human skills." And perhaps it is the same with cricket. "The cricket has got so many good things going for it; the fielding is phenomenal. But as an entertainment, I don't know. Maybe I'm looking at it through the wrong kind of glasses. I find one-day cricket boring in the sense that the skills of the game are not shared between batting and bowling. When you're in a one-day match and you get out, it doesn't matter. It's an exercise to entertain an audience with limited knowledge."

But there is nobody here today in the Arms Park who is not absorbed by this struggle. *'The match was always a battle, and every ball was watched closely by an appreciative crowd which formed the largest aggregate of spectators to attend a county match in Wales for ten years.'* "There's nothing more exciting," Keith says, "than to see a great cricket match on a big ground full of people. We never had that at Northampton." Night-watchman Evans is lbw, Alan Jones touches the ball to Keith behind the stumps, and Bernard

Hedges, venturing on the attack, is caught in the slips. At 36 for three, Tony Lewis and Peter Walker have work to do. They see off Jim Watts, and Keith - between bruises - looks round for his next bowler.

Not Peter Watts, this is not a day to risk leg breaks and googlies. Not Malcolm Scott and his slow left arm, not yet anyway. Not Colin Milburn, his ever-increasing waistline has put an end to his medium pace. And not David Steele, though next May Keith will whistle up David's occasional slow left-arm and see him take eight for 29. "On a cart road at Northampton. He didn't bowl again for some weeks. Then one day I said to him, 'Steele, isn't it? You ought to have a bowl sometime.'" From such moments Keith acquires his reputation not as an all-calculating engineer but as an unpredictable Walter Mitty. "I had the chance of going to university, and I didn't take it. Cricket was such an adventure. You can't speak for when you're twenty-one, can you? The world at your feet and a beautiful girl for your wife. I might have made more money, been a director of this or that, but it gave us another dimension to our lives. Life is as it is. And that was a magic time. I think the captaincy was my university."

It is August 1965. Construction is almost complete on the 620-foot Post Office Tower, Britain has decided to adopt metric measurements, and new universities are opening at Kent and Warwick. Meanwhile in the United States I.B.M. is filing a patent for its computer.

Keith looks round. "Come on, Albert, you can take over from Jim." Lightfoot, in his ninth first-class game, marks the run-up for his sixteenth over of the summer. "Albert used to be quite a useful bowler, but he was a bit lazy at times." *'Peter Walker took fifteen minutes to get off the mark, but then he sent Albert Lightfoot's first delivery to the boundary with a well-timed square cut.'* But Walker is soon lbw to a creeper from Albert and, with Pressdee falling in the leg trap off Brian Crump, it is 57 for five. Another 82 runs for a Welsh victory.

For forty minutes, Tony Lewis and Alan Rees *'watched every ball with the greatest care, the scoring shots few and far between'*, but 20 vital runs are added to swing the pendulum a little back their way. "Tony Lewis was looking a little bit of a threat," Keith recalls, but on the stroke of lunch Albert gets one to pop, and Lewis fell *'to a diving catch by Milburn at short leg'*. And how many people who saw Colin Milburn in Tests know that he holds the all-time record for most catches in a season by a Northants fielder? He held 43 in 1964, two more than Peter Walker, and this one here in Cardiff sends his team to lunch in happier spirits than their opponents. "He was a brilliant catcher. He used to catch pigeons. When he played for England, they had him in the out-field. When he ran with his weight, he ran vertical. He couldn't run leaning forward, or he'd fall. I used to get angry when they went on about his fielding. They'd got people criticising him who couldn't lace his boots."

Jack Mercer reads the bowling figures from the scorebook, 24 overs unchanged at one end by Brian Crump. He may seek relief from his travelling chemist's shop, but he knows that there is still work to be done.

Northants have won eight and lost just one of their last fourteen games. They have stormed all the way to the top of the table, and they are four wickets from a crucial victory now. "Winning can get a habit, just like losing can." And Keith knows what it is like to play in losing sides. "I once went in the Notts dressing room. They'd just lost ten matches on the trot, and they were all making jokes and laughing. And these were professional cricketers with families. I thought, there's no way I'm going to go down that road. I applied a technical view to winning. We liked playing for fun, we had many a laugh, but I didn't want plaudits for entertaining and losing."

In the first over back Euros Lewis hits Lightfoot for two, then pushes a quick single, only to find his wicket broken by a direct hit. And who should be the fielder? Why, Brian Crump, loosening up for his 25th over. When Miller is caught by David Steele, the ball bouncing off bruised Keith's knee, the score is 86 for eight, and the 53 runs still wanted must seem like 253 in the Glamorgan dressing room.

But Don Shepherd is never one to give up the fight. He has already taken eleven for 83 in 65 overs in the match, and his 22 not out was enough to give Glamorgan that slender first innings lead. He joins Alan Rees, and *three quarters of an hour of swelling tension followed as they took the score past 100 and onward. Defensive strokes were clapped, singles acclaimed, and when Rees suddenly hooked Crump into the crowd, their applause knew no bounds. Every ball was watched and criticised as though it might decide the championship - which, in truth, was quite likely.'*

Brian Crump has bowled 34 overs unchanged for 55 runs, but his 35th goes for ten, and it is time for Keith to think of a change in the bowling. You never know with Keith who is going to bowl. Some days like this there are 68 overs and just one change. Other days it seems there is a new bowler almost every over. David Steele recalls the time he was the sixth bowler in nine overs at umpire Cec Pepper's end. "What's going on here, mate?" Cec enquires. "Does your captain think I've got BO or something?" Keith finally turns to Malcolm Scott, his slow left-armer, "All right, Malcolm, have a bowl," and, with just 24 still to win, he knows that Don Shepherd can win the match with a few hefty blows. Malcolm floats up the ball, and Don swings it away into the deep.

The ball hangs in the air for a seeming age, long enough for the crowd to make *'discouraging shouts'* and long enough for the close fielders to realise with a sinking feeling that the figure speeding towards it is Roger Prideaux, not the first man any of them would choose for such a catch. "Don Shepherd hit it miles up in the air." As high as Jack Mercer's hit, perhaps, though not as far. "And I'll never forget Roger. He went three sheets of white, and everybody was backing the ball. But, to his eternal credit, he caught it. And I thought, that's won us the game." The bowling change has been a masterstroke of captaincy. "You remember the brilliant decisions along with the bad ones." Brian Crump's rest lasts just one over as he returns at the other end to trap Alan Rees lbw, a fourth wicket in his 36th over, and in the euphoria of victory they chair him off the field.

Ken Turner is the secretary back in Northampton. He is the man who has raised the money to guide the county to this new-found success. "On my way back to the dressing room I phoned Ken up. There used to be a telephone box just outside the pavilion. I went straight into it."

It is 1965. In the past ten years, the percentage of private households owning television sets has risen from 40 to 88, washing machines from 20 to 56, refrigerators from 10 to 29. But the mobile phone is years from invention, and only 22 per cent of homes have their own telephone line. Keith inserts his pennies and presses button A. It is 33 years ago now, but he can still hear his voice talking down the line. "Get the flag up, Ken, we've won the championship." "Nobody will believe I can remember that long, but I can certainly remember that."

It is Keith's last game at the Arms Park ground, Northamptonshire's last game there, too. At the end of 1966 Keith will return to his engineering career, and the Arms Park ground will be lost to the development of the Welsh national rugby stadium. Yet it remains for Keith the focus of so many happy memories. His debut for the Combined Services in 1952. A young man with no expectation that he will make a career in the game. And now this moment of glory when little Northamptonshire have all but clinched their first championship. Plans are hatched for a great banquet for the team. Crumpy and Steele, the Milk Machine Kids. Colin Milburn with his pints of beer and his infectious grin. Roger Prideaux, stylish batsman and now the holder of the most important catch in the county's history. The Watts brothers and 'Waddy' Reynolds. And Keith, their captain, engineer and dreamer. Their names will live on from this season of triumph. Or will they?

At Wellingborough next day they have Notts five for four, and by the time they have added victories against Kent and Lancashire, five wins in a row, it is only the reigning champions Worcestershire who can catch them - and that only if they win their last four games. The football season starts, and here in Wales Cardiff City play Bury in the second division, a match refereed by Dennis Howell, taking a day off from his duties as Minister of Sport. But away at Everton Northampton Town discover the reality of their first division dream with a 5-2 defeat. Rain falls at the County Ground, too, and despite a whirlwind 152 by Colin Milburn their last match is left drawn, leaving the door ajar for Worcestershire with two games left to play.

But then rain falls at Dean Park, Bournemouth, too, and the lunchtime cricket scoreboard on Friday brings joy to every Northamptonshire supporter's heart. Keith is out playing golf with Lawrie Johnson, the second team keeper, and he still recalls the shock of the news as it comes through during the afternoon. Colin Ingleby-Mackenzie, Old Etonian, lover of racehorses and all-night parties, is in his last days as Hampshire captain and, to liven up a dead, rain-ruined game, he declares as soon as he saves the follow on. Nought for nought declared is the Worcester reply, and suddenly Hampshire are chasing 147 on a wet wicket drying under brilliant sunshine. Worcestershire's Roy Booth remembers the chain of events. "Ingleby misread the situation completely. Just before lunch it was wet, but the sun had come out, not brilliant but it was hot. We came in for lunch, and Ingleby had declared. We were in a tent, and it was getting hotter and hotter, and the pitch was literally steaming. The ball was coming right up. Roy Marshall was fairly wild about Ingleby declaring. He just had a great whack at it, and it went up in the air. They were all out for 30-something. It was really nasty."

"I never could come to terms with the way Ingleby played that match," Keith reflects. "Rightly or wrongly I felt the championship was at stake. And I didn't feel that was the thing to do." Hampshire make just 31 all out. Then Worcestershire wrap up a victory at Hove, and Northamptonshire's banquet is quietly abandoned. "I became quite friendly with Ingleby later, but I never ever let him feel that I was very thrilled about that game. I can imagine the uproar that would go on now if a match was played in that way with the championship at stake. And of course for Northamptonshire it was a huge match. We'd never won the championship in the history of the game." And 33 years on they still never have.

By next summer the football team has begun the quick descent back to Division Four, though the fairy tale of their season of entertaining Tottenham and Manchester United still lives in the folk memory of the town. Just as the triumph of that day at the Cardiff Arms Park lives still in the memory of Keith Andrew. Along with Colin Milburn, "I'll have two halves, please, guv," and Jack Jennings, "Have an aspirin, lad, run it off', Frank Tyson with his tie cut off, Peter Watts with his collar up like Ossie Wheatley and throwing four tails, Brian Crump bowling Tom Graveney, "Oh, I'll have to go to the doctor," and Jack Mercer with his ever-shrinking playing card. "You've given me a tonic today, talking about these people."

GLAMORGAN v NORTHAMPTONSHIRE

Cardiff. 4, 5 & 6 August 1965

NORTHAMPTONSHIRE WON BY 18 RUNS

NORTHAMPTONSHIRE

M. Norman	lbw b Wheatley	4	b Miller		3
B.L. Reynolds	c & b Wheatley	9	c Miller b Shepherd		14
C. Milburn	c E. Lewis b Shepherd	16	c Pressdee b Miller		0
R.M. Prideaux	c Walker b Shepherd	40	b Miller		2
D.S. Steele	lbw b E. Lewis	55	b Shepherd		0
P.J. Watts	b Shepherd	26	c Walker b Shepherd		51
B. Crump	c Hedges b Shepherd	5	lbw b Pressdee		31
P.D. Watts	c & b Wheatley	25	c Evans b Shepherd		10
A. Lightfoot	c E Lewis b Shepherd	0	c Walker b Shepherd		17
M.E. Scott	c Walker b Shepherd	1	c Walker b Pressdee		3
*+K.V. Andrew	not out	0	not out		0
Extras	lb 3, nb 2	5	b 4, lb 6		10
		186			**141**

1-8, 2-15, 3-29, 4-115, 5-139, 6-144, 7-164, 8-166, 9-186, 10-186
1-13, 2-13, 3-19, 4-19, 5-19, 6-32, 7-78, 8-131, 9-139, 10-141

Wheatley	16.3	9	16	3	9	6	23	0
Miller	15	5	45	0	12	4	21	3
Shepherd	34	20	32	6	31	15	51	5
Pressdee	10	3	20	0	11.3	5	14	2
E. Lewis	24	8	68	1	8	3	22	0

GLAMORGAN

B. Hedges	lbw b Steele	47	c P.D. Watts b Crump		12
A. Jones	st Andrew b Scott	21	c Andrew b P.J. Watts		13
P.M. Walker	c & b P.J. Watts	55	lbw b Lightfoot		10
H. Miller	c Steele b Crump	1	c Steele b Lightfoot		1
A.R. Lewis	c Reynolds b P.J. Watts	20	c Milburn b Lightfoot		15
J. Pressdee	c Steele b P.J. Watts	0	c Steele b Crump		2
A. Rees	c P.D. Watts b Crump	2	lbw b Crump		37
E. Lewis	c Steele b P.J. Watts	0	run out		2
+D.L. Evans	lbw b Crump	3	lbw b Crump		9
D.J. Shepherd	not out	22	c Prideaux b Scott		9
*O.S. Wheatley	b Crump	10	not out		0
Extras	lb 6, nb 2	8	b 4, lb 6		10
		189			**120**

1-27, 2-83, 3-84, 4-129, 5-133, 6-138, 7-143, 8-150, 9-158, 10-189
1-22, 2-26, 3-36, 4-54, 5-57, 6-77, 7-79, 8-86, 9-115, 10-120

Crump	41.2	15	77	4	35.1	11	65	4
P.J. Watts	28	9	43	4	15	4	17	1
Scott	13	5	43	1	1	0	4	1
Steele	10	4	18	1				
Lightfoot					20	8	24	3

Umpires: John Langridge and P.A. Gibb

STUMBLING INTO HELLFIRE ALLEY

Somerset v Leicestershire

May 1966

chosen by Peter Robinson

with Mick Norman

Peter Robinson was born in Worcester in 1943. A slow left-arm bowler, he began his career at Worcestershire, moving to Somerset in 1965 where he played till 1977. He turned into a good enough opening batsman to score 1000 runs in 1970. After retiring from playing, he has stayed on the county staff in various roles, including Coach and Assistant Groundsman.

Mick Norman was born in Northampton in 1933. A right-hand batsman, he played for Northamptonshire from 1952 to 1965 before moving to Leicestershire where he played till 1975. In his later playing days he trained to be a teacher, a career from which he has recently retired.

They remember a game with a dramatic finish at Taunton.

"Taunton was my favourite place to play cricket," Mick says. "The welcome there was always so lovely, it was like a home game. And when you looked from the wicket, there was this lovely church over the pavilion. The Somerset team were always such a friendly lot. Even the pavilion itself, where you got splinters in your bottom every time you sat down, even that made it feel like a friendly place."

Mick is a religious man, an occasional visitor to Taunton, and in his memory he sees the red sandstone tower of St James's Church. For Peter, though, the town has been his working home for the last 34 years and, as he sits in one of the new hospitality boxes, he looks to the less picturesque end of the ground.. "You can see where I worked in winter. The railway goods yard. Off-loading wagons. I started at half past five in the morning. I couldn't wait to escape at the end of March. There were some miserable old buggers working up there. I thought, 'If I finish up doing this for forty years, I'll probably be a miserable old bugger.' It doesn't make your noughts quite so bad, you know."

It is May 1966. Somerset are playing Leicestershire at Taunton, two unfashionable counties each looking for their first championship victory of the summer, and there is barely a reporter in sight from the national press. The day is bright, the air is chilly, and Bill Alley crouches in the gully as big Fred Rumsey runs in to bowl.

Bill Alley the evergreen Australian, born in 1919 and still going strong. "The selectors reckoned I was too old to tour England in 1948," he tells, and here he is, eighteen years on, the heart and soul of this Somerset side. Soon he will write his autobiography. 'My Incredible Innings', he will call it, and he is never short of a story: oyster-catching, welter-weight boxing, training with Stanley Matthews, chicken farming outside Taunton. Everything makes a great yarn. "Back in Sydney, in a little back-street where they don't take kindly to strangers, there's a dimly-lit alleyway leading from a dance hall where I used to earn two pounds a night as a bouncer. There was this Scotsman, I can see him now, a ginger-haired wild man lurching up to the ballroom. We slugged it out solid every week until the blood must have flowed down into the harbour. When I left, I told them, 'You want to sign on that bloody Scotsman, rather than have him kill us.' And when I went back years later, there he was. The new chucker-out. 'Are we going to finish this brawl of ours?' he said. But I declined, and we ended up the best of friends. He wasn't a bad scrapper, you know."

Bill loves nothing more than a scrap, and for this match he is up against Leicestershire's skipper Tony Lock, back for the summer from his new home in Australia. Somerset and Leicestershire may not be contending for the championship, but the scrap here at the end of this game will remain in Peter's memory thirty years later. "They were made for each other. The situation was ideal for them."

Somerset and Leicestershire. From the end of the war to the start of this match no two counties have suffered more championship defeats, and no two counties have achieved fewer Test caps. Is it any wonder that there are no selectors here and so little sign of the national press? Yet, for all their poor starts, there is a flicker of hope in both camps that this summer of 1966 will mark an upturn in their fortunes.

Somerset are already over the worst, finishing in the top half of the table for the last four years, and they are enjoying their second summer under the captaincy of the Millfield schoolmaster Colin Atkinson. "He was trying to smarten everybody up," Mick recalls, "to make Somerset very un-Somerset-like. With Bill there, I think he struggled a bit." At Leicester Tony Lock has taken over from the genial Maurice Hallam, and the culture change is even greater. "He was very good for them," Peter says. "He made them so enthusiastic. The big fives, the huddling together, he got them doing that in 1966."

Maurice Hallam cuts the day's first ball for three, then watches as his partner Booth *was beaten by the remaining five deliveries.* "Brian Booth," Peter laughs. "He used to whistle all the time while he was batting." Peter is at short leg, and the whistling soon ends as *in Rumsey's second over Booth was caught at the wicket with the score seven.* There is early life in the pitch as Mick steps out from the pavilion.

"It used to leak like a sieve in the old pavilion," Peter remembers. "We had a bucket catching the drips. And an old gas fire. I've even sat in the bath with rat poison by the holes. I'm probably one of the few who's glad it's been kept. It's part of Taunton for me, that."

It is almost all that does remain of the Taunton ground of thirty years ago. Certainly there is nothing left of the dog track round the perimeter. "They say rugby and football don't go together," Peter reflects. "I can assure you dogs and cricket don't. We had all the lights hanging down, and the bends were all sandy. They'd be setting up on Tuesdays and Fridays. It was quite chaotic at times."

'Hallam and Norman took easy leg side runs off Palmer,' the Leicester Mercury reports. *'Then Hallam edged Rumsey through the slips for four.'* Soon the muttering begins in the gully. "Big Fred had probably had a few pints of cider the night before," Peter explains, "and he used to sweat profusely. I would be fielding bat-pad at short leg, and Bill would be in the gully. With those great bucket hands of his. 'Look at the big tart,' Bill would say. 'He's knackered already. He's only been going three overs. Look at him there.' And Fred would start, 'Is he talking about me? What's he saying?' Bill used to call him Myrtle. 'Well bowled, Myrtle. You're going well. Keep going.' Then he'd turn to us. 'Look at him. I'll be on in three overs.'"

"Fred was a tremendous bowler on his day," Mick tells. "Very aggressive, slanting it across you. He could always bowl you the unplayable delivery. 'I'm not going to waste my energy running up, faffing around. I'm going to bowl you out.' Great fun." It is a long time since Somerset have had a genuinely quick bowler like Fred, and Peter remembers the words of Fred's new ball partner Kenny Palmer. "You suddenly found that some of the batsmen weren't as good players as you thought."

This morning Fred tests the skills of Mick and Maurice Hallam. A few edges through the slips, "they used to call me Nicker Norman", and gradually the batting becomes more fluent, and by lunch it is 100 for one. *'Although needing some good fortune,'* Eric Hill writes in the Western Daily Press, *'they seemed to have weathered the worst of their troubles.'*

It costs thirty-eight thousand pounds to run Somerset in 1966, and the income is almost ten thousand short. "We had three in the office: Richard Robinson the secretary, Tommy Tout the scorer and one more. Bill Andrews was the coach, and there were two on the ground. That was the staff. Now there's all manner of people, including this vast catering empire. We just had Bill Moor. 'Another horse died in Blagdon,' he'd say as he served up steak and kidney pie. The potatoes would all be in dishes in water, with the eyes left in them. We always reckoned the pies had done at least two race meetings."

Hallam and Norman may think they have weathered the hardest session, but *'How wrong they were! Rumsey, fast, straight and hostile, and rushing back to bowl as if expecting all ten wickets, changed the situation. Threatening to take a wicket every ball, he ripped out Norman's middle stump. Soon after Hallam's leg stump bit the dust.'*

"The crowd loved to see the stumps go cartwheeling," Mick recalls. "Fred would be pitching the ball up with slips and gullies. You would play and miss, the crowd would ooh and aah, and every so often you'd put your foot up the wicket, play a super shot and you'd get four for it." It is a different game from the one he watches at the players' reunion in 1998. "It was just seam, seam, seam, to defensive fields. Dropping the ball just short of a length. And the batsman on the back foot. BOING, a single. BOING, another single. It was so boring."

Fred Rumsey's after-lunch burst, *'forcing the batsman to play every ball'*, is not boring but, as Bill observes, he is "knackered" after six overs, and he gives way to Ken Palmer. "Kenny was a very good bowler," Mick reckons, "but if you saw him in a club game you wouldn't say, 'Gosh, this is a superb bowler.'" But then Kenny is a medium-pacer, looking to hit the seam consistently where Fred is striving for that extra yard of pace. "What do you mean?" Fred retorts. "I hit the seam." And one damp morning they go off to the net together: Bill, Kenny and Fred. Peter remembers it well. "Bill bowled his six, every one of them on the seam. He was very good at it. Then Kenny ran up. I think he had five on the seam and one he just clipped. Fred had five on the shine and one little clip."

Norman, bowled Rumsey for *'an infinitely patient 33'*. Hallam, bowled Rumsey for *'a tidy 72'*. 100 for one at lunch, now 115 for three. "Maurice played a very good knock," Mick remembers. "He batted a long time. Usually he was a bit of a dasher." Off-spinner Brian Langford *'nagged and teased his way through 31 immaculate overs'*, and he picks up the wicket of Marner, then it is the turn of Kenny Palmer's seamers. *'Great bowling by Ken Palmer put Somerset right back into the picture.'* He captures two cheap wickets, it is 138 for six, and for the rest of the afternoon the crowd watch with *'some mild barracking'* as *'David Constant and the Devon lad Roger Tolchard stopped Palmer from causing complete devastation.'* The total creeps to 173.

"In those days you had to be a more disciplined bowler," Peter reckons. "You had low scores so you had to get the ball in the right place as often as you could. And uncovered pitches taught you the difference of length. Now the wickets are always dry, and there's a little more pace in them. So the bowlers get excited and think they're quicker than they are. With low scores you had to bowl with discipline."

Kenny is certainly a disciplined bowler - or at least he usually is. His first spell this morning was *'inaccurate'*, but then so was his first spell that day at Trent Bridge in 1963. Peter tells the story. "It absolutely poured down all the way there. They drove into the ground in the evening, and it was like a lake. So Ken decided to have a good night, and he had more Guinness than was good for him. Then, when they got to the ground in the morning, it was glorious sunshine, and the mowers were going. He went for 23 in his first two overs and was taken off. When he came back at the other end, he got the first nine." Nine for 34 in his second spell, but "he got knackered," Peter says, "and he couldn't get Bomber Wells."

Kenny Palmer returns for a third spell after tea, and his last eleven balls bring four more wickets for just three runs as Leicestershire are all out for 178. Best of all is the *'brilliant gully catch'* by Bill Alley that dismisses Tony Lock for three. Tony is due to spend the evening at Bill's house, eating better steak than they have had for lunch here, and Bill is delighted to have drawn first blood in their scrap.

Kenny Palmer, six wickets for 28, his season's bowling average down from 36 to 21. "He liked his figures," Peter tells, and his memory runs on to the game at Leicester in the following summer. "It was a real turning wicket, and Merv Kitchen got a very good hundred. I should have won the match, but I got smacked, got the hundred up in each innings. We used to have the odd argument in the dressing room like you do, and Ken hadn't bowled well at Northampton in the Gillette Cup. I said, 'What about Northampton?' And I'll never forget what he said. 'That doesn't count in the averages.'"

Leicestershire and Somerset. They may be unfancied counties, but their contests throw up some wonderful finishes. Not just here at Taunton but next year at Leicester, too. Eight wickets down, one over remaining, and Tony Lock facing Fred Rumsey with two to win. *'The tension was unbearable,'* Wisden will record. *'Lock drove the fifth ball square to the boundary, tossing his bat aloft in triumph.'* "A stupid declaration," Bill will complain as he drives out of the ground.

There is half an hour left this evening as Tony Lock leads his players out. "Tony was a tough competitor," Mick recalls, "but his competitiveness was always on the field. He was a soft old thing really, but he introduced this great ebullient style. He'd field in the most outlandish positions, without a helmet or anything. And the language was absolutely awful. If an opposition player didn't walk, there'd be a great F word. He was really volatile. Bald and shouting and screaming." Mick is a religious man. "I'd spent two years in a seminary. I was shattered by it."

Tony Lock is a veteran of Surrey's great side of the fifties. Seven consecutive championship titles, five of them under the equally ebullient Stuart Surridge. "Locky did introduce a lot of Surrey to Leicestershire. I admired him tremendously. He had so much charisma, and he made everything such fun." Bill Alley may stand at gully and mutter about the shortcomings of his bowlers, but Tony Lock at short leg "galvanised everybody, even the opposition. He would talk in such a loud voice. 'This chap doesn't like it round his legs ... Why don't you go round the wicket? He's not going to like that.' He'd tell the batsman that. 'Bowl straight. He only needs a straight ball.' It was terrifying."

It is May 1966, and English cricket is used to gentler ways. "I remember walking out to bat at Lord's first thing in the morning. With Bob Gale at slip, and Eric Russell. 'Morning, Mick,' they'd say. 'How are you keeping?' And if they knew your dog's name, they'd ask about that. It was that friendly."

There is not such a friendly welcome for Roe and Virgin as they *'survived a bombardment from Spencer and Marner, runs coming mostly off the edge.'* At 24 for no wicket, it is Bill Alley who has the greater grin as he and Tony Lock depart for their evening together.

It is the Spring of 1966. "There are only three diversions in Taunton," a café-owner tells a shocked Chamber of Commerce meeting. "The pictures, the pubs and the prostitutes." At the Gaiety Cinema, there is 'The Spy Who Came In From The Cold'. At the Gaumont, 'Life at The Top'. Meanwhile, the Gazette reports, *'pep pills are on sale among teenagers out for kicks.'*

"Somerset used to take us to a pub," Mick remembers. "That was the highlight of the day. You couldn't really afford to do much else." "We stayed at the County Hotel in Taunton," Maurice Hallam recalls, "and we had to have Table d'Hôte. They had this twelve and sixpence limit. Then one year we were allowed A La Carte, and Jack van Geloven went a bit over the top and ordered scampi. And had it stopped. We still call him Scampi."

"The meal allowance was a pound," Mick recalls. "We always had fish and chips so we could make a bit of a profit. But I remember one year walking along with Brian Booth after the first day's play. He said, 'Why don't we eat in style tonight?' And we went in this gambling place, with a roulette wheel. Boothy was a great gambler, he owned greyhounds in Blackburn, and he put our meal money on ODD. And the wheel came up ODD. So we walked out with four pounds. And we had a proper meal in a proper restaurant."

Mick Norman and Brian Booth. They are not the most likely men to find in a casino. "I used to cart them around every Sunday morning," Maurice Hallam recalls, "trying to find a Catholic Church. Brian would go to the dogs on a Saturday night, and he'd go to Church on Sunday to get back in His good books."

"Dogs and cricket don't go together," Peter says, and Mick discovers this some years later in Hull. It is another Sunday morning away from home, and Leicestershire have an even more illustrious skipper: Raymond Illingworth, captain of England. And a distinguished overseas player, the great Australian fast bowler Graham McKenzie. "After Mass I went with Brian in his old Morris 1000 to Hull Docks. We were playing a limited over game in the afternoon. We drew up at the barrier, and there was a man there. He put up his hand. 'Sorry,' he said. 'No visitors on a Sunday.' Brian put his head out of the window, and the bloke said, 'It's Brian Booth, isn't it? Blackburn. I see you at the race track.' He didn't mention cricket at all. 'Come on in.' A few seconds later, as we're going along the wharfside, we see Illy's Jaguar at the barrier. With Ken Higgs and Graeme McKenzie inside. 'Sorry, sir, no visitors on a Sunday.' 'Wait a minute,' Ray says. 'You let them in.' 'Ah yes, but they're on official business.' 'But I'm Ray Illingworth.' 'I don't care who you are, sir. I'm very sorry.' And we saw the Jaguar backing out."

Brian Booth, like Peter Marner, has come to Leicester from Lancashire, part of the clear-out at Old Trafford that has brought wicket-keeper Geoff Clayton here to Taunton. Geoff is another who likes the dogs, and Peter shares a room with him in the Princess Royal. Merv Kitchen and Fred Rumsey are in the other room. "Geoff would drink his Guinness and smoke Park Drive." *'I like them - a good smoke. Cool and satisfying,'* the quarter-page adverts read in the County Gazette. *'Tipped, 3/6. Plain, 4/2. Good value for money.'* "The furniture would always have little burn marks."

Peter's main memory of life at the Princess Royal is his struggle to hold on to his clothes. "He was very thick-necked, Clayton. I had a 15 collar, he was probably 16½. 'Cor, these shirts are tight,' he'd say, and I wouldn't have any shirts at all. He'd wear my shoes, too, if he could get his hands on them. It used to cost me a fortune."

It is May 1966. The Times carries news on its front page now, and on Thursday morning it is all of the seamen's strike: the congestion at the ports, the threats of a General Strike if the Navy are called in.

The morning is *'windy and miserable, flecked with rain and a little sun'*, and Tony Lock - "he would dictate the course of the game," Mick recalls - switches his bowlers' ends and immediately has both Somerset openers back in the pavilion. *'Worse was to follow when a brilliant throw from Norman beat Atkinson's attempt at a quick single.'* "I was supposed to be one of the outstanding fielders of my time," Mick says, "but I would be nothing special now. The fielding has gone through the roof." It is 36 for three, time for that buzz around the ground as Bill Alley strides out.

Bill is forty-seven years old, and he still has this and two more summers to play. Last Spring Sir Stanley Matthews retired from first division football at the age of fifty, and Bill will be all set to match his old training partner in 1969. But he will lose patience with the contract negotiations and will opt for umpiring instead. What another world it is from 1998! Mike Gatting the oldest county cricketer, retiring at the age of forty-one. How much entertainment would the people of Somerset have lost if Bill had called it a day at forty-one?

They would have lost that golden summer of 1961, his testimonial year when he became the last man to score 3000 runs in a season. "He probably got more runs than money in his benefit year," Peter reckons.

They would have lost the summer of 1962, when he came within a hundred runs of that rare double of 2000 runs and 100 wickets. They would have lost his six years of Gillette Cup cricket: three man-of-the-match awards and a string of telling all-round performances, leading of course to the great day out at Lord's. "We played in the '67 final," Peter recalls. "Kent versus

Somerset, the hops against the cider. I remember them chanting Bill's name around the ground before the start. ALLEY - ALLEY - ALLEY."

Here at Taunton *'Alley got off the mark luckily,'* the Leicester Mercury records, *'snicking Marner to the fine leg boundary. He was then beaten as he flashed outside the off stump.'* As he struggles for his touch, Tony Lock, his guest from last night, is perched at short leg. "I fed him royally on the best steaks I could find in town," Bill writes. "I treated him like a long-lost brother. We had a rousing evening." When Bill bends down to throw the ball back to the bowler, "Locky turned on me. 'Do that again and I'll have you for handling,' he snapped. There was a mate for you! I reckon he must have picked that up playing for Western Australia."

At 42 for three the rain sets in, rain that seeps through the roof of the old pavilion, and it is three o'clock before the match resumes. Merv Kitchen fails to beat Birkenshaw's *'beautiful throw'*, Colin Atkinson is bowled by Spencer, and it is 61 for five when Kenny Palmer joins Bill at the wicket.

Bill and Kenny are Somerset's all-rounders, but they approach their batting very differently. Bill the belligerent left-hander. "He had a tremendous eye," Peter tells. "He wasn't a driver, he was more of a pick-upper. He could pick a ball up from off-stump and hit it over leg. Amazing. And he never wore a thigh pad. In those days they were only little bits of felt with shammy leather round. 'You kids are soft,' he used to say. 'Use your bat.' Against Fred Trueman even. 'That's all I've got for you today, Fred,' he'd say, and he'd wave his hankie at him." *'Alley provided Somerset's moments of audacity, cutting, pulling and hooking Marner for four, four and six in one eventful over.'* And Ken Palmer? "He hated giving his wicket away. He got over a hundred not outs in his career. I've seen him play a maiden in a run chase." *'Palmer applied himself seriously,'* the Daily Telegraph reports, *'and kept his head down in making 42 not out.'*

Maurice Hallam stands at slip, relieved perhaps to have shed the burden of the Leicestershire captaincy but not so easy with his new skipper's ways. "Bill liked to chat at the crease, and I was fairly like that. You've got to get relief from somewhere. But Locky gave us all instructions: 'You don't even say good morning to him.' He'd got this theory that Bill was nervous, and that's why he was talking. Well Bill got to thirty or so, and he said, 'I don't give a bugger if nobody speaks to me. It doesn't make any difference.' And I said, 'Thank Christ, Bill. How are you doing?'"

It is a tactic that several captains try but never with much success. Peter remembers how Bill always has a way of breaking it down. "'They've told you not to speak to me, haven't they?' he'd say. They didn't know what to do." Today he reaches 41 when *'he tried to hammer Tony Lock and was caught.'* It is a moment for great celebrations and, as Eric Hill reports, *'Lock greeted each wicket with a display of emotion befitting a last minute winning goal in a cup final.'* "He was the one who started it all," Maurice reflects. "They do wheelies round the pitch and all sorts now. It's unbelievable when you see the old footage, how people just put their hands in their pockets and had a chat." There is even a story on the circuit of a Leicestershire player spilling a vital catch and turning to a team mate: "I just can't face any more of Locky's kisses."

It is May 1966. The Queen takes tea with Anthony Wedgwood Benn, the Postmaster General, in the revolving restaurant of the Post Office Tower. Myra Hindley lodges notice of appeal against her murder conviction, and gas is found in the North Sea. "I can see no reason for any gloom," Lord Robens, Chairman of the Coal Board, says.

Ken Palmer continues to keep his head down, but wickets fall at the other end, and the best of the afternoon's entertainment has gone with Bill's departure. Forty-seven years old and still the great attraction. "If he got some runs," Peter explains, "he'd say his back was bad, and he'd sit in the pavilion. But if he hadn't got any, he'd be out there. 'Give us the ball,' he'd say." Next week at Trent Bridge he will hit a *'devastating'* century and sit on the balcony with Reg Simpson, the Notts chairman, while Peter takes seven for ten, the best bowling figures of his career. "It wasn't turning," he admits. "They all just seemed to get out. And Bill was sat there with Reg Simpson, who was tearing his hair out." "We're installing a lift here soon," the dressing room attendant will tell Bill. "Why's that?" "To get you up here when you're playing in a wheel chair."

Two hours have been lost to the rain, yet *'the seemingly tireless'* Terry Spencer has still managed to bowl almost thirty overs in the day. "He was an honest-to-goodness trier," Mick says. "The salt of the earth. What tremendous service he gave Leicestershire!" He returns before the close to trap Langford lbw, and at 160 for nine Somerset are still 18 runs short of Leicester's total. *'The match will enter the third day with neither side in possession of a point.'* Leicestershire have just four points from four games, and Somerset are at the foot of the table with none. Even these two points for first innings lead will be welcome.

Mick has come from Northampton. "At the time Northants was on the rise so it was a step down. The chance of winning the championship was much less." But with Tony Lock, then Ray Illingworth in charge, he experiences a team coming together. "It was the best move I ever made."

Six of this Leicester side have played for other counties. Then there is Roger Tolchard from Devon and Clive Inman who has come from Ceylon via Penzance. "They were something like us at times," Peter says, "A bit of a multi-coloured swap shop."

Peter has come down from Worcester. The nephew of the great leg-spinner Roly Jenkins, he has joined Worcestershire in 1957 to find himself the fifth slow left-armer on the staff. "The make-up is totally different these days," he says. "Here at Somerset, out of twenty-five there's at least ten who are seamers, and for spinners you've just got Mushtaq and Adrian Pierson. Because of the one-day game, you've got all these bits-and-pieces players."

Worcestershire won the Second Eleven championship in '62 and '63, and Peter took wickets galore. They were set for a third title when Peter went for a trial with Lancashire seconds. "I got twelve wickets in the match, and it gave them the title. When I got back, Joe Lister, the secretary, said to me, 'I don't know how you've got the nerve to set foot on this ground.'" He was offered terms at Old Trafford, but he signed for Somerset and he has no regrets. "I like Taunton. It's a bit like Worcester, lovely places all around. I don't think you can be in a better part of the world. Taunton's quite big enough for me."

It is May 1966. A new mortgage rate of seven per cent is referred to the Prices and Incomes Board, and at Heal's Kitchens Exhibition a waste disposal unit is on sale for £33, the new Philips microwave oven for £360.

"Geoff Clayton and I were on three-year contracts. Mine was for 525 pounds in '65, then 550, then 575. Spread over twelve months. I was better off in winter, when I had another job. We were all a bit skint. Tommy Tout, the scorer, used to lend us a fiver and take it out of our wages. I've known two players here who've had nothing to come at the end of the month."

At the end of 1967, their three years almost up, Geoff and Peter will play at Lord's in the Gillette Final. "They gave us fifteen pounds a man, taxable. For the final." And Lord's does not bring out the best in Geoff. "He trapped a couple of balls thrown in with his foot." The season will end the following Friday, back here in Taunton. "We went up the Princess Royal for a drink. 'Don't sign anything,' he said. 'We're worth a few bob more.' We parted like that. Then I got the Evening Post on Saturday. 'CLAYTON SACKED.' I didn't bother asking for the few bob more."

Geoff returns to his coal round in Mossley, a great keeper lost to first-class cricket. Over thirty years after this game, though, Peter will still be on the county staff. "I've done almost every job in this club. I've had more titles than there are in Debrett's." Years later he will be shown the 1964 minute, delegating the secretary to travel to Worcester to negotiate terms with him. "'Go as high as 600,' it said. It took me four years to get to that figure."

The seamen's strike plunges Harold Wilson's government into crisis, and Fred Rumsey sets up a players' association to campaign for better pay. "He wanted a fiver out of us all. I don't think any of us paid up. We were all a bit dubious." But thirty years on, even a newcomer on the Somerset staff will have a sponsored car with his name on it. "The only thing we were given were the club sweaters. I think it did make us hungrier to succeed."

It is May 1966. Off Whitstable and Frinton pirate radio stations play the Rolling Stones' latest single, 'Paint It Black':

'If I look hard enough into the setting sun,
My love will laugh with me before the morning come.'

Friday morning brings more settled weather, gentle sunshine once a partial eclipse of the sun has passed, and Terry Spencer bowls Fred Rumsey to give Leicestershire a lead of eleven. It leaves Kenny Palmer treasuring a not out fifty to go with his six wickets, but Somerset are still without a point. There are five-and-a-half hours left for the teams to play out the two second innings, but *'Leicester's progress was ordinary enough.'*

Maurice Hallam *'steered Palmer twice to the leg-side boundary,'* but with the score on 26 *'Alley came on and removed him by means of a leg-side catch at the wicket.'* Another success for Geoff Clayton. "Bill liked Geoff stood up," Peter remembers, though it does not always happen. "I'll have a quiet day today," Geoff says. "I'll stand back." "They would have great rows. But then Geoff was a great one for getting the bowlers going. If he didn't think Fred was bowling quick enough, he'd say, 'Do you want me to stand up today?' Or he'd throw the ball back at dear old Brian Langford. 'You're not bloody spinning it.' He had a good cricket brain. He'd gee you up a bit."

Twenty-one wickets have fallen in the match, nineteen of them to seamers, but *'the pitch is dry and wearing'* and Somerset have variety in their bowling line-up. Brian Langford's off-spin - "A real craftsman," Mick reckons. "I'd like to have seen him bowl in Test matches" - and Peter's slow left-arm. "I wasn't bowling very well at the time," Peter recalls. "Before play I had a session with Tony Lock in the old nets at the back. My front leg was collapsing a bit, and he was trying to get me up nice and tall. Out on the field he played like it was war, but in the nets he was very helpful to me."

So helpful that *'after Leicestershire had reached the comfort of 63 for one, Robinson and Langford wove a spell over them'*. Brian Booth advances down the track to Peter, game for a gamble, and Geoff Clayton performs *'a smart stumping'*. Then, with Mick Norman playing Brian Langford carefully, Peter has Marner caught at extra cover and Inman bowled off his pads, both for ducks. "I could bowl at Micky," Peter recalls. "He used to run it around. But Inman and Marner liked to smack it. It was either them or me." With Tony Lock's coaching, this morning it is undoubtedly 'me', three for 13 in 14 overs, and when Fred Rumsey returns to uproot Birkenshaw's leg stump, Leicester take lunch at 70 for five. A lead of just 81.

It has taken Tony Lock to spot the fault in Peter's action, and within little more than a fortnight Peter will take 36 wickets at an average of 10.5 each. The best spell of his career, though he does have the advantage of three matches at Bath. "It did turn that day at Taunton, which was unusual. Taunton was a bit of a graveyard for bowlers. We used to look forward to Weston and Bath. It levelled it up a bit."

Bath certainly levelled it up last year. Two days before the first fixture there, the county staff arrived to find an untended field. "The council thought Somerset were looking after it. Somerset thought the council were. They had to take scythes to the outfield. And gang mowers. Then they flooded the square with marl." Worcester the county champions were the first visitors - or should one say victims? "We had a lead of 47 and won by an innings."

But who is Somerset's coach that he has not spotted Peter's collapsing front leg? "There's more coaching now than there ever was in the whole history of the game. We just had Bill Andrews. 'Oh well, you know best,' he'd say."

Bill Andrews. "He gave so much to Somerset cricket, going round the schools and the clubs, speaking every night at meetings and raising money. He had such a tremendous love of the game. I had to speak after him at a dinner in my benefit year. It was like trying to follow Morecambe and Wise. I was a very sad act." 'Shake the hand that bowled Bradman,' is his favourite greeting, and everywhere he goes he is looking to sell equipment from his car boot. "Dear old Bill," Peter laughs. "He's the only person I've known who could sell a pair of wicket-keeping gloves to an off-spin bowler. What a marvellous character."

But this is not coaching as we now know it. "I remember we were playing Wiltshire down here in the Minor Counties, and we were getting a bit of a smacking. A few minutes after the start Bill would nip out the back and go into the Ring O' Bells. He came back just before lunch, saw the score and started having a go. John Martin was the captain. 'John, you bowled like a pr-pr-proper idiot.' He used to stutter. 'But I haven't had a bowl yet, Bill.' 'Don't you argue with me.' We saw him a bit later, and he'd nodded off."

There is no immediate breakthrough after lunch, as Leicestershire add twenty careful runs. 90 for five, a lead of 101. Then Peter takes a hand in four more wickets: Constant caught in the covers, Tolchard *'with six men breathing down his neck'* caught in the leg trap. *'Then Robinson the bowler became Robinson the fielder'* He *'held a beauty'* to remove Mick Norman and *'a one-handed catch'* to see off Spencer. Then Fred Rumsey has Tony Lock caught behind, and Somerset's target is 139 in 112 minutes. About four runs an over, and the rate so far in the match is 1.86.

The target is 139 at about four an over. To the modern player, trained for one-day cricket on covered pitches, it is not such a demanding task. But Mick knows well how different the game was thirty years ago. Maurice Hallam will be Leicester's leading batsman in 1966, and his average of 31 will put him 25th across the whole country. By 1996, the 25th batsman will be averaging 51. "The kids at school say, 'Your first-class average isn't very good, is it, sir?'" Mick tells. "I try to tell them about uncovered wickets and some of the out-grounds where we played, but it doesn't mean a thing to them."

The Somerset openers lay the foundations for the chase, and Bill Alley watches from the old pavilion. "I'll take three pounds ten for my seven pounds now, we're not going to get these runs." "For somebody who was such an attacking player," Peter reflects, "he was a terrible pessimist." But then Bill is not one to see the positives in his fellow players. "You could always get

Bill going by rating somebody. We were playing at Worcester one time, and Tom Graveney was batting. 'What a beautiful player!' I said. 'Ah you say that,' he said, 'but he can't slog.'" And nor can the Somerset early order, only Mervyn Kitchen who *'spanked 21 in 20 minutes'*. But when he is out it is 70 for four and 63 more are wanted in 40 minutes. About six an over. *'Bill Alley stalked in with crisis - as usual - dogging his determined footsteps.'*

His captain Colin Atkinson *'slogged a couple of useful boundaries'* and is run out. 76 for five. Then Kenny Palmer falls to Tony Lock, and it is 87 for six. 52 to win and just 28 minutes left to score them. *'Clayton then joined Alley, and they set about the task in splendid form.'*

No over limits, no fielding restrictions, no covering of wickets or banning of the heavy mower. This is old-fashioned cricket at its best, sprung out of a match that for two-and-a-half days has seen the teams jockey cautiously for advantage.

It is May 1966. In London Henry Cooper prepares for his fight with heavyweight boxing champion Cassius Clay. Graham Hill wins the Indianapolis 500, and Alf Ramsey picks his team for England's last warm-up match before the World Cup.

'Some hair-raising escapes from run outs, some mighty belting and some glorious shots brought 46 runs in 26 minutes. The game was now wide open.' According to the Daily Express, Leicestershire have *'stumbled into Hellfire Alley'*, and Geoff Clayton is *'Alley's ally in the helter-skelter rush.'* "You couldn't have had a better player out there at that time than Bill," Peter reckons. The last over arrives, to be bowled by Terry Spencer, and there are six still wanted to win. "We desperately needed a wicket," Mick remembers. With the first ball of the final over they get one. "Geoff Clayton blasted it to extra cover, and I caught it."

The batsmen have crossed, and Peter makes his way out to the non-striker's end. Number nine in this Somerset line-up, with only Brian Langford and Fred Rumsey to come. "It took me a while to get up the order. I was always what they call a yo-yo batsman. Top or bottom. I worked my way up by being a night-watchman."

Bill and Peter. The Taunton crowd's hopes rest with the two of them. "Bill was very good to me. I used to go with him in his Morris 1000 van. If we had a whole day to travel, he'd say, 'Get out to my place at twelve.' Adsborough, where he had his chickens. We would go over the road and have a pint in the Star. Then we'd go back, and Betty would give us lunch."

But a day to travel is a rare event on the Somerset fixture card. More often, it is a mad scramble at the close of play. "Get those bloody bags packed, get them loaded." "If you travelled with Bill, before all the roads were built, he wouldn't stop. The bags would be hitting the back of your head, and he'd pull up and say, 'Go and get the fish and chips.' And he'd have them on his lap, dropping them as he drove along. You could be two hours getting to

141

Bridgwater. The A38, that's all it was. I think we reached Bradford at half past four once."

It is summer 1966. The Severn Bridge opens, but a local train drivers' leader says that "the spine road through the South West is a pipe dream."

This evening it is Leicestershire's turn to travel. Somerset are playing Yorkshire here in the Gillette Cup tomorrow. Bill will wave his hankie at Fred Trueman as he makes a match-winning fifty, and he will follow up with three wickets, including Fred for a duck. How he will enjoy that! But for now he wants to put one over on Tony Lock, who is "shouting and screaming" more than ever in the field.

'Alley took a single, then Robinson hoisted mightily at the next and missed.' Three balls left, and still five to win. Peter changes tactic. *'He tried to push the next for a single but razor-sharp Leicester fielding stopped that.'* Five to win off two and maybe this is a moment for Peter to look across at the railway goods yard and to realise that there are worse fates than failing here this afternoon. *'He swung bravely and powerfully over mid-wicket.'* "I slogged it out to the old scoreboard, right out in the corner. There used to be an old brick wall there. It must have gone a long way. We ran a three."

One ball to bowl, two runs to win, and Bill back on strike. Terry Spencer returns to his mark, and Tony Lock sends every man bar the keeper back to save the two. Especially on the leg-side. "That was Bill's favourite side. His drive was only a little punch, but he played the pick-up shot brilliantly. I remember Locky, he took so long to set the field."

Leicestershire and Somerset. Next year there will be one ball to spare when Tony Lock hits the winning four and tosses his bat aloft in triumph. What celebrations will he unleash here if he can prevent his old mate Bill from snatching victory?

"In theory," Bill writes, "no more than a single could be scored, provided Terry Spencer pitched up the ball straight." But Terry thinks differently: "A length ball was out of the question," he says, "because he could have carted that." No, there is only one place to put it, short and wide of the off-stump, and that is where the ball goes. And there is only one thing for Bill to do, and that is to flash at it. "He didn't middle it," Peter explains. *'With a tremendous heave, he edged the ball high over the wicket-keeper's head, straight to the sight screen, beating the desperate efforts of two chasing fielders.'* "I remember it very well," Mick says. "Third man and fine leg converging on the ball." "Over his head," Peter chuckles. "It was the only gap, really."

In a Sydney back street Bill has sent the wild, ginger-haired Scotsman sprawling. Now he has seen off the "bald and screaming" Tony Lock. "The match was ours," Bill writes. "I didn't have the heart to look in Locky's direction." Somerset have won their first championship victory of the summer, and it will prove the first of thirteen. Never before nor since in its

108-year history has the county won so many games in one season. "It was probably as close as we ever got to winning the championship," Peter says.

Leicestershire will soon start winning, too, and by the end of next summer they will be finishing just ten points away from winning their first championship. "Leicestershire's history starts with Tony Lock," Mick says. "He taught them how to win, that losing wasn't just a matter of fact. We went into every match, thinking that we were good enough to win." They would have won here at Taunton - if they had not *stumbled into Hellfire Alley*.

"Bill was an incredible cricketer," says Peter. "A wonderful character," says Mick. Forty-seven years old, he will get his thousand runs this summer, just as he will when he is forty-eight and forty-nine. And his fifty wickets and his twenty catches. How many more years could he have gone on if he had not turned to umpiring? "He wasn't the best umpire," Mick says. "He got too involved. 'Come on, Mick,' he'd say. 'Hit the ball, will you? I'd have pruned those trees up there by now.' But he was a super chap."

Peter smiles at the memory of his journeys in Bill's van. "If you were travelling with Bill, you were all right. But he'd probably have mentioned six of the others by the time you got out of the gate. 'Langy doesn't spin it … Kenny bats for his average … Fred's knackered after three overs.' And when you got to the other end, if you travelled with Bill, the others would all ask you, 'Who got the first mention?'"

Thirty years later, Peter looks across from the hospitality box to the railway goods yard, and he laughs as he recalls Geoff Clayton struggling into his shirts and Fred Rumsey wanting a fiver for his players' association. "The Somerset team were always such a friendly lot," Mick recalls. But when the two of them talk of Somerset and they tell the story of this game, there is only ever one player who gets the first mention.

SOMERSET v LEICESTERSHIRE

Taunton. 18, 19 & 20 May 1966

SOMERSET WON BY 3 WICKETS

LEICESTERSHIRE

M.R. Hallam	b Rumsey	72	c Clayton b Alley		18
B.J. Booth	c Clayton b Rumsey	2	st Clayton b Robinson		25
M.E. Norman	b Rumsey	33	c Robinson b Langford		35
P. Marner	c Roe b Langford	17	c Palmer b Robinson		0
C.C. Inman	c Clayton b Palmer	6	b Robinson		0
J. Birkenshaw	lbw b Palmer	0	b Rumsey		0
D. Constant	c Clayton b Palmer	14	c Roe b Robinson		12
+R.W. Tolchard	c Kitchen b Palmer	21	c Kitchen b Robinson		0
*G.A.R. Lock	c Alley b Palmer	3	c Clayton b Rumsey		14
C.T. Spencer	not out	0	c Robinson b Langford		10
J.S. Savage	b Palmer	0	not out		2
Extras	lb 9, nb 1	10	b 7, lb 3, nb 1		11
		178			**127**

1-7, 2-102, 3-115, 4-133, 5-137, 6-138, 7-173, 8-177, 9-178, 10-178
1-26, 2-63, 3-67, 4-67, 5-68, 6-90, 7-92, 8-94, 9-116, 10-127

Rumsey	22	10	35	3	13.4	3	29	2
Palmer	14.2	3	28	6	3	1	14	0
Alley	16	7	24	0	4	1	8	1
C.R.M. Atkinson	11	3	22	0				
Langford	31	11	42	1	28	12	37	2
Robinson	8	2	17	0	23	15	28	5

SOMERSET

R. Virgin	c & b Marner	18	c Hallam b Marner		23
B. Roe	lbw b Spencer	15	c Tolchard b Spencer		15
M. Kitchen	run out	11	c Inman b Marner		21
G. Atkinson	run out	0	c Tolchard b Marner		2
W.E. Alley	c Booth b Lock	41	not out		42
*C.R.M. Atkinson	b Spencer	10	run out		8
K.E. Palmer	not out	51	c Marner b Lock		6
+G. Clayton	b Spencer	1	c Norman b Spencer		18
P.J. Robinson	c Lock b Marner	12	not out		3
B. Langford	lbw b Spencer	0			
F.E. Rumsey	b Spencer	4			
Extras	b 1, lb 3	4	lb 3		3
		167	(7 wkts)		**141**

1-33, 2-33, 3-36, 4-51, 5-61, 6-109, 7-110, 8-156, 9-157, 10-167
1-22, 2-47, 3-49, 4-70, 5-76, 6-87, 7-133

Spencer	34	10	50	5	10	1	40	2
Marner	31	13	84	2	16	1	68	3
Lock	14	4	29	1	7	1	30	1

Umpires: C.G. Pepper and A. Jepson

David Allen

I had to fend off Wes Hall for two balls while Colin stood there watching me with a smile on his face. Not only that but he still gets fan mail for his brave knock, and no one ever mentions D.A. Allen.

Gordon Barker

*I always called him Albert. He loved singing. He'd been right in the middle of the
Pontardulais Male Voice Choir, and he was the man we thought we had to get out.
'Albert,' I said to him, 'if ever you needed to lose your wicket this season, this is it.'*

Fred Trueman

Fred, as much as his greatness was, he never really knew where the ball was going. He used to tell you he did the off-cutter, the leg-cutter, this yorker and that yorker, but we all knew that Fred was Fred. He just ran up and bowled. And he was absolutely brilliant.

Alan Dixon

I was having a pre-match knock, and I came back into the changing room. 'Oh, don't take your pads off,' somebody said, 'You're batting seven'. And he was right. It wasn't long before I was in.

GUESS WHAT

Northamptonshire v Kent

August 1968

chosen by Alan Dixon

Alan Dixon was born in Dartford in 1933. A bowler of medium pace and off-breaks, and an attacking middle order batsman, he played for Kent between 1950 and 1970. In winters and after retiring from playing, he worked in insurance, from which he has recently retired.

He remembers a match against Northamptonshire at Wellingborough.

"We played at Dover near the end of one season," Alan recalls. "A wonderful ground, like an amphitheatre. We were changing after the game, and Colin Cowdrey came in. 'I want you all to stay in your whites, smarten up and come out on top of the pavilion.' It was set in a bank, with a flat roof, and he gave the most remarkable speech. He brought in the crowd with a microphone, and he said that here was the nucleus of a Kent side that was going to win the championship within five years. It was one of the most uplifting ten minutes in my life. Not many people could do that off the cuff. It was a big moment in Kent cricket."

It is the summer of 1968, and the five years are almost up. Last year they were runners-up to Yorkshire. "I dropped such an easy catch at Canterbury, and it gave them first innings lead. It seemed to change the whole course of the game." Now they are chasing Yorkshire again. Six matches left and 22 points behind. A win here at Wellingborough could prove vital.

'Summer 1968 has been a tragedy,' the Kent Messenger records. *'Too much rain and too little sun - that has been the recipe for failure on the farm and at the seaside.'* August is only in its tenth day, and already Maidstone has had more than twice its average rainfall for the month. The county's players have made their way up the M1, and everywhere about them it was grey and damp. Christopher Wordsworth of the Observer sits on the train out of St Pancras, and his spirits are low as he gazes out of the carriage window. *'Viewing cocoa-coloured streams and flattened crops from the train, the prospect of cricket at all seemed remote.'*

The Grove, Wellingborough School. Elm trees line the farther sides of the ground, and county cricket's only thatched pavilion has a short flight of steps leading down to an inscribed stone. 'This stone was once the threshold to the home of Dr. W.G. Grace at Downend,' it reads. 'Not of an age but for all time.' Among the spectators who gather today is the retired schoolmaster Murray Witham, who back in 1939 read of the demolition of Grace's home and drove through the night to preserve this memento.

Wellingborough School, 1968. The Sunday Times prints league tables of exam results, and the heyday of masters like Murray Witham is over. His pupils may not have passed their 'A' level Geography, but all their lives they will remember his eccentric love of cricket: the dormitories named First Slip, Second Slip and Gully, the painted quotations above the staircase. 'Thou shalt not pitch short,' one instructs. 'Consider the Lilies in the Field,' reads another. 'They toil not, neither do they spin. No! But YOU should!'

It was Murray Witham who persuaded Northamptonshire cricket to come here in 1946, and each Hallowe'en till 1965 on the stroke of midnight he led a procession of masters out to the square and buried in a whisky bottle the autographs of the twenty-two players of that summer's county match. The bottles are down there, together with the remains of a master's dog, as Alan looks down at the green wicket and tosses up with Northants' Brian Crump. To the amazement of Christopher Wordsworth, *there was a prompt start, with the sun making steady headway through the clouds.*

A summer of damp weather has brought its share of niggling injuries. Kent's captain Colin Cowdrey is nursing a strain, and Alan's first task as stand-in skipper is to check the fitness of his various bowlers. John Dye limped off last week at Dover with a pulled hamstring, Norman Graham is not fully fit, John Shepherd has groin trouble, and even Asif Iqbal has ricked his ankle in the showers. The only seamer fit, it seems, is Alan Brown.

Northamptonshire versus Kent. There is a whisky bottle that contains the autographs from their 1964 meeting here. Back when Northants were a formidable side, third and second in successive summers, and Kent were just beginning their revival. Now Northants are in the doldrums, and Kent are hoping for easy points to maintain their championship challenge.

What a team Kent have assembled! Mike Denness and Brian Luckhurst the opening batsmen, Alan Knott the wicket-keeper, Derek Underwood the slow-medium left-armer, John Shepherd and Asif Iqbal the overseas all-rounders, and Colin Cowdrey himself still in his prime. But who are the opening bowlers? Since Dave Halfyard's tragic car accident in 1962, they have permed two from the quartet of Graham, Dye, Brown and Sayer, and every game there is a choice to be made.

"In those days," John Dye remembers, "Colin used to arrive about twenty minutes before the start of play. He'd park his car, walk straight to the middle, toss up the coin and tell us what we were doing. But none of us knew who was playing. The most common thing was to go and buy the scorecard to see if your name was on it. The problem with that was that sometimes there were fifteen names printed so you were none the wiser. There was even one game at Canterbury when we took the field with twelve men. 'Colin, we've got twelve here,' someone said. 'Oh, have me? Oh, oh, um, Browny, do twelfthers for me, old boy.' Colin was a hell of a nice man, but he was in cloud cuckoo land."

146

Colin may not be a down-to-earth professional like John but, Alan recalls, "he always had time for people." Ordinary people, too, like the workers in the Canterbury pavilion that he gets chatting to one day. Their children's names, where they go on holiday, they tell him everything. Then one of them turns to Colin: "And you? Who are you? What do you do?" "That was his greatness," Alan says, and he draws the contrast with another England captain, another of the old amateurs. "He sat in the passenger seat of Peter Richardson's car, all the way from Smarden to Canterbury. I was in the back seat, and he didn't as much as turn his head or say good morning to me. I was just a professional, I hadn't played Test cricket. I found that unacceptable, I'm afraid. Can you imagine Colin Cowdrey doing that?"

It is the summer of 1968. It is six years since the end of the amateur in cricket, and now the Lawn Tennis Association has followed suit with its first Open Wimbledon.

"I'm a great believer in professionalism," Alan explains. "I get very upset by things like players not having a cricket bat, borrowing one on the way out. It sounds lovely, doesn't it, but it's totally unprofessional. You need to know what your bat does." He has been on the Kent staff since 1950, and he has known the bad days when the team had no fight in it. "I remember one of my early games. I was having a pre-match knock, and I came back into the changing room. 'Oh, don't take your pads off,' somebody said. 'You're batting seven.' And he was right. It wasn't long before I was in." He has known the seasons when the less established professionals only played till the end of the university term. "Colin Page got twelve wickets in a match, and two games later he had to make way for the boys from Oxbridge." There will be no confusion about the team when he is in charge.

"I'd been injured," John Dye recalls. "A hamstring. They're buggers, aren't they? I was running about down at Canterbury, and I was fine. So they said, 'Okay, off you go to Wellingborough.' So I drove up on my own. The boys were already at the ground, and I know Browny was expecting to play. He and Dicko were great mates, and Dicko had to leave him out for me. Because I was doing well that year." John has only played half the games, but he is high in the national averages and, faced with Wellingborough's damp, green wicket, Alan opts for the variety of his left-arm action.

At Dover last week, John pulled up after three overs of the first innings and, with a bowler short, Alan set Notts 186 to win in two and a quarter hours. An unsporting declaration, Gary Sobers called it, "he was ranting and raving," and he took out his anger on the Kent bowlers, scoring the fastest century of the summer and winning with 25 minutes to spare. But, for all the boundaries, it is a dot ball off his own bowling that remains in Alan's memory. "He had this 360 degree take-up and follow-through. The bat went up, I heard the hit, I saw the bat come through to me, but I couldn't see the ball. Then I heard this tremendous clatter behind me. The ball uprooted two

147

stumps at my end, and it bounced back so hard it ended up back at Gary's feet. He didn't even get a run. Then the next ball went about three feet above my outstretched hand, and I think they're still looking for it in the bank."

Among that Notts side last week was the burly figure of Dave Halfyard. From 1957 to '62 he carried the Kent attack, travelling everywhere on a Lambretta moped, then a Messerchmidt bubble car. "We were at Worcester," Alan remembers, "and he drove all the way home on the moped on the Saturday night. Then on Monday morning he appeared at ten to eleven, stiff as a corpse, absolutely blue. 'You can't expect to turn up like this and bowl,' Colin said. Well, he'd had a net in his garden. 'I've had a bowl already,' he said, and somebody said, 'a bowl of cornflakes.' His first over went for 16, but he finished with five wickets. You had to prise the ball out of his hands.'"

In 1962 his legs were wrecked in a car crash but, after a spell of umpiring, he is back as a leg-spinner at Nottingham. "A hell of a guy," John Dye says, and here at Wellingborough John recalls his advice. "'Always remember one thing, Doc,' he told me. 'If you can walk, you can play. If you come out of the side, some other bugger will get in and you won't get back.'" John is the man in possession, and Alan Brown is once more twelfth man.

For Northants, Roger Prideaux is out of action, suffering from 'a touch of bronchitis', and Brian Crump is in charge. 'Never ask Crumpy about his health,' they say, 'you'll never get away', but he is another Dave Halfyard. He loses the toss, and he takes the new ball against Denness and Luckhurst. *'Skidding footholds and the slow bounce made the going hard for everyone before lunch,'* and the openers accumulate 19 in a *'careful'* half hour.

Denness and Luckhurst. "What runners between the wickets!" Alan says. "They could show our boys today how to score another thirty runs before lunch. Trust in each other, great backing up, and they knew where the ball was going and at what pace." But the damp surface makes running difficult, and *'the tendency to play too early undid them both. Luckhurst was bowled round his legs, and the lofted drive that put paid to Denness would have been a boundary on any normal wicket.'* Both fall to slow left-armer Malcolm Scott, whose faster ball traps Asif Iqbal lbw for a duck, and Kent are struggling at 63 for three.

It is August 1968. Wellingborough is a small market town, but the plan is to increase its 30,000 population to 80,000 by 1981. The Chairman of the Urban District Council has just opened the thousandth development house, there is a new public swimming pool, and industrial estates are starting to appear as the town spreads out towards the ever-busier M1.

In The Grove the batsmen are Alan Knott and Stuart Leary, who *'navigated the spinners Sully and Scott till lunch when Kent were 97 for three.'* Alan is established as England's wicket-keeper, will be for the next ten years, yet only four years ago here at Wellingborough he was a nervous eighteen-year-old, playing his second championship match. "The bounce was variable," he writes, "with the ball often skidding through at ankle height instead of lifting sweetly into my gloves." In that first innings he let through 13 byes and felt terrible till, at the end of the Kent innings, Keith Andrew's head appeared round the dressing room door, 22 byes against his name. "I beat you," he grinned, and together they sat and discussed their craft.

Leary and Knott. In those days Alan was the quiet youngster, humping his kit onto buses and trains, and Stuart the legendary Charlton Athletic goal-scorer with the smart Jaguar and the confident quips. Now Alan is the famous one, but not for him the glamorous life-style. "He was a dedicated, professional cricketer," Alan Dixon says, "to the point of nausea. He even had this American adviser. All the pop stars had gurus at that time so Alan had to have one." It is another world from that of most cricketers in 1968, and among the professionals there are some who look at Alan and his stretching routines, his glasses of orange squash, his boxes of vitamin supplements, and think him 'a strange lad'.

'The short boundaries on the tree-lined school ground offer a tempting harvest to would-be six-hitters,' Michael Tebbitt writes in the Northampton Chronicle. 'Knott was the first to take advantage of the situation by pulling a full-toss for six over mid-wicket.' But Stuart Leary is bowled by Scott for 29, 'sweeping at a ball that deserved more respect', and at the other end David Steele's slow left-arm bowling induces 'a little dab-cut' from Knott that has him caught in the gully, Johnson is bowled for a duck, and Kent are in trouble again at 126 for six.

"I liked to get out and play at different grounds," John Dye says, "and Wellingborough was a lovely place to play cricket. All the leaves out on the trees, the sun shining, the grass so green and the marquees. It was much nicer than Northampton." John is on the revised scorecard at number eleven, and wickets are falling in the middle. How is he preparing for his batting?

"Dear old John," Alan laughs. "He'd had this hamstring injury and, whilst we were batting, he was round the back, playing football with some children. 'John,' I said, 'that's one of the worst things you can do for a hamstring. You're playing cricket for goodness' sake. Come and get organised for your game.'" Thirty years on Alan shakes his head, and the stories about John Dye start to flood back. "David Nicholls gave him a lift one day, and the coppers pulled him over for speeding. 'Do you realise, sir, you're doing fifty-five miles an hour in a forty mile an hour limit?' And John leant over. 'I just told him that,' he said. That was John."

Out in the middle John Shepherd, Kent's Barbadian, is taking the attack to the bowlers. 'He got off the mark with a wild stroke over slip's head.' "He used to whack the ball in places where fielders aren't," Alan recalls. "In the air, wide of extra cover. Well, you didn't get too many doing that, not in those days." Today he hits three sixes and, with Derek Underwood 'of the same valiant mood', the total jumps to 170 for six. Then Brian Crump returns, and

'Kent's end was abrupt.' 177 all out, with John Dye lbw Crump, 0. "The wicket did have a tinge of green," Alan says. "But 177, that wasn't enough." *'Kent's championship challenge was looking distinctly sickly.'*

It is the summer of 1968, and there are bonus points for batting and bowling. Kent have won one more match than Yorkshire and, if last year's scoring system still applied, they would be 18 points clear at the top. Instead, they trail by 22. For all the strength in their upper order, they have not yet adapted their game to these bonus points, and today's score of 177 adds just one to their meagre tally.

Norman Graham and John Dye will open the bowling, with Alan Brown on twelfth man duties. Let's hope that there is no repetition of the scene at Canterbury when he brought on the drinks. "It was sweltering," Alan Dixon remembers, "and he'd got this tray loaded with orange juice, beer, lemonade shandy, gin, and it was too heavy for him. Halfway out from the old pavilion he dropped the whole lot. There was glass everywhere. Then five minutes later he reappeared with another tray, and he'd picked up this young lad who was walking alongside him with a dustpan and a brush."

It is the summer of 1968. Bonus points, overseas players: more changes designed to bring the crowds back to cricket. How much easier it would all be if there were a few more Colin Milburns. In June he set the Lord's Test alight, but in the next match he was hit on the wrist, and he returned only last week. He takes strike to face the six foot seven Norman Graham.

"The majority of us were very conscious that it was our job to entertain," Alan recalls. "You would involve the crowd. Like if you dropped a catch, god forbid, you'd turn round and pull the chain. It was a vital part of the game."

"Big Norm would be the first out of the hat as a team player," Alan says. "He bowled thirty-odd overs for me at Edgbaston one year. He came off at tea, took off his size thirteens, and the skin was all off, there was blood everywhere. 'You'd better have a break,' I said. But no, a bit of powder, a new pair of socks. 'I'll bowl for you,' he said. He was a great line-and-length bowler, and he had this ability to angle it in at you." *'Milburn's reappearance added to the pleasures and pangs of an eventful day,'* Christopher Wordsworth writes. *'He took two agile catches, but his batting was of the briefest.'* Milburn, bowled Graham, 0, and the Wellingborough crowd groans.

John Dye paces out his run at the pavilion end, preparing to come down hill to the left-handed Albert Lightfoot. "Mark me," Alan says, "John could bowl. He could have played for England." He is high in the national averages, and this is a wicket with some green in it. His first three balls are bowled, and no runs are scored. "He was always happy to bowl dot balls," Alan tells. "If I bowl dots," he says, "somebody will nick one eventually."

"I can see him now," Alan says. "He used to puff away. He got to the end of his run-up, spun on his heel, went one, two, and stopped. Then he looked at me at cover. 'Guess what,' he said."

Guess what. Kent are pressing for the championship, and last week John retired after three overs against Notts. He sat and watched Gary Sobers blaze the summer's fastest century - "I pulled out just in time then," he laughs - and he has driven up here this morning to rejoin his team mates. A kick-around with a football, a quick duck, and now guess what.

"I ran in and bowled the ball," John tells, "but it was no good. 'It's gone, Al,' I said. 'Gone,' he said. 'Gone where?'" Thirty years on, Alan shakes his head, still appalled by the lack of professionalism. "There we were, defending 177, and we were down to ten men, without a key bowler. And he'd been playing football all afternoon. I think I only used the two words, and the second one was 'off'." But John roars with laughter at the memory. "Browny was left out so that I could play, and he had to field for two and a half days. He must have loved that. He could bat a bit, too, he wasn't the world's worst."

Alan Brown can bat. Next month at Folkestone he will hit a *'brisk'* 81, and John Dye has never reached 20. In four years' time John will move up here to play for Northants, and the county's history records the tale of his pulling up at traffic lights behind the Chronicle's cricket reporter. "Oy,' he yelled. 'You've got my batting average wrong in the paper. It's 3.09, not 2.93.'" "I don't think I said that," he laughs, "but I could well have done. It's the sort of thing I would do." Here at Wellingborough he limps into the pavilion, and Alan Dixon throws the new ball to Derek Underwood.

It is the summer of 1968. 'Jumping Jack Flash' from the Rolling Stones, 'Hey Jude' from the Beatles, 'Mrs Robinson' from Simon and Garfunkel. In Kent there are plans for next year's Maidstone Cricket Week to include a pop festival, while here in Northants the county will soon be staging discos in the indoor cricket school. Emperor Rosko will charge more for his night as a DJ than most of the players earn in a month.

Kent's gloom from John Dye's departure soon passes as Northants slump to 23 for four. A duck for Colin Milburn, now a duck for Mushtaq Mohammad. Only their South African Hylton Ackerman prevents a total collapse. "He had such strong forearms," Alan remembers. "He wasn't frightened to hit the ball in the air." The first-class batting averages are dominated by the overseas players - Sobers, Kanhai and Barry Richards - but Ackerman has been having a hard time, just one score over 40 in his first 26 innings. Yet at Northampton on Tuesday he hit an aggressive 78, and his confidence is starting to flow. "It's very difficult to set a field when a man's in form, and he was in form. He picked Derek up and kept wafting him wide of mid-on. And at this stage of his career Derek found it very difficult to bowl to anybody who did that." By close Northants have recovered to 125 for six and Ackerman is 69 not out. *The first innings issue looks simple,'* Christopher Wordsworth writes. *'Kent versus Ackerman.'* Meanwhile at Lord's rain has reduced Yorkshire's day by five hours.

151

It is August 1968. Barclay's Bank merges with Martin's, the National Provincial with the Westminster. The first decimal coins are in circulation - five new pence for the shilling piece, ten new pence for the florin - and there are plans to replace the ten shilling note with a seven-sided coin.

In 1968 there is championship cricket on Sundays, with counties able to charge at the gate, but the plan is to play a forty-over league next summer and to attract a new audience. "The football supporters," Alan says. "The niceties of the game, the artistry of the bat versus the ball, started on its downward trend." The hope is that the excitement created by these Sunday League games will feed into a revival of interest in the championship, but "I think perhaps that was always an unrealistic point of view."

Here at the Grove Northants' biggest Sunday crowd of the summer arrives for the two o'clock start. *'There was, I think, no empty seat in the ground,'* Alan Gibson writes in the Times, *'though to be sure there are not many seats here to begin with.'* The gate money totals 375 pounds, on top of yesterday's 204. *'However, the gilt was taken off the gingerbread,'* the Northampton Chronicle writes, *'when one remembered that it costs an extra 300 pounds to stage matches at Wellingborough.'*

"Even in the worst days in the fifties," Alan says, "we had a tremendous following of honest supporters. We had a milkman in Sittingbourne. He used to get up early for his round, then come to watch us. I remember going out at Old Trafford, and he was there. 'I wouldn't miss this,' he said."

Ackerman is *'not able to recapture his dominant mood of the previous evening'* and, when he reaches 82, he steps out to drive Alan's off-spin and is stumped by Alan Knott. It is his highest score in England but, when Sully follows for a duck, Northants are 152 for nine, still 25 behind Kent's total. *'The sun was warm, the colours bright, the crowd eager to be appreciative.'*

Ackerman, stumped Knott, bowled Dixon. Alan Knott only stands up now when Alan Dixon is bowling his off-breaks. "My medium pace was very gentle," Alan says, "but early in his career he dropped a catch off me standing up, so he went back. He reckoned that, for every stumping he got standing up to the medium pacers, he'd miss two catches." Alan Knott is a modern keeper, with stretching routines and an American guru, and perhaps the influence of his standing back will hasten the decline of the traditional stumper. From Ames to Evans and now to Knott, Kent have been blessed with three of the great wicket-keepers of the century, but gradually the stumpings have provided a smaller share of their victims: 37% for Ames, 23% for Evans, but less than 10% for Knott. Didn't Leslie Ames make 64 stumpings in one summer? And isn't that more than in the whole of England in 1998? "Godfrey was the greatest, standing up," Alan Dixon says, "but, standing back, there's never been a better keeper than Alan Knott. He was so nimble."

Godfrey the greatest standing up. Is that what Alan Dixon thought when he made his debut in 1950, that Friday afternoon at Clacton? Scores of three and nought, Essex chasing 60 to win, he had just two overs to make his mark as a bowler. "Sonny Avery nicked one that went straight up. Godfrey went to catch it, and Arthur Fagg ran round. 'Leave it,' he said. 'Leave it to me.' They both stopped, and the ball fell about three yards in front of Godfrey. 'I'm sorry about that,' Arthur said as we came off, 'but, if Godfrey had caught that, we'd never have made the 2.30 train.'" It was five years before Alan took his first championship wicket, ten years before he won his cap.

Within that ten years there was even a winter when Alan handed in his notice to Leslie Ames the secretary, "I just wasn't getting the opportunities, so I took a job, selling Furniglos french polish." But the next spring he stopped his car by a village ground, "and you'll laugh at this, but they were mowing the outfield, and the smell of that new-mown grass, it meant so much. I rang Leslie. 'It looks as if I've made a mistake,' I said."

Ten years have passed since then, Kent have risen to be championship contenders, and today Alan is captain, trying to tease out this final Northants wicket. But *'Johnson cheerfully threw his bat around, taking 12 in an over off Underwood,'* and the last wicket pair takes the score to 183 and a lead of six. There will be three overs of Durose's fast medium bowling, then for the rest of this Sunday afternoon the spectators will watch Brian Crump's gentle seamers in tandem with Mushtaq's leg breaks and googlies. *'This was a marked change of tactics, but it proved effective.'*

Denness and Luckhurst are gone with only 28 on the board, Luckhurst *'beautifully caught low down at short leg'* and Denness *'bowled with a top spinner that kept a little low'*. "Mike had the greater stroke-play," Alan says. They still talk of his two innings at Bath in 1966. "On a square turner. Brian Langford said it was the best batting he'd ever seen." Such class will take him into the England team next summer, and in time he will captain his country, but for Brian Luckhurst it is a harder road. "I had such a great admiration for Brian," Alan says. "When he was fifteen he came on the staff as a left-arm spinner, with a lovely flight and loop. But he went into the army for two years, and he grew and lost it. 'I'm going to get sacked,' he said to me. 'I can't bowl like I used to. I'm going to have to bat.'"

"He was a very determined guy," John Dye says. "Having a net with Lucky was like having a proper game. We all queued up to bowl at him." And they don't say that about Stuart Leary. "He was hopeless, just wanted to whack it all the time. He had to discipline himself to get somebody to bowl at him." "Brian grafted his way," Alan says, "and he ended up opening for England. That's got to take some spirit." Four Test centuries in nine months in 1970/1. "And most of all," John says, "he didn't come back from the Tests, playing the great 'I AM'."

The Wellingborough wicket is still recovering from all the recent rain, and *'Mushtaq was making about three balls every over turn and squat.'* Denness and Luckhurst have grafted in vain, now it is the turn of Knott and

Asif. "I was in the office at Canterbury once with Les Ames," Alan Dixon recalls. "The wicket was slow and dead, and he sent for me. 'Alan, you're the captain, what's going on out there? You're here to entertain the crowd. It's not good enough, they've got to play shots.' I had my back to the window, and I didn't realise that a wicket had fallen and Asif had gone out. 'It's one of those wickets, Les,' I said. 'It's so slow and low, it's almost impossible to play shots.' 'Well,' he said, 'would you like to turn round and watch Asif bat?' And he was smashing it to all parts." Here at Wellingborough *'Asif, who relishes an awkward situation, attacked boldly. He played firm front foot shots, and he twice pulled Mushtaq for six.'*

Asif and Mushtaq. Five years ago they toured England with the young Pakistani Eaglets side. Asif knows Mushtaq too well to fall to his leg spin, *'but Crump's accuracy was too much, and he was three short of his 50 when he was lbw hitting across the line.'* After this there is nobody who can fathom Mushtaq, and 105 for four becomes 130 all out, Mushtaq seven for 67. *'A good leg-spin bowler is rarely seen in first-class cricket today,'* Roger Fowle writes in the Kent Messenger. *'No fewer than six Kent wickets fell to the Pakistani's googly.'* "Did he get me?" John Dye asks, and he smiles as he reads the scorecard. Dye, not out, 1. "Well, he couldn't have bowled at me then." The day is over, and Northants have all Monday to score just 125 for victory. Meanwhile at Lord's Middlesex have only just started their reply to Yorkshire's first innings.

Dye, not out, 1. He has played his last part in this match, his last part in Kent's season. But he will be back next summer, and in the second match he will take five for 32 in 23 overs on "a flat 'un" at Lord's. The sequel at Brentwood will be typical John Dye. "It was Mike Denness's first match as captain, and the wicket was a bloody green, wet lifter. I was getting changed, and he said, 'You're not playing.' I was raving. I jumped in the car, drove all the way back to the Dartford Tunnel, and I realised I hadn't got any money. I had to write out a cheque for half a crown for the toll."

Sunday night in the little market town of Wellingborough. "We stayed at The Plough," John Dye remembers. "It was like a Trust House Forte, only not a very good one. It was right on the cross-roads, with all the traffic going by." "I had dinner on the second night with Brian Luckhurst," Alan remembers. "We've really made a bit of a balls of this," Alan says over the meal. "If we had a lead of 160, I'd fancy our chances. But 125, that's about thirty too few." But Brian is not so sure. "I'll tell you what," Alan says. "Get a bit of paper, scribble down the result and put it in your pocket. I'll do the same, and we'll see who's right."

Kent, all out for 177 and 130. How they could have done with the batting of Colin Cowdrey - as long as he was not in the grip of one of his more fanciful experiments. "Colin was a great theorist," John Dye says. "That's what I remember him for more than anything. I'll never forget this shot he

154

tried to play. The drap, he called it. It was a stand-up sweep." "It was a cross between a lap and a draw," Alan explains. "He'd seen Mike Smith doing it, and he wouldn't give it up, no matter how often it got him out. In the end the team delegated me to speak to him about it. The best time to catch him always was when he was on the throne. 'Colin,' I said, 'we've had a meeting. It's been decided you're above all this Mike Smith business.'"

On Monday morning Alan stands in the Wellingborough dressing room. "I said to the boys before we went out, 'There's one thing in our favour. They've got too long. Our only chance is if we get them pushing and prodding. If they play normal cricket, they'll walk it." He steps onto the Grace stone as he takes the field, and Brian is by his side. In Brian's pocket, the paper reads 'Kent, by 15 runs.' In Alan's, it says 'Northants, by 3 wickets.'

Behind them comes Colin Milburn, and an hour of him will make a nonsense of both pieces of paper. *'Wellingborough again provided a large crowd,'* Alan Gibson reports, and the early arrivals have been treated to some pre-match activity on the square. Movie cameramen have been filming Colin Milburn playing his famous hook. Behind the stumps Alan Knott has squatted down, and Colin has crashed away ball after ball that they have lobbed at him. But, Alan Knott writes, "they decided it would be far more realistic if the film were made during the actual match."

Colin Milburn on film. They set their cameras in readiness as he walks out of the pavilion and steps onto the Grace stone. 'Not of an age but for all time.' He clips the last ball of Graham's first over for a single and prepares for action against Shepherd. The first ball, Alan Gibson reports, *'he pushed amiably to short leg where Denness almost dropped the catch from sheer surprise.'* It is one for one, the cameramen pack up, and it is left to Steele and Lightfoot to build the innings with batting that is *'sensible'* in the Daily Telegraph, *'sedate'* in the Guardian, *'resolute'* in the Times. *'They took time to get used to the pace of the wicket and then collected runs where they could.'* At 45 for one, there are just 80 wanted for victory.

Lightfoot. "I rated Albert," Alan says. "He always played his shots," but *'Dixon turned a delivery back across this batsman whose late shot gave Johnson a simple catch.'* Mushtaq. "He was another who could win them the match in no time," but *'he was unlucky to get a delivery which popped up alarmingly, took the shoulder of the bat and carried into the hands of Luckhurst.'* Scores of nought and one in the match, the same as Colin Milburn. "The same as me, too," John Dye points out. All morning, though, Steele has been batting, two hours for his 34 runs. *'Now Shepherd produced a straight ball which went through his guard, and the verdict was leg before.'* "Steely," Alan smiles. "Never been out in his life."

In the privacy of the pavilion David Steele may think he was not out, but he knows better than to show his feelings on the square. "I remember nicking a ball onto my pads," Alan Dixon tells. "Frank Chester gave me out, and all I did was to drop my jaw in amazement. Colin Cowdrey hauled me out later, and he made me apologise. Perhaps if they did that today, there'd be more respect for the umpires." Steele has batted with patience, now Reynolds tries a more direct approach. *'Two balls later he too was lbw, attempting a wild pull.'* Perhaps Alan is right. The batsmen have got too long, and they are not playing normal cricket. *'It was 69 for five at lunch, with the pitch, though perhaps less awkward than the day before, always holding the threat of the unexpected.'*

"It was a low-scoring game on an interesting wicket," Alan recalls. "A good cricket wicket, not dangerous. A nice-sized ground, a proper county out-ground." Northants will come here every year till 1989, but by then another generation of cricketers will take a different view of its merits. "They complained about the wicket being low and slow," John Dye tells. "And of course the ground's not geared up to all the hospitality they have now."

"You'll probably think I'm jaundiced," Alan says, "but the game today comes second to the money that's made from it. The trend was there by the late sixties. I don't blame the players. We were fortunate to play in the right era. We'd have done it anyway, but to be paid for it was incredible."

Now there is the task of removing Ackerman and Crump, and Alan Dixon's thinking is clear. "When Hylton Ackerman came in, Derek Underwood was off." *'For Underwood does not like bowling at left-handers, and Ackerman's assault upon him had changed the course of the first innings.'* There are ten bowling changes in the first hour after lunch, and *'though usually in action from one end or the other, Underwood did not bowl a single ball to Ackerman.'* Alan turns to the pace of big Norman Graham, and *'Ackerman hit the first ball for six, the second for three, and Northants sailed past the 100.'* Just 23 to win and five wickets still in hand.

At Lord's the Yorkshire slow bowlers have made up for lost time and are bowling their county to victory. Defeat here at Wellingborough will leave Kent 32 points adrift with just five matches to play. Perhaps Colin Cowdrey's vision on the pavilion roof at Dover is not to be.

John Shepherd. "What a fine cricketer," John Dye says. "We called him Walter, I can't remember why. He had this lovely infectious laugh." He may have arrived on Saturday with a groin strain, but he has bowled over twenty overs today. "He had this ability to hit the deck and make it go," Alan says. "Colin used to say, 'you're either a digger-inner or a skidder-onner,' and John was a skidder-onner." *'At 102 Shepherd bowled Ackerman with a fine ball which moved away sharply from the pitch.'* The South African is gone at last, and Alan no longer has to switch his bowling from over to over. It will be Shepherd and Underwood from now on. "Unders would give you nothing," John Dye says, "and Walter would be bowling straight, you wouldn't hit him anywhere, not on that pitch."

102 for six, 102 for seven when Scott is *'brilliantly'* caught in the slips. But *'Johnson was in a properly stubborn mood and, with Crump taking the full weight of a deputy captain's responsibility, the score crept up slowly.'* Will they eke out the runs and bring the three-wicket victory that Alan guessed on the paper in his trouser pocket? Or will they collapse to 110 all out as Brian Luckhurst guessed? The two fielders look at one another, but they do not reveal their secrets. *'Then two snicks for four off Underwood brought a sparkle to Crump's eye,'* and with eight to win Brian's guess is eliminated.

Derek Underwood. "He was the best bowler I've ever seen on a wicket that's doing a bit," John Dye says, "but he was very defensive-minded. He was there to get wickets, and he reckoned that if he could stop the batsmen scoring, sooner or later they'd get frustrated and whack it up in the air." It is another style from the other great slow left-armer of John's career, Northants' Bedi. "Bishen used to drive us mad. They'd hit him for six, and he'd stand there and applaud. 'Oh, good shot.' But then, crafty sod, a couple of balls later it would be, 'Thank you very much.'"

'At 117 for seven victory was again but a breath away,' Alan Gibson writes, *'but Underwood bowled Johnson.'* The time goes on, and the tension mounts. *'One run but several overs later Crump was stumped by Knott off Underwood, and Durose, last man, came in with seven runs needed.'* It is not going to be Northants by three wickets, as it says in Alan's pocket.

Mushtaq and Milburn have each scored one run in the match, and now Sully and Durose must find their way to scoring another seven. Will they graft or will they try to hit? The age of one-day cricket has begun, and it will not be long before the batting of such tail-enders is put under the microscope. "You have six or seven batsmen to get runs," John Dye says. "It isn't for nine, ten, jack to get you out of the mire, they're there to take wickets. I mean, I don't hear anybody asking why your opening batsmen don't bowl."

It is four o'clock in the afternoon. The score is 118 for nine, and there are seven runs wanted for victory. *'One leg-bye later Durose swung wildly at Shepherd and was lbw.'* "His leg was quite a long way down," Alan recalls, "and it looked a bit dubious, but we didn't worry about that. It was just a wonderful feeling. We'd all been so hyped up, trying to finish the game." They have not missed John Dye's bowling after all - as nine of the ten wickets have fallen to Shepherd and Underwood. *'The two of them crossed W.G.'s memorial together.'* Behind them, Alan exchanges pieces of paper with Brian Luckhurst, and in this second contest he is happy to concede defeat.

Kent are still in the hunt for the championship, and they have a day at home before Colin Cowdrey returns to the helm. A month out of action and with just one net behind him, he will score a classy century. Then later in the month Derek Underwood will become the hero of all England as he takes seven Australian wickets to bring off a breathtaking victory on a rain-drenched Oval pitch. But the title that Colin Cowdrey predicted on the Dover pavilion roof will not be theirs this year, though it will come to them in 1970.

Alan Dixon, Kent, 1950 to 1970. He has played in a side where they told him, 'Don't take your pads off, you're batting seven,'' and he will play in a side that wins the championship. Three first-class centuries, 100 wickets in a season three times, figures of seven for 15 in a Gillette Cup semi-final: none of it would have happened if it had not been for the smell of that cut grass.

"It was great fun," Alan reflects. "I'd love it to start again tomorrow."

The Grove, Wellingborough, a first-class ground from 1946 to 1989. Dutch elm disease has destroyed the best of the trees, and in 1997 vandals set fire to the pavilion. But there is a new thatch now, and they have planted fast-growing poplars to replace the elms. W.G.'s memorial is still in place - 'Not for an age but for all time' - and there are many who yearn for the return of county cricket, not least the school's cricket professional.

Wellingborough, 1968. Kent have beaten Northants by five runs, and John Dye has bowled four balls and scored one run. "Poor old Browny," he laughs. "I got my win bonus, and he didn't." At Kent he is remembered as an awkward character - "Looking back, there were times when I should have bit my tongue" - but, when he moves to Northants, he comes into his own, a key part of the midland county's revival.

Wellingborough, 1998, and guess what. In his office in the school's sports centre sits their cricket professional, John Dye. Does he ever tell the boys about his achievements? "No, it's like a Dark Age to them. Except when they re-run the Gillette Final on the box, and they all come in. 'Hey, John, you were on TV.'"

Canterbury, 1998. On Alan Dixon's wall there hangs an oil painting of the Kent team that won the Gillette Cup in 1967, the work of Joan Lyons, a local artist. "It's your benefit next year," she says. "Can I do you a picture?" He thinks she means a photograph, and "to my amazement Colin came into the dressing room the next August. 'Don't rush off, Alan,' he said. 'We've got a little meeting.' And there were all the boys, and she was stood there with this framed picture. I was knocked out. It was the last thing I expected."

The portrait hangs on his wall, the eleven of them walking together onto the Canterbury ground. Colin at the front: "he was an artist with the bat; you don't get many like him now." Derek Underwood with his splayed-out feet: "I bowled at the other end from him, and I picked up the crumbs when he got the sevens and eights." John Shepherd: "we were very lucky with our overseas players." Brian Luckhurst, "he had so much spirit," little Alan Knott and big Norman Graham, "first out of the hat as a team player." They are all there. Mike Denness, Stuart Leary, even "dear old John Dye".

"I can see him now. 'Guess what, Al,' he said, 'it's gone.'"

Gone but not forgotten.

NORTHAMPTONSHIRE v KENT

Wellingborough, 10,11 & 12 August 1968

KENT WON BY 5 RUNS

KENT

M.H. Denness	c Steele b Scott	26	b Mushtaq		15
B.W. Luckhurst	b Scott	11	c Steele b Crump		12
+A.P.E. Knott	c Milburn b Steele	43	c & b Mushtaq		12
Asif Iqbal	lbw b Scott	0	lbw b Crump		47
S.E. Leary	b Scott	29	b Mushtaq		3
J.N. Shepherd	c Johnson b Crump	44	b Mushtaq		15
G.W. Johnson	c Milburn b Steele	0	lbw b Mushtaq		1
D.L. Underwood	c Crump b Steele	19	lbw b Crump		1
*A.L. Dixon	b Crump	2	b Mushtaq		13
J.N. Graham	not out	0	b Mushtaq		1
J.C. Dye	lbw b Crump	0	not out		1
Extras	nb 3	3	b 7, lb 1, nb 1		9
		177			**130**

1-19, 2-59, 3-63, 4-112, 5-116, 6-126, 7-170, 8-176, 9-177, 10-177
1-24, 2-28, 3-59, 4-85, 5-105, 6-112, 7-115, 8-119, 9-129, 10-130

Crump	11	5	19	3	26	6	48	3
Durose	7	2	13	0	3	1	6	0
Scott	29	10	80	4				
Sully	15	2	32	0				
Steele	18	9	30	3				
Mushtaq					23	7	67	7

NORTHAMPTONSHIRE

C. Milburn	b Graham	0	c Denness b Shepherd		1
D.S. Steele	c Denness b Underwood	5	lbw b Shepherd		34
A. Lightfoot	lbw b Dixon	14	c Johnson b Dixon		18
Mushtaq Mohammad	c Denness b Underwood	0	c Luckhurst b Underwood		1
H.M. Ackerman	st Knott b Dixon	82	b Shepherd		35
B.L. Reynolds	c & b Shepherd	19	lbw b Underwood		0
*B.S. Crump	b Shepherd	13	st Knott b Underwood		22
M.E. Scott	c Dixon b Graham	5	c Johnson b Shepherd		0
+L.A. Johnson	c Asif b Underwood	28	b Underwood		4
H. Sully	c Knott b Underwood	0	not out		1
A.J. Durose	not out	11	lbw b Shepherd		0
Extras	b 2,lb 3, nb 1	6	lb 3		3
		183			**119**

1-0, 2-21, 3-21, 4-23, 5-82, 6-116, 7-140, 8-148, 9-152, 10-183
1-1, 2-45, 3-47, 4-61, 5-63, 6-102, 7-102, 8-117, 9-118, 10-119

Graham	16	5	33	2	11	4	29	0
Dye	0.4	0	0	0				
Underwood	23.5	9	75	4	22	14	28	4
Dixon	19	7	38	2	15	5	25	1
Shepherd	16	9	31	2	26.5	11	34	5

Umpires: R.S. Lay and W.E. Phillipson

FRED'S LAST STAND

Worcestershire v Yorkshire

August 1968

chosen by Roy Booth

Roy Booth was born in Marsden, Yorkshire, in 1926. He kept wicket for Yorkshire from 1951 to 1955 and for Worcestershire from 1956 to 1968, returning briefly in 1970. Twice he claimed 100 victims in a season, and his final tally of 1126 dismissals places him twelfth in cricket's all-time list. An engineer after cricket, he is now Worcestershire's President.

He remembers a low-scoring match against his old county at Worcester.

Worcester County Ground on a hot Wednesday morning in August. The fourteenth-century cathedral tower rises high above the marquees and trees that line the meadow's edge, and the river Severn races along, full from all the recent rain. *'On Monday,'* Brian Chapman writes in the Guardian, *'half the playing area was a lake, and I was assured that a few more showers would have washed out play.'* But today there is only sunshine as the people of Worcester put down picnic baskets and settle in deck chairs. Roy is skippering Worcestershire in Tom Graveney's absence, and he is out on the square with Yorkshire's Brian Close.

Roy and Brian. Twenty years ago they were Yorkshire Colts. Along with Ray Illingworth and Fred Trueman. A new generation of cricketers emerging in a grey post-war world of rationing and reconstruction. Roy's Yorkshire career was brief, and for thirteen years he has kept wicket here in Worcester, "a lovely place to live and a good family club." But Close, Illingworth and Trueman have become the backbone of a great Yorkshire side. They have won six championship titles in nine seasons, and they need just one more victory to make it seven in ten. Roy is retiring in a fortnight so this will be his last encounter with his old county. "At that time we were good friends with all the other sides, but I'd played with most of the Yorkshire team. So it was always a special game for me." Brian Close asks Worcestershire to bat first, and soon Fred Trueman is marking out his run.

Fiery Fred. Ferocious Fred. Or just Fred. "On all wickets and in all conditions," Trevor Bailey writes, "it is doubtful that there has been a more complete fast bowler. He had fire, aggressiveness, pace, control, a glorious action, as well as that limitless confidence in his own ability." In 1968 his 307 wickets stand supreme in the history of Test cricket, more than fifty ahead of any rival. It is sixteen years since that explosive Test debut, when he reduced India to nought for four, and his glory years are over. But there is still a buzz of expectation in the Worcester crowd as he prepares to deliver the first ball.

160

Worcestershire versus Yorkshire. The two most successful counties of the past ten years. Yorkshire is only for Yorkshiremen, they have a stubborn streak, they expect to win and that is their great strength. "Every game they played," Roy reflects, "it was a feather in the cap to beat them. So they were used to playing a hard game. When you went out to bat, it felt like a pack around you, all the chuntering going on." But at times the stubborn self-belief is their weakness, too. "They've had so many needless arguments," Roy says. "If things are going too quiet, somebody somewhere has got to promote some problem. They don't seem happy unless they're having a squabble."

Worcestershire is another world from this. With its hop fields and apple orchards, its salmon fishing in the Severn and hill walking in the Malverns. "You've never been too pressured by captains or committees here." By 1968 Worcestershire is drawing players from all over the world. Emerging from the gabled pavilion, with its hanging baskets of flowers, are Ron Headley and Glenn Turner. From Kingston, Jamaica, and Dunedin, New Zealand. Resting a strain is Barbadian bowler Vanburn Holder, and away at the Oval, playing for England, is their all-rounder Basil D'Oliveira from Cape Town.

It is August 1968. Enoch Powell warns of the consequences of 'coloured immigration', but here at Worcester they are proud of their multi-racial team.

Worcestershire is one of cricket's smallest counties, yet "you could guarantee that there'd be a reasonable crowd," Roy says. Not like some of the other small counties. "One or two times at Northampton and Derby it was nearly bereft of spectators. It didn't feel like you were turning out." "I've played in front of two men and a dog at Northampton," his team mate Bob Carter recalls, "and the dog didn't want to stay."

The morning papers report Russian tanks rolling into the streets of Prague, but that is another world. There are two or three thousand in the ground as Glenn Turner and Ron Headley make their way to the middle. Glenn is a young man who has worked nights in a Dunedin bakery to save the air fare for this shot at county cricket, and he walks briskly forward. Ron is a long-established part of the side, and he prefers to take his time. "He'd sit on the bench," Glenn writes, "and hit himself on the back of his neck with his fist. 'To break down the adhesions,' he'd say. 'They're out there waiting for us,' I'd say, and his response was always the same. 'Don't worry, Budge, they can't start without us.' And when he did appear he wandered out so slowly and took such short steps that I mostly had to wait for him to catch up." *'Headley, in fact, played every ball in Trueman's opening over, off-driving his third, a full toss, for four to open the scoring.'*

It is August 1968. Worcestershire's innings is in the hands of a Jamaican and a New Zealander. Nissan enter the British market with a range of seven Datsun cars, Plessey bid to take over English Electric, and 300 doctors a year emigrate to the United States.

Ron is the son of Jamaica's greatest batsman George Headley, and he has gravitated here during his teenage years in Dudley. "One day I was taken to Worcester by my best friend's father," he remembers. "I fell in love with the ground. I can remember it as if it was yesterday. I was sitting in a deck chair. Martin Horton was batting, and I can remember him hooking Peter Loader. And I'm day-dreaming and thinking, 'I'd give anything in the world to play out there.' It's one of the most beautiful grounds in the world. Even today it's retained that village green. And the supporters, they are very special." *'Headley,'* Alan Gibson writes in the Times, *'made one hook off Nicholson, which had all the older generation nodding their heads in happy remembrance. Then Turner produced a ringing off-drive.'* After ten overs the score is 37 for no wicket, and Fred's new-ball burst is over.

Fred. It is eighteen years now since he first appeared on this ground, the raw nineteen-year-old miner's son. But he is 37 now, and even he must know that his pre-match appearances in the opposition dressing room don't carry the threat that once they did. Bob Carter recalls the patter. "'Who are you? I haven't played against you before.' 'Ah, Ron, hit you on the head last year, didn't I? That's one wicket for me.' He wouldn't have said it was psychology because 'that's rubbish', but that's what it was."

"I remember one game at Bradford," Roy tells. "For some reason we only seemed to have half a side out, and I was skippering. 'Who's all these lads, Boothy? It won't be long before I'll be seeing thee out there.' And Alan Duff, he'd got a Free Foresters hat on. He went down the steps, it was like going down into a little bear pit, and Fred saw him coming. He never liked the jazz-hatters." A.R. Duff, scores of one and two, they are his last runs for Worcestershire, and only stubborn batting by Roy himself prevents a two-day defeat. But that was 1961, and this is 1968. Just ten overs have gone, it is 37 for no wicket, and Brian Close turns to the off-spin of Geoff Cope.

37 for no wicket, and Worcestershire have the good start that they need with such an inexperienced team. It is bad enough that so many of their championship side of three years ago are gone now. But today there is no Tom Graveney, down at the Oval for the final Test against Australia. No Vanburn Holder. And no Basil D'Oliveira. Yesterday evening Basil pulled up at traffic lights in the centre of Worcester, only to be greeted by Fred. "What the hell are you doing here, Bas? You should be at the Oval, old son. Roger Prideaux's dropped out, and you've been named." "I thought Fred had gone off his rocker," Basil recalls. "Okay," Fred says, "come into this pub and we'll check it out with the landlord." For Yorkshire, Geoff Boycott is injured and Ray Illingworth at the Test, but "on paper," Roy recalls, "we weren't a side anything like as good as Yorkshire were. They'd got a good side out."

37 for no wicket. Perhaps Brian Close's decision to ask Worcestershire to bat was not so clever. But then Ray Illingworth is at the Oval, and Brian is having to manage without his master pitch-reader. "Raymond was always

very good on wickets," Roy remembers. "He was still looking after the square at Farsley when he was England's chairman of cricket. I wouldn't think he was wrong many times." Fred is official vice-captain, but he spends the toss in the Worcestershire dressing room. Is Fred a good reader of a pitch? Roy chuckles. "Fred prophesied how they'd play after you'd played on them. 'I knew it'd go like that. I knew it'd turn.' Raymond would probably tell you before. I think that was the big difference."

It is ten past twelve on the first day, and it seems that the pitch is already taking spin. *'Headley, deceived by the amount of turn when attempting a hit to mid wicket, was bowled by the off-spinner's third ball.'* Three balls later Alan Ormrod *'attempted a quick single, only to see a perfect throw from Taylor run out Turner.'* A quick single to Ken Taylor? There is not a lot of experience in this Worcestershire batting.

The openers are gone, and the Yorkshire pack closes in on the batsmen, none closer than their captain. "Brian was so brave," his team mate Don Wilson recalls. "He fielded in this silly short leg position." *'The Yorkshire skipper, in fact, was near to plucking the ball almost from Ormrod's bat.'* Roy knows Brian of old, but it is an unfamiliar world for some of his batsmen. "Some of our younger players had never been in that sort of atmosphere before." *'Seeing what was afoot, Close crowded fielders round the bat and managed to unsettle Ormrod, who was bowled apparently between his legs.'* 53 for three. *'Barker was leg before, sweeping at Cope.'* 62 for four. *'And Fearnley, dicing with imminent death for 70 minutes, succumbed to the last of four lbw appeals.'* 67 for five.

The fielders around the bat, chuntering and creating an atmosphere. Is this what we now call sledging? "Oh no, it wasn't unpleasant or bad-tempered," Roy explains. "And if anybody turned round and said, 'Look, do you mind keeping quiet?', that was invariably sufficient."

Cricket at Worcester. John Arlott, in his days as a poetry producer, captured the scene in verse.

> *'Dozing in deck-chair's gentle curve,*
> *Through half-closed eyes I watched the cricket,*
> *Knowing the sporting press would say*
> *'Perks bowled well on a perfect wicket.''*

Reg Perks has long retired and perhaps, in their glorious championship years of '64 and '65, the Worcester wickets are not so perfect. "In the mid-sixties," Roy tells, "our wickets were very sporting, to say the least. They were made that way because Coldwell and Flavell were as good as any pair of opening bowlers in the country." And what do the players of the sixties think about such wickets? "Nobody seemed to bother too much in those days. We played on open wickets. Up in the North everybody always played on them. Batting is certainly more difficult, but it makes better bowlers and in the long run it makes better batters, too."

163

So here we are in August 1968. A hot sunny morning, a happy Worcester team and a crowd at peace in deck chairs and on benches. Or perhaps not. Perhaps there is an edge today to the bowlers' appeals, a tension in the game that will be understood by those who were at Sheffield last month when the teams last met. Understood by the umpires, especially. Ron Lay and George Pope. "By a strange quirk," Roy tells, "it was the same two umpires."

The Sheffield game was another that Roy captained in Tom Graveney's absence, and Fred was there in the Worcester dressing room before the start. "Lets see what wickets there are for me here today. What's thy name then, lad? How you going, Boothy? Captain, blimey!" But it did not last long. There in front of his own Sheffield crowd, to the shock of the whole Worcester side, Fred was made twelfth man. "He'd not been playing very well, and they thought it would be a spinner's wicket." Who among the rest of us can imagine his hurt? Why, only a fortnight earlier, on that very Sheffield ground, had he not captained Yorkshire against the Australians, taken six wickets and led his team to an innings victory? Fiery Fred, the greatest wicket-taker in Test match history, not picked for a routine county game? "It's a major problem when we finish," Don Wilson reflects. "Because, let's face it, none of us think we've had it." For all the bravado, Fred is a sensitive man.

Roy recalls that game at Sheffield. "He spent most of the time in our dressing room, chatting away. 'A right prat is Close', that sort of thing. Then on the second morning he came straight in to us. 'You know what happened last night. We called at the Sovereign at Shepley on the way back, and Illy's in there with Ron Lay. Ron's staying with Illy at Pudsey. He's stopping with him.'" Then at the end of a hard-fought day Brian Close edged the ball into the slips, and Ron Lay gave him not out. "Basil D'Oliveira's not a demonstrative man, but he kicked the ball right across the ground. Fred, of course, who was a hundred yards away, he said, 'He knocked the cover off it; I could see that.'" *The turning point came on the second evening,'* the Worcestershire handbook records, *'when a confident appeal for a catch was surprisingly turned down.'* "You don't fall out with players," Roy reflects, "but the game didn't finish in the best of spirits."

So here at Worcester, perhaps the crowd can sense that there is "a lot of spirit in the game". It is 71 for five, and Ron Lay is umpiring at the bowler's end. "He was a tall, thin man," Roy recalls, "with a thin, black moustache, a bit like one of those gamblers in Westerns." He is that rare character, a first-class umpire who has never played county cricket, "he was just a club cricketer in Northampton", but he is in his thirteenth year on the circuit and people have grown used to his unusual sense of humour. "I appealed for an lbw once," Somerset's Ken Biddulph recalls, "and he just turned round to me. 'My god, you must be having a bad season,' he said." There is only a fortnight to go now till he retires, and he could do without another three days of batsmen not walking, bowlers appealing for everything.

Geoff Cope spins the ball to Roy Booth, who pushes it out to mid-wicket and sets off for a sharp single. Don Wilson swoops on the ball. He is the other half of that Wilson-Taylor partnership that makes runs so difficult on both sides of the wicket. Ron Lay moves to the side of the stumps, and crack, Don recalls, "I hit him smash on his legs, absolutely finished him." *The jocularity with which a cricket crowd invariably greets a mishap to an umpire was stifled when it became clear that he was hurt.'* "He was a lovely man, and I was so disheartened. I knew I'd hurt him very badly." *'He was so badly lamed he had to be carried off and taken to hospital.'* "He never umpired again," Roy tells. "He wasn't the greatest, but he was a nice chap."

So Henry Horton, the Worcestershire coach, takes over at square leg, *'Horton conducted himself to the manner born and never once joined in an appeal'*, while poor George Pope is left to umpire at both ends for the rest of three long, hot and tense days. He is 57 years old now, and he has already been on duty for 15 days in the last three weeks. "It was the biggest cock-up of a match of all time," Don Wilson recalls. "Poor old George couldn't handle both ends. It all got too much for him."

By half past three Worcestershire are all out for 101, Bob Carter last man out, bowled Nicholson, nought. Tony Nicholson has returned for this second spell, but Fred comes off with just those five wicketless overs this morning. "Fred was fielding down at third man," Roy remembers, "and he was signalling that he'd like to come back on. In his heart he still thought he could bowl them out, but he'd lost that nip and movement and he wasn't effective. I can still remember him waving to Closey, to say 'I'm ready to come back', and Closey was walking backwards, not even looking at him."

Now it is the turn of the Worcestershire opening bowlers. *'Coldwell was rubbing his hands in eagerness to get at the champions in conditions which he relished,'* Brian Chapman writes, *'and indeed had his old sparring partner, Flavell, been on hand Yorkshire might have been hard pressed to see the evening through.'* But this is 1968. Jack Flavell is 37 and retired, and Len Coldwell is 35. "He was struggling a bit by then," Roy says. The golden days of their partnership are memories now. "The ground was close to the city," Roy recalls, "and a lot of people used to come in for an hour in the evening. At the New Road end, where there are offices now, it used to be packed at night. And for some reason, when I look back to that time, all I seem to remember is that we've declared, and Flavell and Coldwell are bowling that last half hour or so. It was a really key period of the game. We must have batted at that time, but I can only remember Flavell and Coldwell bowling. And the crowd roaring them on and cheering. We couldn't wait to get out onto the ground." And today? "We might get a few more in, but you don't get that same influx. A lot of people came out of the city and walked into the St Johns area. Now they all jump in cars and drive over the bridge."

There is more than half an hour to play tonight, and the wickets are soon falling. Len Coldwell has Taylor lbw. Then Bob Carter, *'moving the ball sinfully away'*, has Sharpe caught in the slips. "Bob had a very ungainly run." The Galloping Major, Glamorgan's Peter Walker calls him: "He used to run like a shire horse, and he was always laughing. Most unusual for a fast bowler." "When he delivered," Roy tells, "his arm came right across his body, and his head dropped right down. I'm sure he never saw an lbw appeal." In thirteen overs before tea, Yorkshire score just eleven singles.

Among the crowd are some of the schoolboys of Christopher Whitehead Secondary Modern where Bob Carter teaches Maths and Science in the winter. "Every July," Bob tells, "a boy would come to the pavilion door, ask if he could speak to Mr Carter. 'Mr Bourne would like to know if you want to work at the school next term, sir. Could you give him a ring?' One year we didn't bowl a ball in the last match. So I rang the school. 'If it's like this tomorrow lunchtime, I'll start teaching in the afternoon.' And I did." But then a cricketer's wages do not cover the winter. Alan Ormrod is a hairdresser, Norman Gifford a painter-decorator, Glenn Turner a cardex clerk, Len Coldwell a car salesman, and Duncan Fearnley is making cricket bats in the corner of a fishing tackle shop. It all helps to keep their sporting days in perspective. "You'd come off the park after a terrible day," Bob recalls, "you'd be taking your boots off, and you'd say, 'Could have been worse, lads, could have been down the pit.' You've been doing what other people would give their eye-teeth to do."

It is August 1968. The Post Office advertises its new two-class postal system while the Department of Education announces that there are now more than 500 comprehensive schools.

Teatime for the players, teatime for the members, too. Worcester is a family club, and there with her cakes in the members' tea room is Roy's wife Joyce. "I started in 1965," she remembers, and she tells how she parked the Ford Cortina under the chestnut trees and let out their labrador Candy for a walk. Then, when she called in for a cup of tea, "Can you help out?" they asked. It was the second of the championship years, and her date-and-walnut cakes are still being enjoyed in 1988 when the title is won a third time.

"The thing about Worcester," Bob Carter explains, "is it's a parochial ground, it's a village ground. If we got eight thousand in, I'd probably know two thousand of them by sight. I'd walk into town with the wife, and somebody'd say 'Hallo, Bob'. 'Who's that?' she'd say. 'I haven't a clue, but he sits in a deckchair four places from the chestnut tree.' 'And who's that?' 'I don't know. He works nights at Archdales, he rides an A7 motorbike, and he parks it in front of the pavilion.' You know all these people." In 1968 the world has a slower pace, and in this cathedral city it seems that people are contented with their habits. "The motor car hadn't reached the proportions it has now. People were much happier to go to a spot and spend time there."

It is August 1968. British Rail increases the price of its tickets to London. Two pounds, thirteen shillings from Leeds; one pound, fifteen from Bristol. A plan is announced to extend the M5 into the centre of Birmingham. The Edgbaston Expressway, they call it.

'Coldwell conjured a real beauty which came back at Hampshire and wrecked his stumps.' 18 for three. 22 for four when *'Padgett dragged a ball into his stumps.' 'The pitch became trickier as it dried,'* Alan Gibson writes, *'and the batting had that kind of nervous palsy which overtakes modern Yorkshire sides a couple of times a season.'*

Worcestershire 101, Yorkshire 22 for four, and the game is already 80 overs old. "It was a wicket that wasn't easy to score on," Roy recalls, "and the crowd really enjoyed it. It was more like a Yorkshire crowd watching cricket. They knew there was a battle going on, and they loved that bit of devil in it. If somebody was appealing, they liked to jeer, they liked to give a shout."

If there is a battle to be fought, there is nobody better to fight it than Brian Close. *'Close got his head down in that way that he has, and somehow Hutton stayed with him for 67 minutes.'* Richard Hutton, another like Ron Headley who must suffer the comparisons with a legendary father. "I got 150 at Dudley against Somerset in my early days," Ron recalls. "Tom Graveney and Bill Alley said it was the best precision striking on the on-side they'd ever seen from a left-hander. Then somebody in the bar turned round and said, 'Well played, but you'll never be as good as your dad.'" *'Hutton made a speciality, in defence and attack, of the shot that goes off the inside edge and does not hit the leg stump. Yorkshire might have been grateful enough, but I fancy his father would have disowned him.'* It is 67 for four when he skies a ball in the direction of the Severn Bar. "I think Richard hooked or swept," Roy recalls. "I don't know how far I ran, but I did catch it eventually." In the Evening News' cartoon highlights of the match, *'Hutton was superbly caught by Roy Booth, just before the ball dropped into somebody's beer'.*

Hutton is Brian Brain's second wicket, and a more vital third one follows ten minutes from the close. The New Road end is full of late arrivals from the city, roaring their bowlers on, when he raps Brian Close on the pads and appeals to a hot and tired George Pope. *'It seemed to observers behind the arm to be inches high and missing the off stump. But umpire Pope, after a day of unremitting and unaided devotion to duty, could be pardoned a lapse.'* It is 80 for six at the close, and there is still all to play for.

Brian Brain and Bob Carter are the best of mates away from the game, but for most of the sixties they vie for a single place in the team. "We had this wonderful love-hate relationship," Bob reflects. "When we were bowling together, it was good. 'He's got a wicket,' I'd be thinking. 'Come on, I've got to get another one.' And he'd be thinking the same down the other end."

Brian and Bob, the drinking mates who compete for the one place. The ageing Len Coldwell, supping his beer and persuading the young Glenn

Turner to forget the early nights. The youngsters, Roy Barker and Jim Yardley, still reeling from the raw competitiveness of this fixture. Roy Booth, laughing with all his old Yorkshire pals. And Ron Headley, always the last to complete his showering and changing. "We were a disparate bunch," Bob Carter remembers. "There were definitely cliques. We'd drink with the opposition, then everybody would star burst. But usually by eleven o'clock you'd find the whole team together, nattering away around the bar."

It is August 1968. Thursday morning's newspapers tell of Russian troops occupying the major cities of Czechoslovakia, but "I don't think we'd even taken it in," Roy says. "We had tunnel vision for that game."

Brian Brain and Bob Carter. Brian bowls Binks. Bob bowls Cope. Then Bob has Fred lbw. What is it Roy said? "When he delivered, his head dropped right down. I'm sure he never saw an lbw appeal." Then Brian bowls Wilson. Yorkshire, 126 all out. Their lead is just 25.

It is the summer of 1968. A new epidural technique relieves pain in childbirth, the first abortion clinics open, and Pope Paul's encyclical forbids the use of artificial birth control.

Ron Headley and Glenn Turner make their way back to the middle after lunch. It is ten years now since Ron came for trial, and he relives the memory of watching Alan Spencer batting. One of those great talents who never achieve their potential in the middle. "I'm green and raw. And I'm standing outside the net, watching this guy hooking and driving. It's like I could be watching Tom Graveney. And I'm thinking, 'I'll never become as good as that.' So I said, 'Who's that?' And somebody said to me, 'Oh, he's a second teamer.' That was a shock to the system, I can tell you."

First impressions. Last summer Glenn Turner spent his night-time bakery earnings on a one-way ticket to England, and at Edgbaston David Brown bowled to him. "All he did was hit the ball back to me," David recalls. "Mentally he was on the back foot. I thought he hadn't a hope of playing county cricket.' It is much the same here at Worcester, but they see something different. "I bowled at him for forty minutes," Bob Carter remembers, "and I don't think he played one attacking shot. It was total concentration all the time." "He was a slip of a lad," Roy recalls. "He'd never weigh above ten stone. But you could see he had something a bit different. His stance was really good for a young chap. He stood up straight and faced the bowler." Here at the weekend he made his maiden hundred in nearly five hours. But who can guess that in fourteen years' time, on this same ground, he will be completing his hundredth hundred, a blistering 311 in less than six hours? "He'd got a little bit of hardness about him in his own way," Roy reflects. "People thought he was going to come good. But I don't think we ever imagined he'd be able to score quickly like that."

Quick scoring is on nobody's mind here against Yorkshire. Fred's new ball spell is just three overs this time, and it is Richard Hutton who traps Ron

Headley lbw. Then Alan Ormrod joins Glenn Turner and painstakingly they compile a fifty partnership. For Brian Chapman, it all makes for a grim day out. *'W.H. Davies once lamented that in this life "we have no time to stand and stare". For six and a half hours there was little else to do but stare - and precious little to stare at.'* The sun beats down, Fred is out to grass in the deep, and Tony Nicholson retires to the pavilion, *'overcome by the unaccustomed heat'*. Eventually Don Wilson has both batsmen caught, and on the stroke of tea Roy Barker comes out of his shell to sweep two leg-side fours. *'It was sensible of Trueman not to run after them,'* Alan Gibson writes, *'though perhaps he might have made his immobility less ostentatious'*.

After tea Barker plays on to his wicket, *'the ball, in the prevailing lazy mood, barely trickling into the stumps'*. Duncan Fearnley bats for an hour and a half for 13 before George Pope gives his eighth lbw. Fearnley is in the middle order now that Glenn Turner has taken over the opener's spot, and he has just one more game to play before his first-class career is over. Here in 1968 he resents the young New Zealander, but "in the long term," Glenn writes, "he said I did him a favour". With a prospering bat-making business he will soon take great pleasure in driving past the ground in a Rolls Royce.

It is 126 for five, a lead of 101 and only Jim Yardley is left of the specialist batsmen. And Jim only has one shot. "A squirter," Roy calls him. "Jim was a left-hander. He scored more runs behind the wicket than any other batter I've seen. I've seen them put two or three gullies in, and he'd still get them through." Bob Carter remembers a fifty against the great West Indian off-spinner Lance Gibbs. "He'd got two slips and two gullies, and the ball was going through them like a rocket. Lance took the bat off him to look for all the edge marks. 'Christ!' he said. 'They're all in the middle.'" But Jim is a gutsy player, and cricket is about more than style. Alan Spencer, a Tom Graveney in the nets, plays just 27 games in five years. But Jim plays 260, and he is still playing for his second county Northants in 1981. Even in that last season he is good enough to battle out a draw against the touring Australians. "Jesus," Rodney Hogg explodes after yet another squirt. "Are you really a first-teamer?" And Jim looks calmly back at him. "If I said I wasn't, would you bowl any slower at me?" Here at Worcester he comes off with a career-best 43 not out, and the total is 161 for seven. *'The crowd strolled homewards over the Severn bridge, no doubt happy enough to recollect that they, like the swans and the anglers, had at last been able to bask for a whole day under blue skies.'*

At the Oval England have reached 272 for four, and Basil D'Oliveira is 24 not out. In this year's Wisden he is 33 years old, a man in his prime, and he longs to be picked for the tour of South Africa, to step out onto the Newlands ground in his native Cape Town, to play for England, the country that has taken him so much to its heart. "When he was first picked," Roy recalls, "he was playing a benefit match for me at Beaconsfield. He was chaired off the field."

Basil. In next year's Wisden he will be 37. Born not in 1934 but 1931. "And that's where it's staying," he writes, "although I can assure you I'm a little older than my birth certificate states." Older probably than Fred, who is sitting with George Pope in the bar. "Which way are you going back tomorrow, Fred?" George asks. He lives near Chesterfield, and he is on duty there the next day. "Will you give us a lift?" "Yes, of course I will."

"George was a very honest bloke," Bob Carter tells. "Blunt. To the point." In the previous match Ron Lay stayed with Illy at Pudsey, and he gave Brian Close not out. Now George Pope is to travel home with Fred.

"At that time," Roy says, "there was a great respect from players to the umpires. They always had a drink with you in the bar, and sometimes they'd say a little word to you." Like Charlie Elliot at Portsmouth last month. Roy Booth, acting skipper again, is facing Hampshire's Peter Sainsbury. "He turned one, and he wasn't noted as a big spinner. 'If Sains can turn one,' Charlie whispered, 'I should declare.' 'Right, I will,' I said." Worcestershire are batting comfortably at 257 for six, but Roy has Basil bowling off-breaks and Hampshire are soon out for 83.

It is August 1968. Worcester Rep presents 'A Taste of Honey' at the Swan Theatre while Rex Harrison appears as Doctor Dolittle at the Scala cinema. Top of the Pops is the Crazy World of Arthur Brown with 'Fire'.

So to the final morning. Fred is there in the Worcester dressing room again. "All of a sudden," Bob Carter recalls, "the door burst open. Closey's there. He hurls a great big leather bag in. 'You've been in there for two bloody days,' he says. 'You can change with the buggers today.'"

At least Fred gets to bowl. Tony Nicholson hits Brian Brain's off stump with the third ball. Then with his second ball Fred delivers a great appeal to George Pope, his passenger for the journey home. The finger goes up straightaway, the ninth lbw of the match. There is only Bob Carter to bat, and at this point in his career Bob has 311 wickets to his name and just 194 runs. "After the first day," Roy reflects, "you got the impression that a score of 200 in the last innings would be a lot of runs to get. But we were only 130-some ahead, and we were thinking, 'Well, this is a little bit on the light side'."

Bob Carter. His top score this summer is six; "he'd be delighted with that," Roy chuckles. Is he an old-fashioned tail-ender, going out for a whack? Does he back away to leg? Or what? "I never remember what Bob actually did. He just missed the ball all the time." Off the fifth ball of the over, he is clean bowled by Fred, a pair in the match, and the teams come off. Yorkshire need 139 to win, and they have got till half past five to get them.

"I was Fred's last victim in championship cricket, wasn't I?" Bob Carter says. The last wicket Fred ever takes for Yorkshire. Nobody here at Worcester knows it, not even his team mates, but he will play three more wicketless matches, then in the winter he will quietly call it a day. At the end of the Scarborough Festival, the band strikes up a haunting, mellow version of 'Old

Man River', and "he started crying," Don Wilson recalls. "We all knew that was the end of him. He was a very soft man, you know." It is the end of an era: for Fred, for Yorkshire, for English cricket. But he has not played his final part in this game here at Worcester.

Yorkshire, champions six times in the last nine years. Kent, their main challengers, are losing so victory here will clinch the title. And the prospects for next year? Fred has taken his last wicket, Ray Illingworth is in a contract dispute, and Ken Taylor is retiring. Don Wilson expresses his anxieties, but Richard Hutton remains optimistic. "Ah, Fred's past it, anyway." "Well, Fred was past it," Don says, "but he'd been there, and that meant such a lot." And what does it mean to Don? "Playing with a man like Fred has got to be one of the great honours of my life. Not just because of his bowling. Fred was an enormous character wherever he went. He was such a well-loved man."

Roy Booth leads out his team. "I did enjoy captaining, I must say. I liked watching what was happening with the bowlers and the fielders, and I seemed to get a good response." A lead of only 138, a stiflingly hot sun, and Roy at 41 years of age has to combine this captaincy with keeping wicket. In the first over he lets through four byes. "Yes, it was a bit arduous in this game."

The days of Flavell and Coldwell in their prime are over. Len coughs and splutters his way back to his mark, and young Glenn Turner crouches at short leg. Not as silly as Brian Close fields and not as innocent since Len confided in him. "There was a time I'd bowl two balls a season that put bat-padder in danger. I reckon now it's two an over." At the other end Bob Carter runs in, the Galloping Major whose head drops away in the delivery.

Sharpe, Taylor, Padgett, Close. They have all played for England, and Hampshire and Hutton will soon follow them. Boycott and Illingworth may be missing, but this is still a formidable batting line-up.

The first wicket falls at seven, Sharpe, *'backing up too fervently and too far'*, is unable to get his bat down when *"Yardley with a lightning throw from the cover'* hits the stumps. The second falls at seven, too, with Bob Carter removing Padgett's off-stump. Taylor *'managed only six runs in 50 minutes'*, and it is 24 for three when he edges a catch to Roy. *'Yorkshire's three top batsmen had scored eighteen between them in two innings, hard to excuse even in a steamy, misty atmosphere helpful to Carter's type of attack.'*

At 32 for three, Bob Carter again gallops in to bowl, this time to the left-handed Close. *'The Yorkshire captain padded up, presumably expecting in-swing, but the ball went straight through'* and, according to the Worcester Evening News, *'he was plumb lbw'*. In the Times, though, *'Close seemed to consider the ball was going down leg side.'* He may have got away with a snick to the slips at Sheffield, but he has suffered two lbws from George Pope here. "What a pity Henry Horton couldn't do one end," Don Wilson reflects. "Poor old George couldn't handle both ends. He gave the most appalling decisions." There are 106 runs still wanted, a championship waiting to be won, and only Hampshire and Hutton left of the front-line batsmen. *'Yorkshire were now in distress.'*

Back at Sheffield in July it was the *'vigorous on-driving'* of Hampshire that saw Yorkshire to victory, and he soon looks to dominate the bowling. Brian Brain *'all but grazed his off stump but, like the splendid fellow he is, Hampshire struck the following ball with lovely speed through the covers.'* Next summer he will be the first Englishman to score a century at Lord's on Test debut, and many think that he has more natural talent than Geoff Boycott. But he does not have the same single-minded concentration. Lunch at 61 for four will leave all to play for in the afternoon, but alas for Yorkshire Gifford's final ball before the break draws a fateful shot. *'It threatened no danger at all, but Hampshire leaned to cut it and chopped it into his stumps.'* Brian Chapman is in no doubt about the quality of his batting - *'his 31 was emphatically the only innings of thoroughbred class in the match'* - but his dismissal changes the atmosphere at the lunch table. "That was a good wicket to get," Roy says. "The stand was getting worrying with such a small total. And obviously, with Jack Hampshire being out, it encouraged the bowlers again." 61 for five, another 78 for victory and the championship.

At the Oval Basil is batting, and Charlie Elliott is the bowler's end umpire when he runs the single to complete his fifty. "Well played," he whispers out of the corner of his mouth. "My god, you're going to cause some problems." *'D'Oliveira set himself on automatic steering. He batted with the minimum of effort, never a hair out of place.'* When he completes his century, Charlie's whisper is louder. "Christ, the cat's among the pigeons now." But his team mates in Worcester know nothing of such politics. "We just thought, he's booked his passage," Bob Carter says.

It is the summer of 1968. The Queen opens the new Hayward Gallery, an American oil tycoon buys London Bridge, and in East London a 22-storey system-built tower block, Ronan Point, collapses.

The five-minute bell rings, and Yorkshire return to their task of scoring 78 more runs to clinch their seventh championship in ten years. Every single is hard-fought, and Hutton has just 19 in 97 minutes when *'Coldwell found one that dipped in to bowl him'*. 60 to win, and *'Cope merged motionless into the haze for 40 minutes in scoring a single.'* He is caught at bad-pad, and there are still 45 to win. *'Meanwhile Binks settled into the sort of sturdy rescue operation which is his speciality. If anybody could bring it off, he and that other cunning man, Wilson, would. His defence was rocklike, his sweeps firm and safe. After four mortal hours the score was 111, and umpire Pope's waving hat indicated the last 20 overs.'* "The crowd was absolutely on hot pins all the time," Roy recalls. 111 for seven, just 28 to win in 20 overs.

It was Jimmy Binks that took the wicket-keeper's place from Roy in 1955, and Jimmy has not missed a championship match since. "He was a useful batsman," Roy says. "He wasn't a hitter, but he could work it around."

There lies a great difference between the two counties. Flavell, Coldwell, Carter: "If they were nine, ten, jack, you thought it won't be long before we're all out." But there are no equivalents at Yorkshire. "Everybody was expected to bat. It was brought out in the coaching." And Roy remembers the Yorkshire committee all sitting behind the Headingley nets in April. "Fourteen or fifteen of them. We never had that pressure here in Worcester."

Perhaps such pressure is what allows Yorkshire to pull so many games out of the fire. As Don Wilson bats today, does he allow himself a moment to remember that innings here seven years ago? Coming out at number eleven with his left arm in plaster from elbow to fingers. 37 to win in 25 minutes, and he smashed 29, the winning hit a lofted drive over Jack Flavell's head. There are 28 to win now, but *'Wilson hung his bat out quite senselessly at Coldwell.'* 111 for eight. *'Then Binks's marathon ended with a slip catch, and his obvious mortification was understandable.'* He has batted for two hours forty minutes for 34, and now it is 123 for nine. Sixteen to win, and just Fred and Tony Nicholson left to score them. "Fred could get runs," Roy says, "and Tony wasn't the worst batter, either."

Fred is giving George Pope a lift home. First ball Len Coldwell appeals for an lbw, and Fred survives. The next over Norman Gifford raps him on the pad, and he survives again. He has still not scored after twenty minutes when Roy Barker throws down the stumps and they all appeal for a certain run out. Not out once more. "It had been a hard job for George," Roy reflects. "The game was always going to be dwelling on a few runs, and there were a few lbws. Towards the end it got keen, and George was really trying to control it. 'Come on, come along,' he was saying."

"Fred was a good striker of the ball," Bob Carter recalls. "A really good striker. Like Darren Gough." "Fred had a fine eye," Trevor Bailey writes. "His pièce de résistance was a belligerent cross-batted mow that was liable to send the ball anywhere." And Trevor should know. At Scarborough in 1963 he shared a partnership of 120 in 67 minutes with Fred, and Fred scored a hundred of them. With six sixes and eleven fours. Today two sixes and one four will be enough to win the championship.

With Tony Nicholson surviving another lbw appeal, *'Trueman was now in charge and, being a man of quite basic ways, he took the one course Yorkshire had neglected. He attacked. Surviving goodness knows how many lbw appeals, he lunged hugely at Gifford for two boundaries to square leg.'* 134 for nine, just five to win.

It is over three hours now since lunch, three hours of heat and tense cricket, and Fred tries to win the game off Brian Brain's bowling. *'How Trueman failed to get a touch when he twice swished at Brain we shall never know.'* Len Coldwell is exhausted, Norman Gifford has been clattered for two fours, and Brian Brain fails to finish the match in his over. *'Booth, trying every move on the board, made his fourteenth bowling change of the innings by bringing back Carter for his fifth spell.'*

"I was a long spell bowler," Bob Carter tells. "I didn't like short spells. I was fielding at deep square leg. I thought, this one's drifted away. I hadn't had a bowl for a while, and I thought I'm not going to bowl again. I was a bit stiff. It got to one to tie, two to win, and at that moment Roy whistled me in. There was no 'Get yourself loose or anything'. It was 'Come and bowl, Bob.' I'm coming uphill, I'm stiff as a board, and I knew if I bowled anything loose on the off-side Fred would go for it. So I thought, until I get loose, I'll take a risk and put it down the leg." Three balls, three dots. The moment of truth is approaching.

527 runs in 298 overs in three days, and it has all come to this one moment. Bob has been Fred's last ever wicket for Yorkshire. Will he now bowl the ball that gives Fred the glory of winning the championship with the bat? "It was the most memorable game I ever played," Roy thinks. "It was a nail-biting game, and the crowd really enjoyed it. There was nothing given. You didn't expect anything given. And that's how it went right to the end."

Roy is retiring in a fortnight. Only twice in thirteen seasons with Worcestershire has he been on the winning side against Yorkshire. What a wonderful finale it would be for him to win today! What a marvellous memory to cherish for the rest of his life!

And Bob Carter, what a moment this could be for him! They are all cheering him on: the man in the deckchair four places from the chestnut tree, the night-shift worker who parks his motorbike by the pavilion, the schoolboys from Christopher Whitehead Secondary Modern. One to tie, two to win. Their Maths master could be the hero of the day any moment now.

But Fred. To win a championship with the bat, that would be a story to tell.

Bob Carter gallops in once more, the fourth ball of the over. "It's muck or nettles time now, I thought. Fred's going to swing. So I thought yorker, leg stick. And I was an out-swinger." He stops the tale to reflect on fast-medium bowlers today. "I can't understand why bowlers today can't swing the damn thing. It's the only thing I could do." The ball is bowled. His arm comes across his body, and his head falls away. Has anybody on the ground got a worse view of what happens next? "It went down, swung, hit Fred on the toe. I turned round to George." George Pope, who has stood at the bowler's end for three days. George Pope, who is getting a lift back to Chesterfield with Fred. George Pope, whose 'not out's have been *goodness knows how many'*. "And I said, 'How's that, George?' And he said, 'That's out.'" *This time umpire George Pope raised his finger to the almost despairing appeal.'*

Out. "We all went off in great ecstasy," Roy recalls. "The crowd were really up on their feet. And Fred's still stood at the wicket. I can see it now. He'd played forward, and it was a good shout. Some of the other shouts were a bit hopeful, but this was a good shout. And George gave him straightaway. Fred stood there. We were all off, and he was still looking at his legs."

George Pope is disconsolate in the pavilion. "It looks as though my lift's gone," he says. "You'll be all right, George," Roy says. "Give him ten minutes to simmer down." Who knows what the conversation is as they set off together for Chesterfield? Worcestershire, meanwhile, go down to Chelmsford. Stopping for a drink at the Clarendon Court Hotel in London, they meet up with the England team. Basil is glowing with his magnificent 158, but Ray Illingworth wants to know about their county game.

"All I've heard is that we lost by one, and it was an lbw on the last one. Who was it?" "It was Fred," Roy replies. "Fred," he laughs. "It couldn't have happened to a better bloke." "They'd lost by one, but Ray was only interested in knowing who was the last man out. That was the humour they had."

But it will all come good for Yorkshire next Friday. Surrey will be hanging on for a draw at Hull, three wickets left, Younis Ahmed batting magnificently and only ten minutes to go. "Fred took the new ball," Don Wilson recalls, "and somebody in the crowd shouted, 'Come on, Fred, Yorkshire expects'. But he couldn't do it. He just had the one over, and we took him off. It was quite the saddest thing I've ever seen." Then Younis plays a full-blooded sweep off Don Wilson that ricochets off Brian Close at silly short leg and is caught by Jimmy Binks. "There was blood everywhere," Don recalls, "but Closey wouldn't go off. 'It's in the mind, this pain,' he said. He was absolutely mental." Pat Pocock is run out, and it is left to Robin Jackman to block out for the draw.

Albert Gaskell is the umpire. "He was a great big man," Don Wilson says. "He drank an enormous amount, and he had this great purple nose. He was from Northallerton, and he was Yorkshire through and through. He was a great character, and everybody seemed to like him. So they gave him a couple of seasons on the first-class list." This is his last assignment and, when Don raps Robin Jackman on the pad, his finger goes up with glee. "Jackman said it wouldn't have hit four sets, but everybody in Yorkshire said it would have knocked out middle. So we don't argue about that anymore, do we?" There are no close-up replays, and Yorkshire are champions once more. 27 championships in 59 seasons this century. Will they really not win another in the next 30 years? "It was the end of a fantastic era," Don reflects. "The tradition's gone now. I don't think the Yorkshire players of today understand what winning is."

But Roy knows all about winning here at Worcester. *'This win was the highlight of my career,'* he declares across the headline of the Evening News report. "No," he reflects thirty years on, "I think that was when we won the championship. But it was certainly the most memorable game." And no picture stays clearer in his memory than the lonely figure of Fred, standing at the crease as they all run off the field.

WORCESTERSHIRE v YORKSHIRE

Worcester. 21, 22 & 23 August 1968

WORCESTERSHIRE WON BY 1 RUN

WORCESTERSHIRE

R.G.A. Headley	b Cope	23	lbw b Hutton		8
G.M. Turner	run out	13	c & b Wilson		31
J.A. Ormrod	b Wilson	12	c sub b Wilson		28
C.D. Fearnley	lbw b Nicholson	11	lbw b Close		13
A.R. Barker	lbw b Cope	3	b Cope		11
T.J. Yardley	b Cope	14	lbw b Trueman		43
*+R. Booth	b Wilson	5	b Wilson		6
N. Gifford	not out	9	b Wilson		3
B.M. Brain	lbw b Nicholson	4	b Nicholson		3
L.J. Coldwell	run out	0	not out		1
R.G.M. Carter	b Nicholson	0	b Trueman		0
Extras	*b 4, lb 2, nb 1*	7	*b 8, lb 7, nb 1*		16
		101			**163**

1-37, 2-37, 3-53, 4-62, 5-67, 6-72, 7-87, 8-96, 9-99, 10-101
1-14, 2-69, 3-70, 4-89, 5-126, 6-147, 7-151, 8-161, 9-161, 10-163

Trueman	5	1	11	0	3.5	2	3	2
Nicholson	17.2	5	36	3	10	3	22	1
Cope	13	5	26	3	19	8	31	1
Wilson	21	10	20	2	35	15	57	4
Close	4	3	1	0	15	8	23	1
Hutton					10	3	11	1

YORKSHIRE

P.J. Sharpe	c Ormrod b Carter	5	run out		1
K. Taylor	lbw b Coldwell	2	c Booth b Carter		6
D.E.V. Padgett	b Brain	4	b Carter		0
J.H. Hampshire	b Coldwell	6	b Gifford		31
*D.B. Close	lbw b Brain	27	lbw b Carter		8
R.A. Hutton	c Booth b Brain	16	b Coldwell		19
+J.G. Binks	b Brain	22	c Ormrod b Brain		34
G.A. Cope	b Carter	13	c Turner b Gifford		1
F.S. Trueman	lbw b Carter	4	lbw b Carter		12
D. Wilson	b Brain	7	c Barker b Coldwell		10
A.G. Nicholson	not out	4	not out		2
Extras	*b 12, lb 3, nb 1*	16	*b 4, lb 4, w 1, nb 4*		13
		126			**137**

1-7, 2-9, 3-18, 4-22, 5-67, 6-74, 7-99, 8-109, 9-110, 10-126
1-7, 2-7, 3-24, 4-32, 5-61, 6-79, 7-94, 8-111, 9-123, 10-137

Coldwell	20	4	32	2	18	8	28	2
Carter	19	5	30	3	19.4	4	36	4
Brain	24.2	10	37	5	17	4	26	1
Gifford	8	4	11	0	19	9	34	2

Umpires: R.S. Lay and G.H. Pope

WE CANNOT GO ON LIKE THIS

Northamptonshire v Gloucestershire

June 1969

chosen by David Allen

David Allen was born in Bristol in 1935. An off-spin bowler, he played for Gloucestershire from 1953 to 1972, achieving the double of 1000 runs and 100 wickets in 1961. He played in 39 Tests for England, becoming with Ken Barrington the first Englishmen to tour all the six Test-playing countries of that time. After retiring from cricket he enjoyed a successful second career with Harvey's, the Bristol sherry merchants.

He remembers a match at Northampton when he was acting captain.

Captains, captains, captains. While Kent have spent the decade under Colin Cowdrey, Gloucestershire have worked their way through six of them. Does success create continuity, or continuity success? Kent have climbed the championship table to be runners-up in '67 and '68, but for Gloucestershire the movement has been the other way: twice bottom, twice one-but-bottom in the last five years.

"Captaincy is ten per cent skill," Richie Benaud says, "and ninety per cent luck." And so far in 1969 Gloucestershire's Tony Brown has had little more luck than his predecessors. Three potential victories in May were lost to the rain, and after a good win against Essex he injured his groin and gave way to David. "I found captaincy hard work," David remembers, "but it was very exhilarating."

Wednesday morning at Northampton's County Ground. A sunny day but a sparse crowd. David looks down at "one of the flattest wickets you could see", and his heart sinks when he loses the toss. "We'll have a bat," Roger Prideaux says. He is in his third year as Northants' skipper and, though they have been years of decline for the county, he started the summer as favourite to inherit the England captaincy from the injured Colin Cowdrey. But runs did not come when they mattered most, and now he is back in the county game, looking for big hundreds on pitches like this one. *'Prideaux got off the mark first ball with a three off long-haired Mike Procter.'*

It is David's fifth match in charge, and his record stands so far at won two, lost two. It began in ignominy at the Oval: all out for 92, chasing 306. "I remember driving on to Leicester with Grahame Parker. He'd just taken over as secretary. 'David,' he said. 'We cannot go on like this, putting up these performances.' And I said, 'Grahame, I don't think it will keep on going like this. This is too good a side.'" But a five-run victory at Leicester is followed by defeat in two days at Middlesbrough, all out for 41 on a spiteful pitch. "I do apologise for the wicket," Brian Close told David. "Behind the scenes we'll get it right, but for the sake of Yorkshire cricket will you please hold back any strong statements?"

Middlesbrough to Bristol is nearly three hundreds miles, a long enough journey for David to wonder whether his interim captaincy is going to be as short of luck as his predecessors'. His team mate David Green remembers his talk to them when they were preparing to bat against Yorkshire. "Come on, lads, this is one of those wickets where you've got to go out and work." At 36 for six he strode out to demonstrate what he meant. "The first ball from Chris Old flew off a length and went past his nose. He didn't work very hard, either, after that." Allen, caught Hutton, bowled Old, 2.

Then yesterday at Bristol his fortune turned. He set Hampshire 266 to win, and Barry Richards took up the attack against his great friend Mike Procter. Two young South Africans, team mates for Natal in the Currie Cup. Their duels are the high spots of their summers in England. "There was no quarter given or taken when Proc bowled to Barry," David recalls. "They were like tigers going at each other. It was absolutely smashing."

Mike is an out-and-out fast bowler, and Barry a batsman bristling with arrogant talent. "I remember it to this day. I was fielding in the gully, Proc bowled a short one, and I saw Barry go to hook the ball. He was far too early, that's how good a batsman he was, and it hit him on the side of the temple. He went down, and he was motionless, absolutely still." This is the summer of 1969, long before the introduction of helmets, and the medical back-up is basic. "Do you know, there wasn't even a stretcher available. There was an old door in the pavilion, and they had to bring that out." Mike Procter might be like a tiger bowling to Barry but, faced with the sight of his mate laid out on the door, "he went white and speechless." The bowling passed to the spinners, and soon Hampshire's 35 for no wicket was 63 all out. "It put the mockers on that match."

"There's a lot more short-pitched bowling in cricket nowadays," David reckons. "If this is tactical, I don't mind. But you just feel it's intimidation a lot of the time. And if people have been at an incident like this, they know it's not a thing to enjoy. It was absolutely frightening."

Yesterday evening Gloucestershire set off in their cars for Northampton. "Fred Dudridge, our scorer, would have insisted that we stopped at the Evenlode pub near Oxford. It had the best Worthington." Meanwhile the results arrive from the other games, and suddenly they find themselves in the limelight. *'Gloucestershire top for the first time since 1947.'*

1947 was the Golden Summer of Compton and Edrich, but it was also the last great year of old Tom Goddard, 238 wickets at the age of 46. How close he took Gloucestershire to their first championship since the days of W.G. Grace. Did his great deeds that summer inspire the young David as he prepared to start at Cotham Grammar School? From Goddard and Parker, through Cook and Wells, and on to Mortimore and Allen, no county has a richer tradition of slow bowlers..

Runners up in '47 and again in '59, but most of this team have known only life at the other end of the table. Who would have thought that this journey to Northampton would pair top and bottom in the championship? Gloucestershire may only have won three matches, but *'members of the team were last night saying that morale has never been higher.'*

This morning Barry Richards is recovering in Bristol Royal Infirmary, and now Mike is bowling to Hylton Ackerman, another team mate from Natal. His third over is full of life and incident. *'Ackerman survived an lbw appeal and then made leg-side shots for four and three.'* It is 18 for no wicket, but *'Procter's whippy action deceived Prideaux and Lightfoot with successive balls,'* and the over ends at 18 for two.

"We never really had a quick bowler," David says. "Then Procter came along, and life changed completely. People used to attack us, and we couldn't fight back. Tail-enders came in and slogged our medium-pacers around. Well, numbers eight and nine soon stopped getting runs against us, and that was a super sight to see." Brian Reynolds pads up to the hat-trick ball, and *'the enthusiastic Procter only just managed to stifle a frivolous lbw appeal.'*

It is the summer of 1969. The Concorde supersonic plane makes its test flight, crude oil is discovered in the North Sea, and the Apollo 10 spacecraft completes a successful rehearsal for July's Moon landing.

Procter to Richards yesterday, to Ackerman today. There is novelty still in these overseas players. Back here in May the crowd saw Colin Milburn hit a wonderful 158 with boundaries galore, and now he is a forlorn sight at the ground, his left eye lost in a car crash. "A jewel that sparkled briefly and was stolen," Matthew Engel writes, and the Northampton crowd is glad at least to have the excitement of these two South African youngsters locked in combat.

'Procter tried every trick in the book in a bid to remove his friend Ackerman,' Michael Tebbitt writes in the Northampton Chronicle. *'He switched to bowling round the wicket and, at one stage, reduced his run up from thirty to three yards.'* Mike has a great swing of the arm to generate pace, but he delivers the ball before his left foot lands and his unorthodox action causes confusion to many a batsman. *'At times Ackerman hardly knew what time of day it was, but he stuck doggedly to the task and made good use of his incredible luck by hitting two fours off the edge of the bat.'* By half past twelve Mike Procter has bowled eight overs, and for David that is long enough. "I was always concerned about him being over-bowled."

'After Procter's onslaught, there was an inevitable lull in proceedings.' It is back to the home-grown bowlers: Jack Davey from Devon and David Smith, Bristol-born and -bred. "Smithy was amazing. He never put himself up as a front man, he was never looking for image. They wound him up on the first of May and he bowled till the fifteenth of September, with that lovely

natural action of his. There were years when he carried the Gloucestershire seam attack." The best bowling action in England, some say. At his peak he was bowling 1200 overs a summer, and he made it all look effortless. "We were fit carthorses. Nowadays they want to be thoroughbreds. And, as we know in racing circles, thoroughbreds break down a lot."

Reynolds is a no-nonsense professional, and he takes half an hour over his first two runs. Then *'Ackerman was caught in two minds, playing forward to a ball from Davey, and was clean bowled.'* It is 60 for three, and Reynolds is joined by David Steele, another who will not give his wicket away lightly. At lunch the score has reached 105, and the players return to the dressing rooms, put on their blazers and walk across the ground for lunch. "That was something I didn't like about Northampton," David reflects.

Northampton is not the most popular venue on the county circuit. The redbrick housing lacks the charm of Worcester's cathedral or Taunton's church towers. The adjoining football ground has seen better days, as has the ramshackle west stand, and there is rarely much of a crowd in midweek. "There'd have been three or four hundred there," David Green says, "and that would have been all right. It wouldn't have been at Bristol, because it's a bigger ground. I liked Northampton. I got my first championship century there. And it was nice weather for that game. The sun was beating down."

But David Allen is not one to dwell on such thoughts. "I tended to put aside personal preferences. We had a professional job to do." And today his job is captaincy. Much of the winter speculation was that he would be the new Gloucestershire skipper, and perhaps this spell in charge is his chance to prove to himself that he could have done the job. He has played under Tom Graveney - "We always said that Smithy bowled the overs he did because Tom didn't like to take him off." - and under John Mortimore - "Meet our new captain, he's led us from bottom-but-one to bottom," one joker said after his first match as stand-in skipper. There have been the ones the committee brought in from outside - Old Etonian Tom Pugh, to revive the amateur spirit, and Ken Graveney, returning at 38 after an 11-year retirement. Then last year the job passed to the obvious choice, Arthur Milton, but he barely lasted the summer. Had they left it too late for him or was he not cut out for the stress? It's like Bill Andrews used to say down at Somerset: "we can't find a captain. They've all had a go. We've had Freeman, Hardy and Willis here."

Won two, lost two is David's record so far, and there is work to be done on this flat wicket to stop Northants putting the game beyond them.

Lunch is over, and Mike Procter once more measures out his long run. Immediately *'Reynolds was brilliantly caught at backward short leg by Mortimore.'* 112 for four. *'Two balls later Procter beat Willey with a ball which just missed the off stump. Then at the start of the next over the unlucky bowler had Steele dropped at second slip.'* Six overs from Procter yield one wicket for seven runs. Now it is the turn of the off-spinners, John Mortimore and David himself. "We did look after each other. I'm sure when he was captain he bowled me first most of the time, and when I was captain I bowled him first. We had a tremendous respect for each other."

It is June 1969. Apollo 11 is being prepared for its Moon landing, and Concorde has taken its first flight. Sixteen years ago, back in June 1953, when it was Everest that was being conquered, and the Comet jet that was being launched, a seventeen-year-old David made his debut. In his fourth match he took six Surrey wickets for 13, and with just two deliveries to spare he clinched victory over the county champions. "There's the ball," he says, 45 years later, pointing across his dining room. The boys of his old school, Cotham Grammar, chaired him off the field.

Yet such were the riches of Gloucester's slow bowling - the off-spin of Mortimore and Wells, the slow left arm of Sam Cook - that it was another six years before he found a regular place in the team. "I went to the committee at the end of 1958. I didn't want to spend ten years in the game and leave with nothing. It was time to go, I thought." The committee persuaded him to stay one more year and, with Tom Graveney replacing George Emmett as captain, he never looked back, an England player by the winter. "I've just heard you're going to the West Indies," George Emmett said. "Well done. But John Mortimore should have gone."

Allen and Mortimore. It is inevitable that they will forever be compared. "I was a big spinner of the ball. John was good in the flight, but perhaps he didn't spin it enough for international level." John takes wickets by bowling his balls in subtle sequences, and it is no surprise when he trains to become an accountant. David rips the skin off his fingers with attacking spin - "the way you played, you should have been a Yorkshireman," Fred Trueman tells him - and after cricket he puts his outgoing personality to use in search of customers for Harvey's sherry.

The nineteen-year-old Peter Willey is already in his fourth summer of first-team cricket, and he decides to take on John Mortimore's flight. *'Young Willey shows signs of maturing into a first-class batsman,'* Pat Marshall writes in the Daily Express. *'He now is able to pick the right ball to hit ... as John Mortimore will testify. He hit him for a glorious on-driven six and next ball hammered him through the covers off the back foot for four.'*

With the score 174 for four Gloucestershire are struggling, but somehow *'on a fine batting wicket they winkled out Northants for 205.'* Two wickets for David, one for Jack Davey, a run out and two more for Mike Procter in a final burst. "They weren't a bad side to have bowled out for 205 on that wicket. And what a strike rate Procky's got! He's only bowled 16 overs, and he's got a five-for."

Now Northants must counter the pace of Procter with their own new ball attack. No David Larter, retired, and no Brian Crump, resting an injury. Their opening bowlers are Peter Lee, "we called him Leapy Lee", and Tony Durose, journeymen medium-pacers, and *'Green and Nicholls with quiet authority gave Gloucestershire the kind of start required if they are going to establish a large first innings lead.'*

David Green has come down from Lancashire, a history graduate who has been lured to Gloucestershire by the offer of winter work with Sutcliffe's Catering. "I had to learn the trade. So there I was at the Port of Bristol canteen, serving on the counter with my Oxford degree." In twenty years' time he will be writing the history of Gloucestershire County Cricket Club, and he will record the 25 years of service of his partner here today. "Ron's graceful strokeplay and his modest and engaging personality were to be a feature of the County's cricket until he retired in 1975." As they will be a feature of Cheltenham Town cricket till he dies in 1994. "He was very poorly on the Monday," David Allen tells. "Isn't it amazing how we know what's happening to us? He said to both his sons, 'Whatever happens, you *will* go and play for Cheltenham on Saturday, won't you? You won't let me down.'"

Green and Nicholls. There are none of the quick singles that Arthur Milton has them running. David is a rugby union forward: *'a big man with forearms like prize-winning marrows.'* "I was fairly quick on the gallop, but I couldn't turn like Milt. He ran me out just before a declaration at Cheltenham, and he was lapping me." "I don't know, Ron, I only go when Milt says. I think we're better off sticking to basics." Green and Nicholls, the basics are all in order here as *'this handsome stroke-making pair reached 79 with 50 minutes of the day's play remaining.'* Pat Marshall looks into the Gloucester dressing room. Top of the table this morning, now they are 79 for no wicket in reply to 205. *'The atmosphere was chatty and relaxed.'*

'But country lad Peter Lee, who a fortnight ago was bowling his pacy out-swingers for the village cricket team of Sibbertoft, stepped in to bring them down to earth. Green failed to get on top of an on-drive and was well held by Peter Willey at mid-wicket.'

"A captain must study his team as individuals," the M.C.C. Cricket Coaching Book instructs, "get to know their temperaments and how best to handle each of them." And this is David's intention here. "I suppose that's why I remember the game so well. I was so concerned about everybody."

David Shepherd is the next man in, a big man from Devon, and David has been sitting beside him, passing on the positive approach he learnt years ago from old George Emmett. "We're on a flat wicket, Shep. I want you to impose yourself. Take charge. Don't let them bowl at you."

Shep strides out, full of purpose, but *'Lee knocked back his leg stump, and before the shock waves subsided Nicholls was gone too, beautifully picked up at backward short leg by Steele.'* It is 104 for three, and David is no longer chatty and relaxed. "I was absolutely furious. It was a 400-wicket, and there was Shep playing over a straight ball."

"What the hell do you think you were doing, Shep? It was a good length ball, and you were trying to strike it over the top?" "You told me to impose myself," comes back the reply. "So I took the offensive early." "You've got to get yourself in first," David groans, and even thirty years later he shakes his head at the confusion. "There was a tremendous lack of communication between the two of us."

'It took all the Northern phlegm and impeccable technique of Geoff Pullar and the calm of Springbok Test man Procter to get the innings back on an even keel.' By close the score is 121 for three, and perhaps in the grim post-mortem of his brief innings David Shepherd lets pass the chance of some fun on 111. "A great guy to have in your side, but a damn nuisance. Whenever the runs got to 111 or 222, we didn't often get to 333, we all had to pick up our feet in the dressing room. They had to be in the air or stood on boxes."

The day's play is over, there are drinks for the two teams, and the Gloucestershire players make their way back to the Angel. "We had a lot of fun there," David remembers. "A few beers at night and off to the cricket next day." In twenty years' time, he will be working for Harvey's Bristol Cream - "a Rolls Royce of a company" - and, when he passes through Northampton, he decides to stay at the Angel. "It looked a bit old-fashioned, not the upmarket pub I once thought it was. I wasn't quite sure if time had taken its toll or if I'd got used to a better standard."

Some of the team have other plans, though. "Procky liked a drink," David Green tells, "and so did I. Milburn was around at the ground, and of course Hylton Ackerman was another drinking mate of Procky's. So we had this tremendous piss-up planned." And what will they drink? "Procky didn't like the English beer, said it was warm and it wasn't very strong, so I suggested we had Black and Tan. A half of Worthington or Bass with a bottle of Guinness poured on top. It knocked you about a bit, but he said it still tasted horrible, it was still warm." And is that what Mike Procter drinks this evening? "He'd hardly made a run all summer, so he decided to have an early night, left us to it." He is six not out, determined to capitalise on this flat batting track. "After two halves of lager," he writes, "I went back to the hotel, had a meal and turned in for the night."

Wednesday the 25th of July, 1969. David Allen recognises the date. "Of course, this is the anniversary of the day Cowdrey joined me to face the West Indies at Lords, with his arm broken." Six years earlier, David has been at the wicket for one of the great moments of Test match history when, with nine wickets down, Colin Cowdrey has come out to bat with his arm in plaster. Wes Hall was the fastest bowler in the world, and, according to Alan Gibson on Test Match Special, he was "bowling out of the background of a dark pavilion on a dark and gloomy evening." David was on strike for the two remaining deliveries: "I had to fend off Wes Hall for two balls while Colin stood there watching me with a smile on his face. Not only that but he still gets fan mail for his brave knock, and no one ever mentions D.A. Allen."

Lord's 1963. Has there ever been a better drawn match in the history of the game? And what on earth happened on the fourth ball of that last over to bring Colin Cowdrey to the middle? England, with two wickets left, needed six to win off three balls, and David was batting with Derek Shackleton. "The idea was to get a couple of singles so that we could have a swing at the last ball. I said to Derek, 'If it goes through to the keeper, I'm going to run it.'" In the feverish atmosphere, Shack played and missed, and David was through in a trice for the single. But his partner had not moved, and Frank Worrell picked up the ball and beat him to the bowler's end, two 38-year-olds sprinting down the pitch together. "It would have looked a pantomime in a club game," David says, "and this was a Test match at Lord's." In the pavilion afterwards, David sat down beside Shack. "Derek, I thought we agreed we were going to run if it went through to the keeper." But the drama of the moment has scrambled even the phlegmatic Derek's brain. "I thought you meant if I hit it," he said. Thirty-five years on, David shakes his head. "Shack, if you'd hit it, you'd have been caught."

Mike Procter wakes on Thursday morning. "I was fresh as a daisy," he writes. "I had a net and felt really good." David Green is not so fresh after his night's drinking, but he sits with his team mates and watches the start of play. "This was the old pavilion, it's hospitality now. We changed underneath, it was fairly primitive, and we watched from above." Mike Procter blocks the first ball of the morning, then he *offered no stroke to Durose's second delivery and looked on helplessly as the ball sent his off-stump cartwheeling towards the wicket-keeper.* "Middle stump," David Green remembers. "He had a face like thunder. We thought, we'd better go down below, get out of his way. We could hear the bat clattering around upstairs." Eventually they decide to go back up. "All right, Proc?" "No," he says, "I'm not all right." There is a pause. "Anyway, Steely's going to get it." David Steele, who was crouching at short leg when his stump went flying. "What's Steely done?" "He laughed." "Proc," I said, "everybody in the bloody ground laughed."

"He was absolutely wild," David Allen explains. "He wanted to prove himself." It is 121 for four, and that becomes 141 for five when *'Pullar was lbw to a ball from Sully which appeared to turn sharply'* and 185 for six when *'Bissex was caught at mid-on.'* Gloucestershire are still 20 runs behind, and they are down to David Allen and John Mortimore.

With Pullar, Procter and Green, the batting is stronger this year than it has ever been during David's time at Gloucestershire. "I remember when I'd only just got in the team. We were up against Derek Shackleton at Bristol. It was 35 for seven when I went in, and Tom Graveney gave me my cap for getting a fifty." Tom has become one of the great batsmen of the sixties, but he moved to Worcester when he lost the captaincy and Gloucestershire's batting for most of the decade has depended on Arthur Milton and Ron Nicholls. "Down the order we were used to backing the batsmen up. We used to call ourselves the Engine Room." David may be used to it, but it does not make his mood this lunch time any more cheerful.

"The team went across the ground for lunch, but Morty and I stayed in the dressing room. We had a sandwich and a cup of tea. 'What the hell's going on in this side, Morty?' I said. 'Here we are on the flattest wicket ever, 180 for six, down to the bowlers. Where are we going?' I was almost crying into my beer, as you might say. You can understand my disappointment, can't you?"

Perhaps the words of Grahame Parker echo in David's mind: "We cannot go on like this, putting up these performances." "And Morty said, 'Well, let's give it our best shot.'" *'Allen, living up to the responsibilities of captaincy, found the ideal partner in Mortimore.'* "He was tremendous," David says. "He could strike the slow bowlers very straight." "He didn't hit it that straight," David Green says. "He liked to drag it round to long-on, mid-wicket, it would go further. He was very, very violent."

Allen and Mortimore, the attacking off-spinner and the thoughtful flight bowler. With the bat it is David who is the patient one and John who favours the instant result. *'Allen played the quiet role, content to cut and glide, and gave Mortimore his head,'* the Western Daily Press reports. *'It was no hit or miss slog,'* Pat Marshall writes in the Daily Express. *'Mortimore made most of his runs by firm, fluent driving off the front foot and then he twice hit superb sixes with glorious punches off the back foot.'* They add 120 before David is out. Then John completes only his second championship century in twenty years. *'The most vital innings of his career,'* the Daily Telegraph calls it. By tea he and Barrie Meyer have scored 58 for the ninth wicket, Shep has even enjoyed the fun of 333, and the lead is 160. "I couldn't see us beating them by an innings," David says, "so I declared." In one session of play the match has been transformed.

John Mortimore. In the whole history of Gloucestershire county cricket only four bowlers have taken more wickets than him, and none of them came within seven thousand of his run tally, let alone hit hundreds like this one today. Perhaps in another age he might have played more Tests. Perhaps with a stronger side he might have been a more successful captain. But he is too much of a team man to dwell on such thoughts. "Cricket now," David Green thinks, "has become too focused on the individual. All these personal interviews, these vignettes of people while they're still playing. 'My views on English cricket, by Ben Hollioake, age 12.' People start believing they're tremendously important when they're not." And nobody ever accused Morty of thinking himself too important.

It is the summer of 1969. Lady Summerskill calls the new Divorce Laws "a Casanova's Charter", Barbara Castle fights for new trade union legislation 'in place of strife', and Bernadette Devlin becomes an MP at the age of twenty-one,

At Wimbledon eighth seed Ray Moore, *'the South African with the hippy hair style'*, is knocked out in the second round, but here at Northampton the *'long-haired'* Mike Procter has no intention of finishing a loser. Three slips, two gullies and two short legs crouch round Roger Prideaux, and David has a word with the bowler. "All I said to Proc was, 'Let the bloody thing go. You ain't going to bowl much, but you're going to bowl quick.' It was an all-out assault. It didn't matter if they got 200 that night. That way they'd get enough runs to give us a declaration." *'Allen used Procter sparingly,'* the Western Daily Press writes. *'He brought him on at crucial moments.'*

With the total on 17 it is Jack Davey who strikes first, having Prideaux caught behind for one. The Northants captain has scored seven runs in two innings on this flat track, and he will never regain his Test place. *'Ackerman thrashed the new ball,'* 37 out of 45 in half an hour, but Procter wins their *'tremendous duel'* when the ball catches an edge and flies into the slips. "And David Smith's gone sideways, caught him left-handed."

David Smith. Smudger, they call him. He may have taken over a thousand wickets and played five Tests for England, but he is not one ever to dwell on his own success. Thirty years on he stands in his shop in East Bristol, and he struggles to recall the detail of any of it. "But I do remember that catch," he says. "It was up above my left shoulder. It was going so fast it knocked me backwards." In his action replay his hands go up together as he falls back towards a display of ladies' bags. "A really great catch," David Allen says. "I can see it now."

Five runs later Reynolds is out, and at 50 for three Steele joins Lightfoot. "If anybody was going to worry us," David says, "it was going to be David Steele. He could bat all day for absolutely nothing, I mean that with a great deal of respect, and the match was all set for him to do that."

Today at Lord's Yorkshire's John Hampshire is playing against the West Indies. On Saturday he will become the first Englishman ever to hit a debut Test century at cricket's headquarters, and he will not let on that he is batting with a little finger broken last week at Middlesbrough by Mike Procter. "It hurt like hell," he writes. "To this day I cannot move it inwards to meet the third finger." In Bristol Barry Richards is recovering from the blow to his temple. "Although I've got very het up sometimes while bowling," Mike Procter writes, "I've never really set out to hurt a batsman - except once."

David Green is not so sure about this. "I think fast bowlers always try to hurt people, even if they regret it when they do." And Mike Procter? "He was a very hostile bowler, so unrelenting. He wasn't the fastest I faced. That would be Wes Hall or Fred Trueman, but he didn't seem to tire. Day after day he would give it everything. He didn't like batsmen. He just liked to get them out, liked to make them hop about a bit."

But David Allen puts it differently. "Some fast bowlers got angry, but he had this cold, calm hatred. You rarely saw him lose his temper. He'd just as soon bowl them out with a yorker as a bouncer. You certainly felt he wasn't there to hurt the batsman. The short ball was just a tactical weapon."

It was David who brought Mike Procter and Barry Richards to England. A telegram from Gloucestershire before the end of the M.C.C. tour of South Africa in '64/5 asked him to sign up a young player, and he made a bee-line for the eighteen-year-old Richards - and not just because he made some runs against them. "He was playing for an Invitation XI, and he came in to bat the over before lunch. He came about three yards down the wicket to whack me over the top, missed it and was stumped for nought. I said to Jackie McGlew, the old South African captain, 'I like the look of him.' He had this outrageous exuberance. 'Take him,' Jackie said. 'I think he'll do well, but I'll tell you what. There's a lad called Procter, he might be even better.' So I said, 'If you think he's better, Jackie, I'll have him as well.' And we took them both back."

Richards and Procter spent that summer in Bristol, and Gloucestershire seconds rose from last place to runners-up. Mike topped the batting averages, and Barry with his off-spin the bowling. They ran riot in the local leagues - "they had a six-a-side tournament among the local clubs, and Proc hit something like 90 in five overs." - and they made the most of the social life. "I remember driving them home, with the pair of them on the roof and the bonnet of our car."

Then in 1968 the counties were freed to register an overseas player without qualification, and Gloucestershire joined the rush for Gary Sobers. But Mike is ten years younger than the great West Indian and, with Barry Richards at Hampshire growing disaffected with the treadmill of the county game, perhaps Mike is the best of all these early signings. In time he will become the next county captain after Tony Brown, and he will still be playing here against Northants in July 1981, the only survivor of this match.

July 1981 will be the month of Prince Charles' wedding. But for now he is preparing to be invested as Prince of Wales, and on this Thursday evening he is interviewed on television. "It is awfully difficult," he says. "You have got to remember that when you marry you are going to marry somebody who perhaps one day will be Queen."

Here at Northampton Mike Procter runs in to bowl his first ball to the bespectacled David Steele, a man with the technique and concentration to bat all day, and it looks as though that is what he will need to do. But Mike has not got over his dismissal in the morning, "I'd looked such a fool padding up to a straight one," and Steele is the Northants player he has caught laughing as he left the wicket. "I never set out to hurt a batsman," he writes, "except once." And alas for Steele, this is that once. "I dug one in at him first ball." *'Steele turned his back on a short-pitched ball and took a crunching blow just above his left wrist.'* "He went to go forward, and Procter bowled a beautiful bouncer," David says. "There weren't many who could have got through his defence like that." Steele retires with a broken left forearm, and unless he plans to copy Colin Cowdrey the score is effectively 52 for four. *'Northants were in big trouble.'*

'The nineteen-year-old Willey, greeted by a bouncer, was later struck painfully on the shoulder when he turned his back on a lifter.' This is the gritty Willey whose name will soon be on the selectors' lips whenever the West Indian quicks are to be faced. *'Despite that bruised shoulder he stuck to his guns bravely, and he and the veteran Albert Lightfoot battled out the last 85 minutes.'* "Dear old Albert," David chuckles. "Brian Statham hit him once. 'Albert, Albert, are you all right? Where have I hit you?' 'Where do you think you've bloody hit me,' Albert replied, 'with a hooter like mine?'" At close the score is 133 for three, and Gloucestershire's lead is down to 27.

It is the summer of 1969. The Ministry of Agriculture introduces a new code for factory farming, and a Cambridge laboratory fertilises human eggs in a test tube. The Kray twins are gaoled for murder, and Rupert Murdoch wins control of the News of the World.

It is the summer of 1969, and cricket is bringing in a new audience with its Player's Sunday League. "The orchestra is expected to play Beethoven during the week," Glamorgan's Wilf Wooller writes, "and boogie woogie on Sundays." David may have taken 122 wickets for England, and he may be acting captain of Gloucestershire, but he bowls only once in sixteen Sunday matches. In his place David Green, with his steady medium pace, "I was just a net bowler," is their leading wicket-taker and in the three-day game he does not claim a single victim. Worcester's slow left-armer Norman Gifford learns to adapt to the new game but, as he says, "I push it through on a Sunday to tie them down, and it's not till Tuesday that I get my action back properly."

In the late 1970s, David will watch Fred Titmus and John Emburey bowling in a charity match to the great Australian batsman Neil Harvey. Two different generations of off-spin. "When Fred bowled, the flight was above eye level and Neil was having to look for it. But when John bowled, it was flatter and Neil could just play it off the wicket. As soon as it's below eye level, you see, you can judge the length."

"I just wonder," Basil D'Oliveira says to David years later. "If you or Fred Titmus came on today in a one-day match and bowled like you used to, I think you'd fox them. They don't see good slow bowling nowadays." It is a speculation that can never be put to the test. Fred has long retired, and David plays only occasionally for the Whitbread Old England XI. "The mechanics have more or less gone," he says sadly in the autumn of 1998. "I got through this year, mainly because all but one of the games were rained off."

In any case, it is not a matter of whether David Allen, born in 1935, would trouble the modern batsman, but whether another David Allen, born in 1975, could ever develop these skills. "When I was fourteen or fifteen," David recalls, "I started playing with the men at Stapleton, and we played all time matches, not over limit. I used to get slogged out of the ground, and they'd say, 'That's all right. We'll put another man out there. Pitch it up, he'll get out in a moment.' They had that lovely, optimistic attitude. But then there wasn't the fear of losing. I was brought up in a super age with a super set of people, full of enthusiasm." And now? "The kiddies only play 20-over cricket. Four lads bowl five overs each, and slow bowling's not encouraged too much. Then they come into 46-over cricket.."

It is the summer of 1969. Paul McCartney marries the Kodak heiress Linda Eastman while Brian Jones of the Rolling Stones drowns in his swimming pool.

The teams arrive at the ground for the final day's play, and the players warm up without great exertion. Tony Brown has begun his reign as Gloucester captain with a new fitness regime, but not everybody in his side is taking it seriously. "Before Tony took charge, our pre-season practice would be three hours in the nets and an hour's football. But he decided to run us round Failand, near Redwood Lodge. We'd never been out of the County Ground before. It was quite hilly, and Browny was about a hundred yards in front, leading the way, the rest of us struggling along, with Shep the straggler at the back. A milkman came by - so we put Shep on his float. And as he passed us, he gave us this royal wave. We were all falling about laughing. Browny was furious but, to be fair to him, he did see the funny side of it."

'Mortimore opened the attack, and Lightfoot cut his first ball to the boundary to reach 51.' Mike Procter has another burst, but *'Northants did not surrender meekly.'* "They were fighters," David recalls, and soon everybody on the county circuit will know Peter Willey as one of the greatest fighters of them all. *'The first innings arrears were wiped out, and then Willey became the second member of the partnership to reach his fifty.'* He has passed his highest championship score.

Peter Willey made his debut here in 1966, and he will be playing here for Leicestershire in 1991, the longest-surviving player on the county circuit. Then he will take up umpiring and by his fourth season he will be on the international panel, a tough man able to handle the pressure. For David, though, there is one umpire better than him, and here at Northampton his heavily-built frame can be spotted in the outfield. "Shep's been number one for a long time," David reckons. "He's knowledgeable, he's decisive, and he does it with a sense of humour." Throughout the world television viewers will focus on his feet whenever the score clicks to 111 or 222.

The score here reaches 183 for three, *'then Willey pushed Allen to mid-wicket and was caught by Procter.'* Sully survives three lbw appeals, and with half an hour to lunch the 200 is passed. Albert Lightfoot is in the eighties, the lead is 40, and even without David Steele Northants have five wickets in hand. *'The result seemed to be slipping away,'* the Gloucestershire handbook records. But David has been brought up with "that lovely, optimistic attitude" of the men at Stapleton, and he is still expecting the wickets to fall. "As far as I was concerned, the match was in hand."

Mike Procter returns for his second spell of the morning, and at last *'he grabbed the breakthrough wicket when Smith in the gully caught Lightfoot.'* Not a catch that can be re-enacted among the shoulder bags, but it is one that puts victory back in hand. By lunch Procter has taken three more wickets, his second five-for of the match, and the lead is just 50 with the last pair together. *'Procter gave Northants a harrowing time,'* the Daily Telegraph reports. *'He worked up a speed which few other fast bowlers in the country can generate.'*

It is the summer of 1969. Somerset County Cricket Club are considering the sale of their Taunton headquarters, and Geoff Boycott becomes the first cricketer to sign up with the sporting agent Mark McCormack.

"It was a love of the game that we worked for," David says. "That winter of '58/9, when the committee persuaded me to stay one more year, I rode my bike up to the County Ground every night after work. I took my sandwiches, and I went in with George Emmett, coaching from six to nine-thirty. There were no bowling machines, and quite often it was individual coaching. You'd have to bowl to a bloke for half an hour. You got so knackered that, even if he didn't have a fault, you'd go up and point one out to him, just for a break."

After lunch *'tail-enders Malcolm Scott and Peter Lee hung on,'* and in over 200 first-class matches 'Leapy Lee' will never make a higher score than his 26 this afternoon. Procter drops him off David's bowling, and the stand becomes *'stubborn'* in the Gloucester Citizen, *'breezy'* in the Bristol Evening Post, *'merry'* in the Daily Telegraph. Time slips away, and instead of a whole afternoon to score fifty the target could soon become a hundred or more in less than two hours.

"Suddenly there was this shout coming up from fine leg," David recalls. "'There's nothing bloody wrong with me, you know. I can bowl.' It's Procter. He's getting angrier and angrier, but I'm thinking, 'he's got to be looked after.' I was trying to conserve him." "To make the best use of his bowling resources is the captain's most important task," the M.C.C. Coaching Book says. "'All right, Proc,' I said. 'I haven't forgotten you, mate.' And up he came again." *'And Procter promptly bowled Lee.'* "I could have done that half an hour ago," the fast bowler thinks as he leaves the field, but David is happy enough. The target is only 98 in 130 minutes.

'Allen has shown himself to be a shrewd captain in Tony Brown's absence,' the Western Daily Press declares, and David reflects with pride on the way these Northants wickets were teased out. His wife Joyce joins in. "It's memories, you see," she says. "Ask him when he painted the lounge."

David Green falls for 15, leaving David Shepherd the opportunity to make amends for his impetuous duck on Wednesday evening. Shep is never a man to brood on failure - "all he ever cared about was the team's success,"

David Green says - and there is more to his game than big hitting. He may prefer a ride on a milk float to an uphill run to Redwood Lodge, but here at Northampton *'Nicholls and Shepherd scampered singles as though it was knock-out cricket,'* and the winning runs are scored with nine overs to spare. "Well played, Shep," David says as the batsmen come off, and Gloucestershire's championship lead increases from five to seventeen points.

By Monday evening it will be 27, with Sussex beaten in two days at Lydney, and this time the bowling hero will be David himself, his eight for 34 the best figures of his career. The Lydney pitch will be deemed unfit, and the county will never play another championship match there. "We played on anything and everything in my day," David says. "That was the beauty of the game. It gave you the whole schooling. And that's what it's lacking now."

Anything and everything, from a flat batting track at Northampton to a deadly turner at Lydney - though David has known greater contrasts than this, like in 1962 when he travelled from a Test match at the Oval, England 480 for five, to the Margam ground near Port Talbot, Glamorgan needing 119 to win on the final day and batting till nearly four o'clock for 49 all out, Mortimore five for 10 in 27 overs. "We came off the field, covered in this red tinge from the steel works." *'The game was farcical,'* the Gloucestershire handbook records, *'but the hospitality of our hosts will be remembered by all those who took part.'*

Margam, 1962. Nobody in the match reached 25, and Glamorgan's top scorer was opener Alwyn Harris. "He took about three hours to get 19; he didn't get the ball off the square. At the end of the season there was an award for the Cricketer of the Year, and we all voted for Alwyn Harris." That was back in the days of the amateur Tom Pugh's captaincy, and such funereal batting was not for him. "This is damn silly, Cecil," he told the veteran Sam Cook. "I'm going out to knock these chaps off a length." He flailed his bat wildly for quarter of an hour and returned, bowled Shepherd, 3. Sam watched the quieter efforts of the next batsman as his captain took off his pads. "They don't seem to be having any trouble with that swarm of bees now, skipper."

Tom Pugh's captaincy must seem another age here in 1969, the game fully professional though the captains still come and go. After Lydney Tony Brown returns to take charge, David Shepherd hits peak form, and there are victories over Worcestershire and Derbyshire, then an unlikely triumph over Yorkshire when Brian Close sets them a generous target at Gloucester. Is this his way of thanking David for his diplomacy at Middlesbrough? "These good deeds aren't always forgotten," David reflects, but David Green is less convinced. "No, there was no quid pro quo. It was typical Closey. He didn't mind risking a loss if it gave him a chance to win."

Captains, captains. Between them David Allen and Tony Brown take Gloucestershire to six consecutive victories, and they lead the table by 52 points. Not since the days of W.G. Grace have they known such supremacy.

But "we cannot go on like this," the pessimists say, and for the fifth time in forty years they end as runners-up. "If you'd have put Graveney into this side," David thinks, "we'd have won the championship."

In 1986 they will head the table by 54 points before finishing again in second place. Tony Brown will lead them to the 1973 Gillette Cup, Mike Procter to the 1977 Benson and Hedges. David Green's history of the county will carry photographs of both of them, brandishing their trophies, each time borne aloft on the broad shoulder of a laughing David Shepherd. But the century will draw to a close with no sign of the championship pennant.

"Everyone is working for everyone else," David tells the Bristol Evening Post at the end of his six matches as captain. "This is the best county side I've ever played in." He sits in his dining room, and he reads the article. "That's exactly how I feel thirty years later, how I feel about the boys. Dear old Ron Nicholls, John Mortimore, Smithy, Shep. I loved every minute of it."

"Memories," his wife Joyce smiles. "They don't get the front room painted, though, do they?"

NORTHAMPTONSHIRE v GLOUCESTERSHIRE

Northampton, 25, 26 & 27 June 1969

GLOUCESTERSHIRE WON BY 9 WICKETS

NORTHAMPTONSHIRE

*R.M. Prideaux	b Procter	6	c Meyer b Davey	1
H.M. Ackerman	b Davey	41	c Smith b Procter	37
A. Lightfoot	lbw b Procter	0	c Smith b Procter	86
B.L. Reynolds	c Mortimore b Procter	40	c Allen b Smith	4
D.S. Steele	c Nicholls b Allen	47	retired hurt	0
P. Willey	c Meyer b Procter	43	c Procter b Allen	55
H. Sully	lbw b Davey	0	c Meyer b Procter	8
M.E. Scott	b Allen	12	not out	22
+L.A. Johnson	c & b Procter	6	c Pullar b Procter	4
A.J. Durose	not out	3	b Procter	0
P. Lee	run out	1	b Procter	26
Extras	*lb 6*	6	*b 6, lb 4, nb 4*	14
		205		**257**

1-18, 2-18, 3-60, 4-112, 5-176, 6-176, 7-185, 8-199, 9-203, 10-205
1-19, 2-45, 3-50, 4-183, 5-203, 6-206, 7-210, 8-210, 9-257

Procter	16.2	2	46	5	26.5	7	71	6
Davey	15	0	58	2	23	3	86	1
Smith	17	6	44	0	14	2	38	1
Green	4	1	3	0				
Mortimore	15	8	25	0	6	5	4	0
Allen	9	2	23	2	22	9	44	1

GLOUCESTERSHIRE

D.M. Green	c Willey b Lee	38	c Prideaux b Durose	15
R.B. Nicholls	c Steele b Sully	47	not out	36
D. Shepherd	b Lee	0	not out	40
G. Pullar	lbw b Sully	38		
M.J. Procter	b Durose	6		
M. Bissex	c Sully b Willey	24		
*D.A. Allen	c Johnson b Scott	50		
J.B. Mortimore	not out	124		
D.R. Smith	c Steele b Scott	0		
+B.J. Meyer	not out	21		
J. Davey				
Extras	*lb 8, nb 9*	17	*b 4, lb 4, nb 1*	9
	(8 wkts, dec)	**365**	(1 wkt)	**100**

1-79, 2-85, 3-104, 4-121, 5-141, 6-185, 7-305, 8-307
1-27

Durose	24	6	68	1	12	2	38	1
Lee	29	4	70	2	8	1	29	0
Willey	15	1	45	1	4	1	9	0
Sully	32	5	89	2				
Scott	20	8	62	2	5	1	11	0
Steele	3	0	14	0				
Ackerman					0.4	0	4	0

Umpires: G.H. Pope and P.B. Wight

193

NEVER IN DOUBT, OLD BOY

Glamorgan v Essex

August & September 1969

chosen by Peter Walker

Peter Walker was born in Bristol in 1936. He spent most of his childhood in South Africa, returning to the U.K. after a spell in the merchant navy. A tall right-handed batsman and slow left-arm bowler, he was an outstanding fielder close to the wicket. He played for Glamorgan from 1956 to 1972 and three times for England in 1960. After retiring from playing, he enjoyed a successful career in broadcasting, but he has now returned to cricket as Director of Development of the Cricket Board of Wales.

He remembers a breathtaking finish at Swansea in a year when Glamorgan were pressing for the county championship.

"People undervalued fielding in the sixties," Peter reflects. "Not everybody was expected to be a competent fielder like today. There were a lot of duds around."

"When I played," Worcestershire's Ron Headley says, "it was two to third man, regular. It wasn't an occasion. You tapped it down, it only had to go a yard either side of him, you walked two. Today every quick bowler can run round, pick up and throw."

"You win the game in the field," Peter reckons. "The chap who scores a hundred to put his side in a winning position, if he then drops number eleven, he's wiped that hundred out."

If it is in the fielding skills that the modern game has shown the greatest improvement, then perhaps the genesis of that improvement occurred here in Wales with Wilf Wooller's championship-winning team of 1948. "We cannot compete with Middlesex in batting or Derbyshire in bowling," he said in the after-glow of their success, "but in fielding we give first to no side. We have attempted to make each fielder, be he a deep long-on or a short-leg, an integral part of a machine." Wilf is the driving force of Glamorgan cricket, 14 years as captain, 31 as secretary, but in 1969 he still awaits a second championship. But perhaps at last the machine is again in good shape. "Wilf was very generous," Peter remembers. "He always went on record as saying that the '69 side was the best he'd seen play for Glamorgan."

August the 30th, 1969. The summer of Charles's investiture as Prince of Wales, and Glamorgan sit on top of the table, 13 points ahead of Surrey with just three matches left to play: Essex here in Swansea, Worcestershire in Cardiff, then off to the Oval to play Surrey themselves. "Worcester were a goodish side, but we thought we could take them at Cardiff. But we never did that well at the Oval so we knew we needed to win this game against Essex."

For seven of the past ten summers Yorkshire have won the championship. Now, in this age of overseas cricketers and the John Player Sunday League, they languish in the lower reaches of the table. Just as the Beatles, whose singles have dominated the charts for seven years, have had their last number one. Nobody here quite realises it, but an era has ended.

Alan Jones takes strike to the match's first ball. For a quarter of a century, he is at the heart of Glamorgan's batting. The eighth child of a South Wales miner, he hits a thousand runs in each of the 23 seasons from 1961. And not all Welsh wickets are as easy for the batsmen as the one here at St Helens today. "He was a super bloke," Peter recalls. "Always well turned out, always polite. When he got out early, we often struggled." Yet he will have just one Test cap to show for it. Next summer at Lord's, when the South African tour is cancelled, he will open against a Rest of the World XI. And for nine years his name will appear in the Wisden list of England cricketers. Then it will be gone, the game no longer deemed a Test match. "He's the most generous, gracious guy, but in private I think he still feels it. That Rest of the World team was the strongest side which ever walked this earth. Procter came in at number nine for God's sake. If that wasn't international standard, I don't know what was." Now he must live with the tag of the highest run-scorer never to play Test cricket. Just as Don Shepherd, his team-mate in this Glamorgan side, is the highest wicket-taker.

It is 1969. Glamorgan have been a first-class county for 49 years, and they have provided just seven players for the England side. At times it rankles. But not in 1969, not with a championship to be won. Surrey lose Edrich and Arnold to England, but Glamorgan field the same team match after match. Beyond this eleven, they only turn to leg-spinner David Lewis, for two appearances, and to their ex-captain Ossie Wheatley.

It was Ossie who came here as captain when a 47-year-old Wilf Wooller finally called it a day at the end of 1960. He is a Cambridge man like Wilf, and Peter recalls his six years of captaincy with affection. "Ossie created a wholly different feeling. He brought with him some of the undergraduate freshness, this sense that we've got to take a chance and it doesn't matter if we lose because we've got the ability to win more than we lose. Ossie Wheatley to me created the side that Tony Lewis inherited and polished."

And what polish! When Roger Davis is lbw in the third over of the day, his place is taken by Majid Jahanghir Khan. They still talk of his 147 here two years ago for the visiting Pakistanis. Thirteen sixes in less than an hour and a half of blazing strokeplay. With Wilf Wooller at Cambridge University with Majid's father, and all the counties suddenly free to sign an overseas player, it is an innings of perfect timing, and already in his own quiet way he is an integral part of this happy mix that forms the Glamorgan dressing room.

195

"We gave him the nickname Bearer, because he came from one of the hundred best families in Pakistan and of course they all had servants. So we used to tease him that he was our bearer, and he took it very well. If Tony ever wanted a big innings from him, he would take him round the boundary edge. 'Bearer, if you get fifty today, there's four ice creams for you, six if you get a hundred.' And it was extraordinary how often that worked." Not at Chelmsford in the previous match, though. Peter still recalls his reaction to the shot that got him out. "He was a devout, strict Muslim. He never swore, he was very quiet. He went into the groundsman's hut, borrowed a saw and sawed his bat in half without saying a word to anybody."

'Majid made a quiet start,' the South Wales Echo reports, 'and it was some time before he brought loud appreciative applause from the crowd with a glorious drive through the covers for four.' And his new bat? He has called on Bill Edwards' shop by the ground, and he has taken a bat from the window. "It had been there all summer. It was bleached white by the sun. The rubber handle was starting to perish from the heat of this magnifying glass of a shop window. It was just a plank, like a piece of the Victory." But there are no fairy tale endings today, and no ice creams. 'Majid tried to lift East away but failed to get to the pitch of the ball and skied it to mid on.' With Tony Lewis soon caught behind, it is 65 for three, Alan Jones still there but the Sunday Telegraph wondering about the wisdom of opting to bat first. 'On a wicket of such lasting excellence as St Helens, the toss has only relative merit. There were knowledgeable supporters who would have been happier had Glamorgan extracted what morning life there was from the wicket in terms of victims rather than runs.' And who are these knowledgeable supporters? Perhaps the Sunday Telegraph correspondent is one of them. His name? Wilfred Wooller.

From the high eyrie of the Swansea pavilion Bryan Davis, the Trinidadian, joins Alan Jones. Bryan has opened the batting for the West Indies, but that was in the Caribbean. Over here he has struggled to find his touch, "he couldn't come to terms with opening when the ball moved around in English conditions," and he has had to swallow his pride and drop down the order. Tony Lewis has promised him his county cap if he completes his 1000 runs today, and Alan Jones gains 'solid support from his new partner who picked the right ball to hit - and hit it so hard that he found the boundary five times with his first seven scoring shots.'

Bryan Davis and Majid Khan are the official overseas players. But they are not the only ones who have grown up abroad. There is Tony Cordle, the cheerful Barbadian who has emerged from Cardiff club cricket. Eight years ago he stood on the staircase of the Cardiff Labour Exchange, a new arrival in a damp and strange country, and he spied the green grass and the scoreboard of the old Arms Park ground, "the first friendly sight I'd seen in Britain." Now he is TC, Top Cat, at the heart of the dressing room fun, though the local papers portray a different image. "He had a job with British Railways,

196

and all his career the press used to publish this picture of him in what was a British Railways shunter's cap. He used to get so incensed." And there is Peter himself, who has worked his passage to Cardiff from South Africa. It is a very different mix from the side that Wilf led in 1948. But then so much is changing in Britain in the sixties. In any case, a winner in Wales is soon an honorary Welshman.

"The Swinging Sixties," Peter reflects. "At the time it didn't seem like such a culture shock but, looking back now, it was. We had long hair and sideburns. For a while a lot of us wore these Caribbean shirts - with v-necks instead of collars." What does Wilf Wooller think of that? "Not much, but we told him he wasn't up with the times." Like the current players tell Peter today when he shakes his head at the coloured clothes they wear for Sunday cricket.

Bryan Davis and Majid Khan, the rum-drinking party-goer and the strict Muslim. Whose idea was it to have them share digs in Cardiff? "What a combination!" Peter laughs. The problem is resolved now, and success has bred tolerance all round this dressing room. "For four months of the season we were never out of the top five. We were on a long, ecstasy-type high." *At 156 Jones got a top edge and was caught in the covers, Walker stayed for a while before being caught at mid-on,'* but Bryan Davis comes off at tea to receive his county cap. 78 not out, and the total 210 for five.

Essex versus Glamorgan. Two good social sides, both prepared to lose in search of victory. Essex, led by Brian Taylor, the Cockney sergeant-major. Glamorgan, led by Tony Lewis, the fiddle-playing Welshman. "There was a great camaraderie between Essex and ourselves. So when they came to play at St Helens, the first thing we agreed was, 'Whoever bats first, we guarantee we'll leave a reasonable target, not an easy one but a gettable one.' They were a very amusing bunch, and we delighted in playing against them because they gave it a go." That is certainly not how Peter remembers Glamorgan versus Essex in the days of Wilf Wooller, Doug Insole and Trevor Bailey. "Doug was most amusing and so was Trevor in his own dry way, but of course they had Cambridge as a link with Wilf and we didn't. It was still in the days when that meant something. Wilf's battles with Robin Marlar at Sussex were legendary. It was a huge contest between them, and the rest of us just turned up for their private battle. We were the archers, if you like, in Henry the Fifth's army at Agincourt."

Wilf Wooller may be secretary and press reporter now, but he is as hungry for fresh triumphs, as frustrated by the seasons of failure, as ever. "I remember Wilf once apologising when we finished at the back end of the table," Peter tells. "There was a press conference. 'Well, you've got to remember,' he said, 'that we're in a period of transition.' The players looked at one another. And we weren't sure where we were transiting from or to! For about fifteen of the eighteen seasons I played we were in a transitional period." Maybe this year they will discover their destination.

210 for five at tea, it is soon 239 for nine, only Ossie Wheatley to come. He retired in 1966 to pursue his business career, but each time a fast bowler gets injured they turn to him. In 1968 it was Jeff Jones, finally established as an England bowler, throwing his elbow out at Ilford, never to play again. In 16 matches Ossie took 82 wickets and finished at the head of the national averages. Now it is Lawrence Williams, exhausted at the end of his first season in county cricket. "Lawrence came straight out of the South Wales league. He did us a fantastic job, but he was shot by the end of the season with the sheer physical strain of playing. It left him short of everything - pace, legs, the lot." So it is back once more to Ossie. "He wasn't in sparkling form, but he certainly had the best bowling brain of anybody I've ever played with or against. He was the only example I can think of at first-class level of a wholly coached action succeeding. He was never quick, but he got into all the right M.C.C. positions, and he knew how to bowl at different batsmen."

Ossie is not a batsman, and he is soon remounting the endless Pavilion steps, caught and bowled Hobbs for nought. *'The final total of 241 was disappointing,'* Wilf Wooller writes.

Ossie is not a fielder. "He was a good enough bowler to play for England," Tony Lewis writes, "but his lumbering fielding style must have gone against him." "Poor old Oz," Peter laughs, "he couldn't see very far without glasses, and he never wore them to field. You had to shout if it was on the way to him. He was very tall, somewhat ungainly, and he couldn't bend. A delightful guy, a marvellous bowler, but I can't remember a worse fielder, certainly in our side, possibly in the whole U.K."

Tony Lewis leads the team out, and Ossie goes down to third man for Malcolm Nash's first over. The sun is shining, there is a crowd of six thousand, and Ward and Edmeades open up for Essex. As they did in very different conditions last Tuesday at Chelmsford, when Majid sawed his bat in the groundsman's hut and Tony Lewis set Essex a gettable 199 to win. No ice creams for Majid at Chelmsford, nor would he have wanted any. The rain teemed down, but Glamorgan refused to leave the field. "We were desperate to win. Losing didn't matter, that was the attitude we had. The only side that could have won was Essex, particularly when it became impossible to hold the ball. In fact, I remember this vividly now, Tony Cordle fielded for the last hour holding an umbrella in the outfield. Now can you imagine that happening in modern cricket? 'You can't play in this rain,' he said. 'I'm not going to stand out here and die. I'm from Barbados.' He only put it down when he had to field." Taylor and Edmeades took the score to 72 for no wicket, and "it was only given up because Brian Taylor said it was becoming a farce." Here at Swansea Essex reach 68 for three at close of play, two late wickets for Ossie, and Wilf Wooller declares the game *'evenly balanced'*.

At the Oval, Hampshire have piled up 401 for four against Surrey, but the young Bob Willis, in only his third championship match, does not stay to inspect his bowling figures. Surrey have Sunday free, and he hurries to Waterloo station where he takes a train to Portsmouth, then a ferry to the Isle of Wight. By midnight he is one of a hundred thousand people in a great field at Britain's biggest ever pop festival.

Here in Swansea it is drinks for the teams. "You always had a beer with the opposition on the first two evenings. If you broke that, you were considered a very self-centred human being. The weakest drink you had was a shandy. Nobody had shorts, but it could be pints of black and tan." A soft drink, though, for Majid, and a rum-and-coke for Bryan Davis. "Nowadays they have eleven pints of milk and an orange squash." But the real fun in Swansea is saved for Sunday night.

It is the summer of 1969. Tony Jacklin wins the British Open Golf, Ann Jones wins the Wimbledon Ladies' Singles, and Jackie Stewart becomes motor racing champion of the world. High-grade crude oil is discovered in the North Sea while Neil Armstrong takes mankind's first steps on the moon.

Sunday is another day of competitive cricket. It is the first season of the John Player League, and Essex are in second place. "We considered it to be like baseball," Peter remembers. "It was paper hat and red nose time," Tony Lewis writes. "It was like playing Monopoly the short way, dealing out the properties first." But Essex are taking it more seriously. "We adapted to it quite well," their slow left-armer Ray East recalls. "Some counties started with two slips, a gully and forward short leg." Here at Swansea Essex make 180 in 40 overs, and so far this summer Glamorgan have not managed more than 151. But Brian Taylor, Essex's captain, is not a mathematician; "he found it quite difficult to work out how to get five bowlers into forty overs unless he stuck to his format: 4,4,8,8,4,8,4." Ray bowls his eight overs from the sea end. He is the country's leading wicket-taker on Sundays, but "Majid, Bryan Davis, Tony Lewis could hit the spinners," Ray tells. "They kept hitting me over the stand. I think they were firing warnings on the beach that I was still bowling." He bowls unchanged, and his eight overs go for a record 79 runs. It is thirteen years before a bowler concedes more Sunday runs. "I honestly thought it would never be broken. Now you carry more than five bowlers so, if somebody gets hit around, they just get taken off."

Sunday League cricket is in its infancy. Now that teams set out their stall for totals of 250 or 300, it is not so hard to imagine a bowler going for almost 80 runs. But there is one Essex record that first summer that will never be beaten. "One of the most wonderful records of all time," Robin Hobbs calls it. With eight victories in their first nine games, they travelled to Yeovil in late July and so short-staffed were they that they summoned the long-retired Doug Insole. "He came down by train with his great leather kitbag. A child was sick all over the bag, and he was run out without facing a ball." The pitch turned square and, with the big-hitting Keith Boyce stuck at the other end, Brian Ward decided to see off Langford, Somerset's off-spinner. "I thought he was the danger man," Brian said afterwards. "I thought I'd play him out." Langford, eight overs, eight maidens, nought for nought. "Talk about records like Laker's. That'll never be beaten." They made just 126, but they only lost by two wickets in the final over. And here at Swansea Essex make 180 and, though Ray East goes for 79, they win on the final ball by one run.

On the Isle of Wight, the Times reports, *'one young couple embraced in a mass of soap foam as part of a "happening". Later the girl who said she came from "nowhere" remarked, "It was beautiful."'*

The cricket is not the highlight of a Sunday in Swansea. That comes in the evening. "We used to go to a little village called Pontardulais which was in the Swansea valley. We used to go to a pub called The Fountain Inn which was where the Pontardulais Male Voice Choir adjourned after their Sunday evening rehearsals. We took the Australians there in '68 and '64, we took all the sides we got on well with. On the county circuit the Swansea fixture became the game to play in. We'd go down as one group of cricketers from the two teams and we'd sit there. We'd have a couple of beers, and we'd join in the singing. The Essex boys adored it."

Alan and Eifion, the Jones brothers, are Welsh-speaking miner's sons, "Alan was a very fine singer," and Tony Lewis has played in the National Youth Orchestra. "Wilf never quite trusted him because he played a violin." Don Shepherd is a local from the Gower Peninsula, but what of some of the immigrants? "I can sing in Welsh without quite understanding what I'm saying," Peter admits. "They were all well-known hymns and arias." In any case, this is the sixties, and there are musical cross-overs everywhere. "Tony Cordle always used to lead us in Delilah, that was his forte. Wherever he went, he was always called on to sing it." And the Essex players are not slow to join in. "I wouldn't say that we were up to the male voice choir," Ray East recalls, "but we had a funny trio. Myself, John Lever and Brian Ward. We used to call ourselves the Odd Bods. 'The Green Green Grass of Home', we surprised them that we could sing that as well. Beatles, Rolling Stones. Frank Sinatra. We did 'The Lady Is A Tramp' and 'New York, New York'." Frank Sinatra? His songs are not that easy to sing, are they? "Well, anything's easy to sing when you've had a couple of pints."

'Hey, Mr Tambourine Man, play a song for me,' a white-suited Bob Dylan sings in an Isle of Wight farm field. *'I'm not sleepy and there is no place I'm going to.'* John Lennon and Jane Fonda sit cross-legged two rows from the stage, but Bob Willis is hundreds of yards away. "Probably the worst concert he ever gave," he reflects laconically. In the small hours he heads back to the ferry and the Waterloo train, arriving at the Oval with five minutes to spare. Surrey are all out for 208, and soon after tea they are following on.

Monday the first of September is little better for Glamorgan. When the covers are removed at the start of play, it emerges that the stumps have been stolen, but Essex are 304 for seven before a bowler disturbs the new set. South African Lee Irvine hits his first Essex century, celebrates by pulling Don Shepherd for six, then dances down the wicket and is bowled. His is the steady batting, though, for at the other end Fletcher's *'sparkling 49 bore the stamp of consummate class'*, Boyce made 16 *'with murderous intent'*, and Brian Taylor *'punished the bowling ruthlessly to the tune of 70 runs'*. *'Boundaries came in such abundance that, in the last half hour before luncheon, Glamorgan had the deep field heavily manned.'*

A September Monday in Swansea, and twelve thousand spectators create a record post-war crowd for a county championship game at St Helens. There have been more for tourist matches, but then they are like Test matches for the Welsh nation. Especially here in Swansea. Who will ever forget the scenes here last year when Glamorgan beat the Australians for the second tour running? 'Bread of Heaven', 'Land of My Fathers', 'Ar hyd y nos', they sang them all. Even 'Waltzing Matilda'.

'Some of the Essex side were saying on Sunday,' John Woodcock writes in the Times, *'that if cricket was always played in the spirit of these matches with Glamorgan, the game would have no problems. On a perfect pitch, more strokes were played than one usually sees in weeks of watching. The only trouble, from Glamorgan's point of view, was that the majority of them came from Essex.'* With a lead of 95, Brian Taylor declares. "They could have played us out of the game without any trouble," Peter remembers, "but they gave themselves the best chance of winning by declaring. And we made a bit of a pig's ear of it in the second innings."

Surrey may be following on at the Oval, but Gloucestershire are beating Somerset at Bristol. If they win and Glamorgan do not, they will move to within three points of the leaders. Roger Davis is bowled behind his legs, but *'Alan Jones and Majid rode hell for leather for half an hour.'* Then, his concentration broken by *'a series of announcements that could have waited to the tea interval'*, Majid hits across the line and is bowled. It is 50 for two. Tony Lewis scores a careful 21, *'batting as though suddenly aware of the pressures of their position'*, but he falls before the arrears are cleared, and the match is slipping away.

'Essex looked the better side on the day,' the Western Mail tells, *'to remain Glamorgan's bogy side.'* The Glamorgan players may look forward to their visits from Essex, but they are beginning to need long memories to recall the last time they beat them. This is their eleventh contest since that last taste of victory, longer than against any other county. Twice they have had Essex hanging on with nine wickets down. Three years ago here Don Shepherd needed one off the last ball and he was caught on the square leg boundary. Then there is Robin Hobbs, 34 wickets in his last three matches in Wales and

even a maiden century last summer at Ilford - and he had never hit a fifty in 237 previous attempts. How he must look forward to these Glamorgan fixtures! In three years' time he will arrive here in mid-August with a championship tally of just 11 wickets, a bowling average of nearly 80. Essex are as ever in financial straits, no reserves on their staff. "You never got in and out. You played. There was no pressure on you." And he will have figures of nought for 78 at one point in the second innings, Glamorgan will be chasing runs for a quick declaration, and he will visit their dressing room. "I've had a crap season so far," he will say. "If you're going to get out, get out my end." And he will come off with seven for 118. "Brilliant," he laughs. "I didn't care how I got them." *'A feature of Glamorgan's second innings,'* Wisden will report, *'was the clever leg-break bowling of Hobbs.'*

"Being a first-class cricketer," Peter reflects, "was like being in a protected Masonic-type club, a sort of Brotherhood of Man for pro players. It was a fabulous life, provided you weren't a battler. If you held your own with the bat or ball, it was a super way of wandering your way through from April till September. And it was a wander. It really was. Delightful. I thoroughly enjoyed the sixties. Wouldn't change any of it."

A delightful wander, fifteen years of transition. Now there is a chance to make history, to become part of the folklore of the valleys of South Wales. Robin Hobbs throws up an inviting leg-break, and *'Bryan Davis was caught by Irvine, running back at deep mid-off.'* Four good wickets down and a lead of just 14 as Peter makes his way to the middle. *'Glamorgan,'* Brian Chapman writes, *'found themselves in the Valley of Tribulation.'* Alan Jones and Peter, *'these two steadied the ship,'* but 123 for four at close is no cause for hymns and arias from the twelve thousand who depart the ground.

"People often ask me," Peter says, "if I'd rather be playing now. Certainly for the money I would. But I feel privileged to have played the same game that W.G. Grace played. Three days each, and 32 matches." This is starting to change by 1969. One-day cricket has arrived, and the fixture card is down to 24 championship matches. They do not know it here in 1969, but the great changes of the sixties are but the harbingers of greater changes still to come. "It's become a game with a greater emphasis on instant action instead of the reflective game I played. The cricketer that plays the game now is only a third cousin, twice removed, from the animal who played in my era. The attitude is very different."

It is September 1969. The T.U.C. demands equal pay for women, and Britain's longest-surviving heart transplant patient dies three months after his operation. In Fleet Street Robert Maxwell drops his bid for the ailing Sun, leaving the way clear for Rupert Murdoch, who promises "a much more independent paper."

Tuesday morning. An eleven o'clock start, and Peter sets out to be *'the shield and buckler'* of Glamorgan's innings. Alan Jones on-drives Hobbs for six before falling to a catch behind the wicket. His brother Eifion *'livened up proceedings'* with a quickfire 28, Tony Cordle hits two great sixes in his 30, but it is almost lunchtime before Peter sweeps his first boundary. *'An impatient crowd gave him the slow handclap,'* Brian Chapman reports, *'but, without his innings, Glamorgan would have been harried out of the game.'* They reach lunch at 236 for seven, a lead of just 141, and Peter knows that once he and Malcolm Nash are parted, there is just Don Shepherd and Ossie to come. "Malcolm was essentially a hitter, yet he played this wholly uncharacteristic innings. He blocked it out while I fenced away. We just ground it out really, trying to waste time. We were effectively out of the game." Essex take the new ball, the score somehow reaches 284 for eight, "and that's when Tony came up with this inspired declaration." 190 in just under two hours. "Whoever bats first," the captains have agreed on Saturday morning, "we'll leave a gettable target." It must be gettable if Glamorgan are to have any chance of bowling out Essex on this *'perfect batting wicket'*.

Swansea's last afternoon of cricket in 1969. Malcolm Nash and Ossie Wheatley sharing the last new ball. Just as they did in the last game of 1968 - with a ball that now sits in the Trent Bridge museum. A ball that Gary Sobers despatched for six sixes in one over, the last one so huge that it was not discovered till the next day, somewhere down towards the town hall. Malcolm Nash was the bowler, "he had a heart the size of a cricket pitch; he always wanted to bowl, no matter what the score." Peter remembers his reaction to that fateful over. "He was smiling broadly as he walked off alongside Gary. 'We've gone into the record books, and you couldn't have done it without me.' That was typical of him. He always turned it back into a positive." Don Shepherd remembers the scene in the dressing room afterwards. "Everyone was chiding him, and he sat there quietly with a drink in his hand. 'I'll have the last laugh,' he said. 'Somebody will probably write a book about it.' And young Brian Lewis said, 'What will they call it? 'Gone With The Wind'?'"

Malcolm Nash, three overs for 16 runs. He is top of the county's bowling averages, but his pace and swing are not the answer this afternoon. Tony Cordle replaces him, two overs for 21. "With Tony you knew he was trying. It's just that he didn't always get it in the right parish. If you wanted a tight over, you didn't throw the ball to Tony Cordle. But every now and then he bowled the unplayable delivery." As he did in June at Colwyn Bay. Coming on as seventh bowler, "the last option", he took nine for 49, the best bowling figures of 1969. "What on earth Leicester made of it, I've no idea." But that is the secret of this Glamorgan side. There is always somebody who produces a match-winning performance. "We had massive talents. Every one of those players could look back on that season and see there was a match he'd won."

Here at St Helens Ossie Wheatley takes three wickets with a spell *'whose speed appeared deceptively mild'*. Edmeades, Ward and Taylor are all caught off *'slightly slower deliveries'*, and it is 43 for three when Fletcher and Irvine take up the chase, 89 for three at the call of the last hour with its minimum now of 20 more overs. Five an over to win, and Fletcher *'playing another gem of an innings'*. Ossie has retired to the deep, and the bowling is now in the hands of the eternal Don Shepherd, treasuring his action still in his twentieth season, and Roger Davis who, according to the Guardian, *'deals in gently optimistic off-breaks.'*

"You win the game in the field," Peter says, and at the heart of this Glamorgan team are the quartet of close catchers that crouch around the bat. Bryan Davis and Majid in the slips, Roger Davis and Peter in the leg trap. The leg-side fielders are closer than in the modern game. "People stand deeper now. They're playing on better pitches, quicker pitches as well, and they're armour-plated, that slows you down. It's like carrying top weight in the National. But the closer you can stand, the more balls will go straight at you." A young Peter has stood here between Wilf Wooller and Allan Watkins, and he provides the link with that last great Glamorgan fielding side. "Shep was bowling beautifully all that summer, and we had this pride of close catchers like lions. I was the old bull in the middle. Whenever a wicket went down, I used to call them together and we'd have a competition. We'd stand as close as we reasonably could, and we'd throw the ball amongst ourselves - at some velocity, too. We'd regroup at the next wicket, and we'd keep the score. It was a game within a game."

Catching. "If you think catching a cricket ball is hard, you try catching a potato. All odd shapes. Different sizes, different weights." Peter is the greatest catcher of a cricket ball of his generation. Yet his skill began with potatoes. That spell in the merchant navy after he left home in South Africa. With his Dutch ship mate Benny Le Ross. Three months on a Finnish ship travelling from the Persian Gulf to Los Angeles. On the top deck they threw potatoes at each other, "just to escape the boredom when we were off watch". A great contest, Holland versus South Africa. "And of course the potatoes would regularly disappear over the side. But I learnt how to catch with soft hands, how to fall on the metal deck without giving myself a serious bang, and how to try for everything." They are lessons that he retains throughout his career. "Unfortunately we ran out of potatoes two weeks before we got to L.A."

Holland versus South Africa on the top deck, the game within the game for the pride of lions around the bat. And on rainy days there is Klaverjas, "a horrendously complicated Jewish card game that I brought over from South Africa". Alan Jones, Bryan Davis and Malcolm Nash make up the foursome. "It was a kibbitzing game. You were allowed to stand around and comment on the inadequacy of the players." There are only pence at stake, though sometimes you would not know it from Bryan's volatile play.

The picaresque journey of Peter's life sees him "in perpetual summer", playing cricket all year in the U.K. and South Africa. His father was a journalist who emigrated to the warmer climate when he contracted TB, an educated man with liberal values, but "in South Africa he was described as a communist". By 1969 Peter is feeling the same contradictions. "I found myself increasingly embarrassed in going to South Africa and coming back to play in a team with Majid Khan, Bryan Davis and Tony Cordle. I became very left-wing by South African standards."

It is the end of the summer of 1969. Police evict squatters from a 100-room mansion at 144 Piccadilly, and Catholics in Northern Ireland cheer the arrival of British troops.

It is 109 for three. *'Then, as Essex appeared to be sailing merrily to victory, Glamorgan struck again to revive once more the tension and excitement that only cricket can bring.'* Fletcher hits a *'full-blooded pull'*, and Bryan Davis dives at full length *'for a catch that surely bruised his knuckles and knees'*. 'Try for everything' is Peter's maxim, and by half past four *'the cool head and cunning'* of Don Shepherd have outwitted Lee Irvine, and Tony Lewis has backpedalled for a third *'awkward catch'* to dismiss Keith Boyce. 125 for six, 65 still to win, and the sight of Boyce climbing back up the pavilion steps brings fresh heart to the vast Swansea crowd. "Keith had all the shots," Ray East reflects. "And when he hit it, it stayed hit. If he'd have come off, we'd have won easily."

On Sunday Glamorgan failed by one run to match Essex's 180 in 40 overs. With no need to take wickets to win and a maximum of eight overs a bowler, it is a form of cricket that the players are still trying to fathom - those that take it seriously, anyway. But here on Tuesday Essex need 190 in 37 overs, and Glamorgan need ten wickets. Both teams know exactly how to play this game. "Gordon Barker went in to close up the shop," Ray East remembers, "but Glamorgan realised this and brought the fielders in. So he thought, 'If they're in, I'll go for it.'"

'Barker was the man who mattered,' John Woodcock declares in the Times, and he faces Shep with Peter's pride of close catchers all round him. "I always called him Albert," Peter tells. "He loved singing. He'd been right in the middle of the Pontardulais Male Voice Choir, and he was the man we thought we had to get out. 'Albert,' I remember saying to him, 'if ever you needed to lose your wicket this season, this is it.' 'I'm not going to do that,' he said, 'but I'll tell you something. I'm not going to stop playing shots. So if I hit in the air it could be your day.' And he was absolutely true to his word." He skies Shep to deep square leg, and the crowd gasps with horror as Alan Jones loses the ball in the sun. Then he celebrates his escape by hitting a great six off the ever philosophical Shep.

Turner is snapped up in the leg trap, but Robin Hobbs enjoys another encounter with his favourite opponents. *'He profitably patented a looped swing like that made famous by Bruen the golfer,'* Brian Chapman reports. *'Any weapon that came handy would do now.'* At five to five, there are four overs left, and the score has reached 163 for seven, just 27 to win. Robin is a great social cricketeter, and it wins him more selections for overseas tours than many a player of similar ability, and in ten years' time he will be lured out of retirement to take on the captaincy of Glamorgan. "He liked the lifestyle," Ray East says. "He liked the way they played their cricket." He is certainly not one who will block out the draw and, when he dances down the wicket to Shep, *'he was stumped so far out of his ground that Eifion Jones waved him goodbye with the gesture that removed the bails.'* Ray East joins Gordon Barker, and there is only John Lever to come. "I'd been playing since '66," Ray says, "so I'd just about learnt what batting was about.". By the start of the final over, there are seven to win, and Gordon Barker is on strike to Roger Davis, with his *'gently optimistic off-breaks'*. "I wouldn't say he was a big spinner," Ray says kindly, "but he was very tight on length and line."

Seven to win. A single first ball, another second. *'Then Barker strolled two yards down the wicket, missed and was stumped.'* A single for John Lever, a single for Ray East, and there are three to win with one ball to bowl. "We could have blocked it out for a draw," Ray remembers, "but, because the game had been so exciting, we met halfway up the wicket and decided to go for it." There is no pride of catchers around the bat now, the boundary is manned everywhere by fielders, so where should they look for their runs?

"There were a lot of dud fielders around in the sixties," Peter says. And who is the worst of them here? The worst possibly in the whole UK, if Peter is to be believed. "We had this devious plan," Ray tells, "that we were going to get the ball to Ossie Wheatley." John Lever is a right-handed batsman, and Ossie is on the third man boundary, down near the sight screen to stop the edged four. "I think you'll find that John played some sort of reverse hit," Ray remembers. "And we decided that, if he made any contact whatever, we were going for two." "No, that's not right," Peter says. "He ran it down through the gully." *'Lever chopped it down almost intentionally to third man,'* the South Wales Echo reports, *'as if realising that Wheatley is weak on his fielding.'* What a cruel game is cricket! Two runs will bring scores level, with five points to Essex as the side batting last. The ball runs down, well to Ossie's right, and all the results are possible as the batsmen set off on their first run.

"Poor old Oz," Peter laughs. "He couldn't see very far without glasses. You had to shout if it was on the way to him." His team mates watch with sinking hearts as he lumbers towards the ball. "He runs to his right, towards the Cricketers' pub. He picks it up, and at full gallop bangs it back. A very awkward bounce to Eifion Jones, wide of the wicket, and he beats John in by several yards. Because John, seeing it was Ossie, has coasted the first run." *'Glamorgan and Essex are good friends,'* John Woodcock declares, *'but without difficulty they could disprove any charge of collusion. It was simply a wonderful finish to a glorious match, and it was followed, I need hardly say, by the wildest jubilation.'*

"We all raced over to Ossie to congratulate him. 'That was amazing,' we all said, and I'll never forget his reply. 'Never in doubt, old boy. Never in doubt.' But if ever something was in doubt, it was that. There were two runs there every day of the week except the second of September 1969."

"I think people didn't realise that Ossie had a very good arm," Don Shepherd reflects. "And what hasn't come out of the tale over the years is that it was such a good take by Eifion Jones. A terrific take. He was so nimble that he made it look as if it was all part of a day's work."

On Sunday Essex won by one run to be runner-ups in the John Player League. Now on Tuesday Glamorgan have won by one run to make them strong favourites for the championship. "The crowd surged onto the pitch," Peter recalls. "I've seen similar events when English counties have won, but there isn't quite the battle cry that the Welsh supporter has. And Wilf was waiting at the top of the steps. He gave every player he could lay his hands on a great hug - which nearly broke a few ribs because he was a big fellow."

"The crowd carried a few of the Glamorgan boys off," Ray East recalls. "I think they carried us off. They were all singing as well. We had a glass with them, but we had to hit the road." But Don Shepherd remembers differently. "Carried off? No, they wouldn't carry you off. They'd gather round and follow you up the steps. Crowds were much more restrained in those days. Plenty ran on, trying to get a souvenir stump, but we would have beaten them to that."

Surrey have little to show for three days at the Oval and, though Gloucestershire win, they are thirteen points adrift with one game left to Glamorgan's two. *'It will take an unusual combination of the weather and the peculiar points system to give Gloucestershire the mastery,'* Alan Gibson laments in the Times. *'Still it is worthwhile uttering a few prayers beneath the yews of Painswick.'*

"Alan Gibson," Peter sighs. "What a magnificent writer! We played Hampshire at Basingstoke one year. He wrote 750 words in the Times. 740 of them were a tirade against Basingstoke Council's ugly developments around the ground. That was his match report. You wouldn't get away with that today. Now it's just who did what to whom."

So on to Cardiff for the Worcestershire match. "When the openers went out, Majid was sitting with his pads on. He had his bat upright, and he had his head on it. Roger got hit, and I said, 'Come on, Bearer, it's time to bat.'" It has been a long summer, and the emotions have gradually grown more intense. But Majid walks out with his bleached plank, "like a piece of the Victory", and he scores "this magnificent 156. He just hit every other ball for four. The next highest score was 37. He was just a genius." 156 runs, how many ice creams is that worth?

That is Wednesday, and on Thursday there is even higher emotion as Peter holds the catch that gives Don his two thousandth wicket. Play is halted while they bring out champagne on a tray. Don sips with joy - Don, who started his career twenty years ago as a Welsh teetaller. "You'll never be a bowler on orangeade," Wilf chided him. On Friday, there is joy and more champagne as Bryan Davis clings to the slip catch that guarantees Glamorgan the title. It is live on Welsh television, and the commentator's voice throbs with pride. His name? Wilf Wooller, of course. He puts down the headphones and goes out to greet his team with another round of rib-cracking hugs.

Friday the fifth of September. Glamorgan win the championship, and ITV makes its first colour transmission.

Who would have guessed at this outcome back in early May? In that first match at Swansea when, with nine wickets down, Don held out for twenty minutes against the champions Yorkshire. In the year of Charles' investiture, for the first time since the year of the Prince's birth, Glamorgan have won the county title, and they have won it without losing a game. They have played to win, unafraid to lose, and they have become the first side since Lancashire in 1930 to win the title unbeaten.

The transition is over at last, and Wilf dreams of a Glamorgan side that will dominate the seventies as Surrey have the fifties, Yorkshire the sixties. "But, by the end of the sixties," Peter says, "the counties had evened up. The gap had narrowed." A different county will win the championship in each of the next seven summers before Middlesex and Essex emerge to dominate the early eighties. "We might have learnt from Glamorgan," Ray East reflects. "The fact that team spirit was of paramount importance. When we were successful, we were certainly regarded as having the best team dressing room in the championship."

Here at Swansea there are hymns and arias, 'Land of my Fathers', and a cheer for each of the players. All Welshmen now. Even their genius from Pakistan. *'When Majid appeared too shy, the crowd chanted 'Majid, Majid, Majid', and he received a special cheer.'* "You can't live in Wales and not respond to it," Peter says. "Every pub or shop you went into, in the wilds of west Wales or the Lleyn peninsula, you'd be recognised. People would come up and say, 'We're so pleased. We're proud of what you did for Wales.' That still happens 29 years on. People recognise you as one of the '69 side. As they will this team of '97. People will name them."

"I wouldn't believe it," Don Shepherd remembers. "'I'll wait for the papers tomorrow morning,' I said."

'Gwlad, gwlad, pleidiol wyf i'm gwlad,
Tra mor yn fur i'r bur hoff bau,
O bydded i'r heniaith barhau.'

"Wilf made a speech," Peter tells. "Tony made a speech. But the only thing I remember, I was living in Newport, and my father-in-law came down to see the last day's play. He gave me a lift back, and halfway up a hill we had to stop the car and I was violently ill. I had a head like Birkenhead for three days. I don't think I had a pulse."

208

The committee opens a fund for all the players, the office staff, the groundsman. "It got to be about two thousand pounds," Don thinks. "Then somebody said, 'We'd better close it; we don't want to spoil them.'"

The championship pennant flies at Sophia Gardens, Cardiff, and Peter remembers hauling down the old Glamorgan flag. "It had probably been flying for fifty odd years; it was in tatters. I've still got it in my room. When I die, I'm going to give it to the Welsh Sports Hall of Fame. That was the flag that was flying the day we won the championship. Boy, that was a night."

GLAMORGAN v ESSEX

Swansea. 30 August, 1 & 2 September 1969

GLAMORGAN WON BY 1 RUN

GLAMORGAN

A. Jones	c Boyce b Turner	75	c Taylor b Lever	69
R.C. Davis	lbw b Boyce	2	b Lever	2
Majid Jahangir	c Turner b East	23	b Turner	28
*A.R. Lewis	c Taylor b Turner	1	c Irvine b Lever	21
B.A. Davis	c Ward b East	78	c Irvine b Hobbs	5
P.M. Walker	c Barker b Hobbs	14	c Ward b Boyce	50
M.A. Nash	c Edmeades b Lever	14	not out	36
+E.W. Jones	c Fletcher b East	0	st Taylor b Hobbs	28
A.E. Cordle	c Taylor b Boyce	20	b Hobbs	30
D.J. Shepherd	not out	2	not out	2
O.S. Wheatley	c & b Hobbs	0		
Extras	b 4, lb 3, nb 5	12	b 8, lb 2, nb 3	13
		241	(8 wkts, dec)	**284**

1-5, 2-58, 3-65, 4-156, 5-196, 6-210, 7-210, 8-230, 9-239, 10-241
1-8, 2-50, 3-90, 4-109, 5-144, 6-181, 7-227, 8-272

Boyce	18	3	52	2	25	5	79	1
Lever	15	5	38	1	22	4	64	3
East	19	3	63	3	9	3	19	0
Turner	20	8	44	2	11	1	31	1
Hobbs	11.1	2	32	2	36	16	78	3
Fletcher					1	1	0	0

ESSEX

B. Ward	c R.C. Davis b Wheatley	31	c R.C. Davis b Wheatley	21
B.E. Edmeades	lbw b Nash	4	c Lewis b Wheatley	10
G. Barker	lbw b Wheatley	17	st E.W. Jones b R.C. Davis	28
K.W.R. Fletcher	lbw b Wheatley	49	c B.A.Davis b R.C. Davis	44
B.L. Irvine	b R.C. Davis	109	b Shepherd	29
K.D. Boyce	c B.A. Davis b Shepherd	16	c Lewis b R.C. Davis	11
*+B. Taylor	c Cordle b R.C. Davis	70	c Lewis b Wheatley	5
S. Turner	not out	23	c R.C. Davis b Shepherd	2
R.N.S. Hobbs	not out	8	c E.W. Jones b Shepherd	17
R.N. East			not out	14
J.K. Lever			run out	2
Extras	b 1, lb 7, nb 1	9	b 4, lb 1	5
	(7 wkts, dec)	**336**		**188**

1-5, 2-48, 3-63, 4-139, 5-165, 6-294, 7-304
1-29, 2-36, 3-43, 4-109, 5-123, 6-125, 7-131, 8-163, 9-185, 10-188

Nash	24	5	84	1	3	0	16	0
Wheatley	26	3	77	3	10	0	40	3
Cordle	8	2	32	0	4	0	33	0
Shepherd	28	10	78	1	11	0	56	3
Walker	3	0	20	0				
R.C. Davis	10	1	36	2	9	0	38	3

Umpires: D.J. Constant and G.H. Pope

CLOSE OF PLAY

"The Swinging Sixties," Peter Walker reflects. "At the time it didn't seem like a culture shock but, looking back now, it was like a Caesarean birth without the anaesthetic. It was a time of 'try it and see'. There suddenly came a panic on the Test and County Cricket Board that the game was slipping away from them."

"After the war people went back to the cricket in droves," Roy Booth recalls. "During the fifties there was a spin-off from that." John Clay agrees: "People were just grateful to be playing cricket, and that lasted a long time."

By the mid-sixties, though, the crowds are thinning, and cricket is in financial crisis. Somerset consider selling their Taunton ground, and Essex have a playing staff of just twelve. The richest county is Warwickshire, their money comes from a football lottery, and they give Essex an interest-free loan to buy their Chelmsford ground. "We worried that we'd have less opposition," Ray Hitchcock remembers, "that one or two counties would go out of existence if we didn't help them financially."

"We were the cheated generation," Tony Lewis writes. "We had been brought up on Hutton and Compton, we queued up to watch the 1948 Australians, clamoured into county grounds with thousands of others, and when we ourselves made the grade there was no one watching."

It is all change in the sixties: the end of the amateurs and the founding of the players' association, the start of one-day cricket and the removal of restrictions on overseas players. Every year there are alterations to the county championship and to the laws of the game. "One year," Bob Carter remembers, "the first innings was limited to 65 overs. That was a great year for quicks. Three of you bowled twenty overs each, then you came back and sat with your feet up in the pavvy."

"The damn no ball law," Don Wilson remembers. "First they tried putting a disc down for the drag, and that didn't seem to work. Then they brought in this incredible front foot law. You had to have your foot behind the line. It absolutely ruined the likes of Fred. Then you were allowed to break the line. And since then we seem to have had more injuries."

"We enjoyed the limited over cricket when it started," Alan Oakman recalls. "It was an innovation, and people came to watch it." "We had a new era of supporters," Alan Dixon thinks. "The football supporters, if you like, the people who wanted to see the beginning and the end of the game." But even in the first round of matches it becomes clear that one-day cricket is not quite the same thing as Brighter Cricket. Peter Richardson of Kent is batting, and Sussex's captain Ted Dexter moves all the close fielders into run-saving positions and bowls 65 overs of seam. "If this is the way you play it," Peter Richardson protests, "you can stuff this knock-out cricket."

"The cricket they play today is tremendous," Keith Andrew thinks, "but I do find the one-day game boring. When you're in a one-day match and you get out, it doesn't matter. As a spectacle of pure cricket, it's not got the same feel." Alan Dixon agrees: "The niceties of the game, the artistry of the bat versus the ball, started on their downward trend."

"It was fun when the spinners bowled on turning pitches," Les Lenham says. "You had great close catchers round the bat, and you had to work the ball through them. It was interesting cricket. I'd love to go back to uncovered pitches. It would create good batters, and the spinners would come into their own. But the county game now relies on corporate entertainment, and you can't have matches over in a day and a half or two days."

"I liked the out-grounds," Robin Hobbs says. "We looked forward to Wellingborough and Yeovil more than Old Trafford and the Oval."

"We probably played in more adverse conditions," Peter Robinson says. "The umpires would get you out there. If you said you couldn't bowl, they'd say, 'Well, find me somebody who can.' Now it has to be almost perfect." And the out-grounds? "Yeovil was a dreadful place. Glastonbury was better. They used to take us round the factory and give us a free pair of shoes. That was something when you were on the money we were on."

"You often played on wickets that were dicey from the word go," Mick Norman recalls. "Everything now is much more sophisticated." Derek Morgan agrees: "There was such a variety in the games, and that created excitement. Sometimes you were out for 100. That's much more fun than seeing somebody scoring 300 or 400 regularly."

"There was no way you could go in on a Saturday morning with four seamers and a make-believe spinner," Don Wilson says. "You couldn't do that, no matter what the wicket looked like. That was the beauty of the game."

"People accepted the fact that there were bowlers' umpires and batters' umpires," Robin Hobbs says. "And if the umpire was getting the four o'clock train from Southend and you were hit on the pads, you knew you were gone. But you accepted that. The umpires were all nice people, and it was more of a family in those days."

"We never argued," Don Wilson says. "If you were given out, you were out. But there wasn't the replay, was there? I suppose some of us might have complained if we'd seen what they see today, but we were never brought up like that."

"You could talk to the umpires," Peter Walker says, "and they would have a beer with you at the end of the day. The players helped the umpires. There was a feeling that, if I cheat them, I cheat my profession. There was more sense of ethical pride in the sixties." "You could name the so-called cheats, the batsmen who didn't walk, on one hand," Ray Hitchcock says. "I finished in 1974," Don Wilson says, "and that was going by then."

"I shall go to the grave with one real thing on my conscience," Peter Walker says. "I've never told anyone this. We were playing at Leicester on a very bad wicket, and we needed to bat out the day. I somehow survived, and Don Shepherd came out to bat at number eleven. Terry Spencer came racing in. He bowled this ball, and it just brushed my glove. Terry didn't appeal, but behind the wicket they did. The umpire said 'not out', but I knew that I'd gloved it. I couldn't look anybody in the face. Luckily Shep got out in the next over, and it didn't matter. But I carry that now as a stigmata. I feel I let everything down."

"It isn't cricket," people used to say, and perhaps they don't now. Where did that go? "It went with more money," Peter Walker thinks. "It went with the greater emphasis on instant action instead of the reflective game."

"I'm glad I played when I did," Alan Oakman says. "I don't envy the young players now. I don't think it's easy for them. You've got to win now. The members expect it."

"Too many older players are knocking the modern game," Ron Headley says. "Youngsters today play a lot of high pressure cricket."

"A lot of the pressure, they build up on themselves," Roy Booth says. "It's all taken so seriously. They do all this pre-season training, pre-match exercises, then invariably somebody pulls a muscle during the course of the game. There's more injuries now than there ever were."

"We were fairly fit carthorses," David Allen says. "Nowadays they want to be thoroughbreds. And, as we know in racing circles, thoroughbreds break down a lot."

"I go over and coach the boys at Ampleforth," Peter Lever tells. "Mum will come and pick them up, and she'll carry their bag back. You know, these great, big cricket bags, and there's Mum, staggering out with it. And it's cars and cars. When I was their age, if I wanted to go anywhere, I had to walk it. And if it was out of Todmorden, it was the bus."

"I started playing cricket in the back streets of Gloucester in the war," Bomber Wells says. "We grew up in our own little world, free of all this intense commercialism. If we got hold of a bat, we'd drop it handle first onto the pavement, see how many times it bounced. Boom-boom, that's a two-springer. Boom-boom-boom, that's a three-springer. 'That's a better bat, that's a three-springer.'"

"I was born in 1933," Brian Jackson says. "We were different from people today. We were much harder. We didn't expect as much as they do now. The game today, they want much more out of it." Bob Carter has seen the same change: "The work ethic is different these days."

"If you look back from 1969 to 1960," Peter Walker says, "there was a huge change. I can remember about 1960, driving from Cardiff to Sheffield, and the drive taking about eight hours, with a two-hour wait at the Aust

Ferry. Middlesbrough to Llanelli one year, we arrived forty minutes before the start of play, having left at six the previous evening. Four train changes. The two opening batsmen went out, number three was kitted out, and the other eight were asleep."

"The game today comes second to the money that's made from it," Alan Dixon says. "I don't blame the players, but the trend was there by the late sixties."

"I might have made a lot more money as an engineer," Keith Andrew thinks. "I might have been a company director, but I've had a wonderful life. It was the experience of playing in those times that gave me a wider vision."

"I didn't play cricket for the money," Brian Jackson says. "I played cricket because I wanted to play every day, and I enjoyed every minute of it."

"I missed it so much when I retired," John Clay says. "It takes a long time to get over the loss. I still feel it a bit."

"I was brought up in a super age with a super set of people," David Allen says. "They were full of enthusiasm and encouragement. It was a love that you worked for. That's why the technique was so good."

"It was fabulous fun," Don Wilson says. "We used to be a community of men. We were there to play, we were there to enjoy it, and we were there to entertain. The players of that era, we have all got good memories."

Alan Castell remembers his championship debut at Bournemouth, nine wickets down and Fred Trueman bowling him a bouncer. Peter Robinson remembers batting with Bill Alley at Taunton, five to win off two balls, and the miserable old buggers working away at the railway goods yard. Peter Walker remembers his old friend Ossie Wheatley lumbering around the boundary at Swansea, bending to field a ball that could win Glamorgan the championship. Roy Booth remembers the hot and flustered George Pope, turning down goodness knows how many lbw appeals at Worcester. And Alan Dixon remembers his old team mate John Dye, pulling up in his first over at Wellingborough: 'Guess what, Al. It's gone.'

Gone.

"Every two years," Alan Dixon says, "the old Kent players have a day out, and we love to recount the stories."

"You'll search for memories of days gone by," Bob Carter says, "but they won't come back."

"It was great fun," Alan says. "I'd love it to start again tomorrow."

214

ACKNOWLEDGEMENTS

I would like to express my thanks to all those cricketers who were so generous with their time during my writing of this book.

I met in person: David Allen, Keith Andrew, Ken Biddulph, Roy Booth, Bob Carter, Tom Cartwright, Alan Castell, John Clay, Alan Dixon, John Dye, John Elliott, David Green, Ron Headley, Ray Hitchcock, Robin Hobbs, Peter Lever, Derek Morgan, Mick Norman, Alan Oakman, Peter Robinson, David Smith, Roy Swetman, Peter Walker, Bomber Wells, John Wilcox and Don Wilson.

I spoke on the telephone to: Bill Blenkiron, Geoff Clayton, Ray East, Maurice Hallam, Malcolm Heath, Brian Jackson, Les Lenham, Michael Mence, Eric Russell, Don Shepherd, Terry Spencer and Mike Willett.

Their love of the game shone through everything they shared with me, and I hope that I have captured some of that on the pages of this book.

Additionally I would like to thank the following for their help: Dave Allen at Hampshire, Mike Carey at Derbyshire, Jeff Hancock at the Oval, Andrew Hignell at Glamorgan, Rev Malcolm Lorimer at Old Trafford, Andrew Radd at Northampton and Peter Wynne-Thomas at Trent Bridge.

I have made regular use of the following cricket reference books:
Wisden Cricketers' Almanack
P. Bailey, P. Thorn & P. Wynne-Thomas, *Who's Who of Cricketers*
(Hamlyn, 1993)
Robert Brooke, *A History of the County Cricket Championship*
(Guinness, 1991)
Bill Frindall, *England Test Cricketers*   (Willow Books, 1989)
Jim Ledbetter & Peter Wynne-Thomas, *First-Class Cricket, 1932-39*
(Limlow Books, 8 volumes, 1991-7)

I have read and occasionally quoted from the following autobiographies:
Bill Alley, *My Incredible Innings* (Pelham Books, 1969)
Trevor Bailey, *Wickets, Catches and the Odd Run* (Willow Books, 1986)
Brian Close, *I Don't Bruise Easily* (Macdonald & Jane's, 1978)
Mike Denness, *I Declare* (Arthur Barker, 1977)
Basil D'Oliveira, *Time To Declare* (J.M. Dent & Sons, 1980)
Ray East, *A Funny Turn* (George Allen & Unwin, 1983)
Keith Fletcher, *Captain's Innings* (Stanley Paul, 1983)
John Hampshire, *Family Argument* (George Allen & Unwin, 1983)
Ray Illingworth, *Yorkshire And Back* (Queen Anne Press, 1980)
Colin Ingleby-Mackenzie, *Many A Slip* (Oldbourne Books, 1962)
Alan Knott, *It's Knott Cricket* (Macmillan, 1985)
Alan Knott, *Stumper's View* (Stanley Paul, 1972)
J.K. Lever, *J.K. Lever - A Cricketer's Cricketer* (Unwin Hyman, 1989)
Tony Lewis, *Playing Days* (Stanley Paul, 1985)

Roy Marshall, *Test Outcast* (Pelham, 1970)

Colin Milburn, *Largely Cricket* (Stanley Paul, 1968)

Mike Procter, *Mike Procter and Cricket* (Pelham, 1981)

Alan Oakman, *How I Became A Cricketer* (Thomas Nelson, 1960)

David Shepherd, *Parson's Pitch* (Hodder and Stoughton, 1964)

David Steele, *Come In Number 3* (Pelham, 1977)

Bob Taylor, *Standing Up, Standing Back* (Collins Willow, 1985)

Glenn Turner, *My Way* (Hodder & Stoughton, 1975)

Glenn Turner, with Brian Turner, *Opening Up* (Hodder & Stoughton, 1987)

Derek Underwood, *Beating The Bat* (Stanley Paul, 1975)

Don Wilson, *Mad Jack* (Kingswood Press, 1992)

from the following county histories:

Brian Bearshaw, *From The Stretford End* (Partridge Press, 1990)

Matthew Engel & Andrew Radd, *The History of Northamptonshire CCC* (Christopher Helm, 1993)

David Foot, *Sunshine, Sixes and Cider* (David & Charles, 1986)

David Green, *The History of Gloucestershire CCC* (Christopher Helm, 1990)

Andrew Hignell, *The History of Glamorgan CCC* (Christopher Helm, 1988)

David Lemmon, *The History of Worcestershire CCC* (Christopher Helm, 1988)

David Lemmon & Mike Marshall, *Essex County Cricket Club - The Official History* (Kingswood Press, 1987)

Don Mosey, *We Don't Play It For Fun* (Methuen, 1989)

Grahame Parker, *Gloucestershire Road* (Pelham, 1983)

Peter Roebuck, *From Sammy To Jimmy - The Official History of Somerset County Cricket Club* (Partridge Press, 1991)

Peter Wynne-Thomas, *The History of Nottinghamshire CCC* (Christopher Helm, 1992)

from the following biographies:

Ralph Barker, *The Cricketing Family Edrich* (Pelham Books, 1976)

David Matthews, *On The Spot: A Biography of Derek Shackleton* (Blackberry Downs Books, 1998)

Don Mosey, *Fred - Then And Now* (Kingswood Press, 1991)

Brian Scovell, *Ken Barrington - A Tribute* (Harrap, 1982)

from the following other books about cricket:

David Rayvern Allen (ed), *Arlott on Cricket* (Collins Willow, 1984)

John Arlott, *John Arlott's Book of Cricketers* (Lutterworth, 1979)

Michael Marshall, *Gentlemen and Players* (Grafton Books, 1987)

Patrick Murphy, *The Centurions* (J.M. Dent & Sons, 1983)

George Plumptre, *Homes Of Cricket* (Queen Anne Press, 1988)

David Seward & Peter Wynne-Thomas (eds), *Memories of Trent Bridge* (Nottinghamshire CCC, 1987)

A.A. Thomson, *Cricket: The Wars of the Roses* (Pelham Books, 1967)

Frank Tyson, *Northamptonshire Revisited* in *County Champions*
(Heinemann, 1982)
Fred Trueman & Don Mosey, *Champion Times: Yorkshire CCC 1959-68*
(Dalesman Publishing, 1994)
Peter Walker, *The All-Rounder* (Pelham Books, 1979)

and from the following non-cricket book:
Neil Lyon, *Four Centuries: The History of Wellingborough School*
(Wellingborough School, 1988)

I have quoted from the following national newspapers:
Daily Express, Daily Telegraph and Sunday Telegraph, Manchester
Guardian, News Chronicle, Observer, Times and Sunday Times.

from the following local newspapers:
Birmingham Post, Brentwood Gazette, Brighton Gazette, Bristol Evening
Post, Derby Evening Telegraph, Gloucester Citizen, Kent Messenger, London
Evening Standard, Manchester Evening News, Northampton Chronicle and
Echo, Nottingham Evening Post, Somerset County Gazette, Southern Echo,
South Wales Echo, Western Daily Press, Western Mail, Worcester Evening
News and Yorkshire Post.

and from the following cricket magazines:
Cricket Lore, The Cricketer, Wisden Cricket Monthly.

I would like to thank Faber & Faber Ltd for permission to quote from 'Little
Gidding' by T.S. Eliot and the Estate of John Arlott for the lines of 'Cricket at
Worcester'.

I would like to thank everybody who encouraged me to write a sequel to 'Runs
in the Memory'. Writing is a solitary business, and on a bad day I can start
wondering whether there is anybody out there gaining any pleasure from my
labours. I especially treasure the telephone call from a woman in Lichfield.
"My husband's been driving me mad," she said. "He's spent the whole
weekend sitting in the garden, chuckling away at your book." Unlike the man
in London who wrote, "I'm enjoying your book very much. Unfortunately it's
taking a long time to read as I seem to drop off to sleep very easily."

Finally I would like to thank Sue Kendall and Humphrey Keenlyside, who
have read every word and made so many helpful suggestions. Humphrey is
secretary of The Journeymen, a wandering cricket club for which I play, and I
hope to repay him with some sparkling performances during the summer. Sue
is my partner, and she and our daughter Martha have never wavered in their
encouragement for my writing these two books. But then I have had so much
fun doing it. That perhaps has made me easier to live with!

Stephen Chalke
Bath, March 1999

INDEX

Also available from Fairfield Books

RUNS IN THE MEMORY -
COUNTY CRICKET IN THE 1950s
by Stephen Chalke
The stories of twelve county matches
with illustrations by Ken Taylor
and a foreword by Tom Cartwright

I was just seventeen, a little lad walking out to bat at The Oval, trying to grasp what was going on. I think I learnt more in my time at the wicket in that game than I've learnt in any period of any other game.

Tom Cartwright (Warwickshire)

'We want 100 in forty minutes,' Brian said. 'Don't get out, and don't make it look easy.'
Ken Taylor (Yorkshire)

I was sharing a room with a bloke who'd shared a room with Don Bradman. Two o'clock in the morning I'd wake up. Clink-a-clink-clink. 'Colin, what are you doing?' 'Get back to sleep, I'm writing a book.'

Ken Biddulph (Somerset)

I don't know why he did it. I'd never seen him hit a straight six before. There were three to win off four balls. Why on earth did he keep trying to hit sixes?
Dickie Dodds (Essex)

I think you'll find that my run-up was from the start of one of the white lines on the middle of the road to the far end of the second one.

Don Shepherd (Glamorgan)

Limited over cricket? Neville Cardus said to me, it's like trying to play Beethoven on a banjo.   Bomber Wells (Gloucestershire)

It was born in me to play cricket, and they were wonderful days in the sun. The days were never long enough.   Arthur Milton (Gloucestershire)

Also featuring Dennis Brookes (Northants), Bernie Constable (Surrey), David Green (Derbys), Malcolm Heath (Hants), Martin Horton (Worcs), John Pretlove (Kent), Jim Parks (Sussex), Harold Rhodes (Derbys), Terry Spencer (Leics), Bryan Stott (Yorks), Merv Winfield (Notts) and more.

The book is available for £15.95 post free from Fairfield Books, 17 George's Road, Fairfield Park, Bath BA1 6EY.   Telephone 01225-335813.

LES JACKSON - A DERBYSHIRE LEGEND

by Mike Carey

with a foreword by Freddie Trueman

A wonderful whiff of nostalgia. - Michael Parkinson

Available in paperback for £9.50 including postage and packing from
Mike Carey, 5 The Square, Darley Abbey, Derby DE22 1DY

ON THE SPOT

A BIOGRAPHY OF DEREK SHACKLETON

by David Matthews

with a foreword by Colin Ingleby-Mackenzie

Any coherent cricket library must contain this biography. - Robin Marlar
A conscientious study of a bowler of mesmeric, unerring length. - David Foot

Available in hardback for £15.95 including postage and packing from
Blackberry Downs Books, Lincombe, Lee Bay, North Devon EX34 8LL

TRAGIC WHITE ROSES

THE SAD STORY OF YORKSHIRE CRICKETERS
ALONZO DRAKE & MAJOR BOOTH

by Mick Pope

The old James Dean formula: talent perishing before its time. - David Frith
Nothing if not a good read. -- Robert Brooke, The Cricket Statistician

Available in paperback for £5.00 including postage and packing from
Mick Pope, 59 Wood Lane, Treeton, Rotherham, South Yorkshire S60 5QR